W9-CGX-754

Entrepreneurship

ENTREPRENEURSHIP
The Engine of Growth

Volume 2
PROCESS

Edited by **Andrew Zacharakis**
and **Stephen Spinelli Jr.**

PRAEGER PERSPECTIVES

Westport, Connecticut
London

Library of Congress Cataloging-in-Publication Data

Entrepreneurship : the engine of growth / edited by Maria Minniti . . . [et al.].
    p.   cm.
    Includes bibliographical references and index.
    ISBN 0-275-98986-0 (set: alk. paper)—ISBN 0-275-98987-9 (vol 1: alk. paper)—
    ISBN 0-275-98988-7 (vol 2: alk. paper)—ISBN 0-275-98989-5 (vol 3: alk. paper)
    1. Entrepreneurship.   I. Minniti, Maria.
    HB615.E636 2007
    338'.04—dc22   2006028313

British Library Cataloguing in Publication Data is available.

Library of Congress Catalog Card Number: 2006028313
ISBN: 0-275-98986-0 (set)
        0-275-98987-9 (vol. 1)
        0-275-98988-7 (vol. 2)
        0-275-98989-5 (vol. 3)

First published in 2007

Praeger Publishers, 88 Post Road West, Westport, CT 06881
An imprint of Greenwood Publishing Group, Inc.
www.praeger.com

Printed in the United States of America

The paper used in this book complies with the
Permanent Paper Standard issued by the National
Information Standards Organization (Z39.48-1984).

10 9 8 7 6 5 4 3 2 1

Contents

Preface

The editors of this three-volume set are pleased to present readers with insight into the field of entrepreneurship by some of the leading scholars around the world. Babson College, the home institution for all the editors, has been a leader in entrepreneurship education for over thirty years and is recognized by many leading publications as the top school for teaching entrepreneurship at both the MBA and undergraduate levels (thirteen years running by *U.S. News and World Report*). Since 1999, Babson College, in conjunction with the London Business School, has led the Global Entrepreneurship Monitor (GEM) research project. GEM assesses the state of entrepreneurship activity across more than forty countries around the world (comprising two-thirds of the world's population and over 90 percent of the world GDP) and has shown that entrepreneurship can be found in all economies and that almost 9 percent of the adult population is actively attempting to launch a new venture at any given time.[1] While the percentages vary by country, GEM illustrates the importance of entrepreneurship and provides context as we try to better understand the entrepreneurial phenomenon.

We have compiled three volumes focusing on entrepreneurship from three different perspectives: people, process, and place. Volume 1, edited by Maria Minniti, looks at the intersection of people and entrepreneurship. Taking a broad view of entrepreneurship as a form of human action, chapters in this volume identify the current state of the art in academic research with respect to cognitive, economic, social, and institutional factors that influence people's behavior with respect to entrepreneurship. Why do people start new businesses? How do people make entrepreneurial decisions? What is the role played by the social and economic environment on individuals' decisions about entrepreneurship? Do institutions matter? Do some groups of people such as immigrants and women face particular issues when deciding to start a business? The volume addresses these and other questions. Each chapter provides an extensive bibliography and suggestions for further research.

Volume 2, edited by Andrew Zacharakis and Stephen Spinelli, examines the entrepreneurial process. The book proceeds through the life cycle of a new venture start-up. Chapter authors tackle several key steps in the process, ranging from idea, to opportunity, team building, resource acquisition, managing growth, and entering global markets. These chapters identify the current state of the art in academic research, suggest directions for future research, and draw implications for practicing entrepreneurs. What is clear from this volume is that we have learned a tremendous amount about the entrepreneurial process, especially over the last fifteen years. This deep insight leads us to ask more questions and suggest new research to answer these questions. This learning is also applied in the classroom and shared in this book so that students and entrepreneurs can assess best practices.

Volume 3, edited by Mark Rice and Tim Habbershon, examines place. In this volume and in the literature, *place* refers to a wide and diverse range of contextual factors that influence the entrepreneur and the entrepreneurial process. We represent these contextual factors as a series of concentric circles ranging from environmental and global forces, to national and regional policies, industries and infrastructures, to cultural communities, families, and organizational forms. Chapters in this volume address entrepreneurship in the context of the corporation, family, and franchise. We provide insights on ethnicity and entrepreneurship in the U.S. Hispanic, Slovenian, and German context. We look at the impact of public policy and entrepreneurship support systems at the country and community level, and from an economic and social perspective. We also examine the technology environment and financing support structures for entrepreneurship as context issues. By placing this array of contextual factors into an ecosystem perspective, we show how entrepreneurship is a complex input–output process in which people, process, and place are constantly interacting to generate the entrepreneurial economy.

It is our hope that the chapters spur the reader's interest in entrepreneurship, that the academic who is new to entrepreneurship will see an opportunity to enter this field, and that those who are already studying this phenomenon will see new questions that need investigation. We hope that practitioners and students will glean best practices as they work in entrepreneurial ventures and that the prescriptions within these chapters will help them succeed. We also think that these volumes can help policymakers get a firmer grasp on entrepreneurship and the potential it has to spur economic growth within a country, state/province, and town. Entrepreneurship operates in an ecosystem that is reliant upon all the audiences of these volumes. As we gain better understanding of the ecosystem, we all benefit.

NOTE

1. M. Minniti, W. Bygrave, and E. Autio, *Global Entrepreneurship Monitor: 2005 Executive Report* (Babson Park, MA: Babson College and London Business School, 2006).

Introduction

Andrew Zacharakis and Stephen Spinelli Jr.

We are pleased to present the second volume of Praeger Perspectives on Entrepreneurship. *Entrepreneurship: The Engine of Growth* contains the research and thinking of eminent scholars in the field of entrepreneurship. Whereas Volume 1 of this set looks at the intersection of the individual and entrepreneurship and Volume 3 looks at the intersection of the physical place and public policy with entrepreneurship, this volume examines the entrepreneurial process: the pattern of phenomena that starts with creativity and ideas and progresses through growth and harvest. It encompasses opportunity, teams, and resources, and the behavior that brings those components together into a business. The entrepreneurial process is generally viewed from the perspective of new venture creation. However, it is so deeply embedded in the development of our economic and social well-being that the concepts covered in the volume can be applied to most existing businesses and social entities.

The entrepreneurial process is a global experience. Babson College and the London Business School lead a contingent of forty universities in a worldwide study of individuals' propensity to start and grow businesses. The Global Entrepreneurship Monitor (GEM) annually issues forty national reports, a global report, and special issues such as women in entrepreneurship and venture capital (VC) investment.[1] The report continues to show high rates of entrepreneurial activity around the world. In the United States, 9 percent of the population is actively attempting to start a business, termed nascent entrepreneurship. Another 5 percent of the U.S. population are owners of established businesses less than forty-two months old. That means more than 16 percent of the U.S. population are involved in the entrepreneurial process at any point in time.[2,3] These statistics tell us that it is important for both individuals and nations to understand the new venture process if we hope to build and sustain our economic well-being.

This volume is designed to describe the entrepreneurial process in both holistic terms and in its components; from idea to exit and the steps inbetween. Chapter 1, by Spinelli, Neck, and Timmons, lays out the framework in the Timmons model. This model is well defined in entrepreneurship research and has been used in entrepreneurship education for over thirty-five years. Dimov then examines idea generation, described in chapter 2 as intertwined with opportunity recognition and supported by Corbett and McMullen's following chapter on opportunity. Chapters 4, 5, and 6 look at the team and resource elements laid out in the Timmons model. Chandler reviews the research on entrepreneurial teams and provides direction for future research as well as implications for practicing entrepreneurs. Amatucci and Sohl examine angel financing while Zacharakis and Eckermann review VC financing. Wiklund moves us to the next phase after the team and financing are in place; venture growth strategies. Because the factors of influence in entrepreneurship, customers, supply, financing, and so on, are global in nature, Dickson describes international entrepreneurship as an extension of growth strategies and in terms of high potential vision of a firm's impact and scope. Finally, Treichel and Deeds conclude with an overview of trade sale (being acquired) and initial public offering (IPO) exit mechanisms. Exit, sometimes termed harvest, is seen as a liquidity event for investors, not as an exit for the entrepreneur.

Entrepreneurship is sometimes referred to as an *ecosystem*, a network of people, places, and behaviors that seek and exploit opportunities. We expect that the major players in that system, academics, students, support professionals,[4] and practicing entrepreneurs will find this book of use. For academics, the volume reviews the research on significant perspectives of entrepreneurial activity and suggests direction for future research. Students will find that the chapters uncover and explore the underlying mechanisms central to the entrepreneurial process. Support professionals will better understand the expectations and goals of their clients. Finally, entrepreneurs will learn from leading scholars, many of whom have entrepreneurial experience, the state of the art on new venture creation, growth, and launch. We hope that the Praeger Perspectives on entrepreneurship will provide a useful resource that you refer to again and again.

In chapter 1, Spinelli, Neck, and Timmons lay out the Timmons framework of the entrepreneurial process. This model has been widely taught for almost three decades as it has evolved through the various editions of Timmons' *New Venture Creation*.[5] In the chapter, they describe how opportunity, team, and resources are joined in a symbiotic process leading to the creation of a venture. In particular, Spinelli et al. articulate the importance of balancing the opportunity, resources, and team elements inherent in all new start-ups. While this chapter asserts that the entrepreneurial process starts with opportunity identification, it is clear that the model captures the iterative nature of opportunity recognition, team-building, and resource acquisition. The dynamic shaping of the opportunity influences and is influenced by marketplace feedback, team input, and the resources controlled and sought.

We used the Timmons model as a guiding framework to target and identify chapter authors to further explore issues related to the entrepreneurial process. Specifically, chapters 2 and 3 drill into the idea and opportunity recognition components. Chapter 4 adds greater depth on team issues. Chapter 5 looks at acquiring equity capital from angels whereas chapter 6 examines VC. We believe the Timmons model, as asserted by the chapter authors, consistently maps the entrepreneurial process, the texture and complexity of which is increasingly strengthened by continuing academic research.

Dimov in chapter 2 focuses on idea generation, presenting a concise view of the literature. Drawing from a number of process models, the chapter crafts a systematic architecture of how idea generation occurs in entrepreneurship. First, it is a process—typified by the Wallas and other models—rather than a "eureka" inspiration.[6] Second, a product is conceived; third, the role of motivation, cognitive styles, and knowledge; and fourth, idea generation occurs in a context—different situations influence which ideas are developed and pursued. Although exploring the process, product, person, or situation in isolation adds to our knowledge, it may be misleading as much of the variance is left unexplained. Dimov rightly calls for entrepreneurship research to expand and capture this complexity. He explains that loosening the boundaries between the phenomena in entrepreneurship will reveal textured linkages and insights.

Chapter 3 also focuses on opportunity but stresses the power of "mindfulness," being truly cognizant of one's current situation. Mindfulness occurs within the individual and is driven by the opportunity under consideration, the motive for pursuing the opportunity and the means of achieving exploitation of the opportunity. The chapter authors assert that if one is practicing mindfulness, one will discover opportunities through entrepreneurial alertness. These opportunities will be both economically attractive and fit the individual entrepreneur. Corbett and McMullen then suggest that mindfulness is a Zen-like concept that can be taught and learned. The chapter concludes with a concise prescription for how one can increase mindfulness.

Chapter 4 examines the research involving teams and new venture creation. This chapter sets out a uniform definition for new venture teams, which is important for researchers, so that results can be generalized across studies and is important for entrepreneurs so that they can follow the prescriptions of research. Chandler goes on to review a number of the important research questions regarding teams, including how and when teams form, and how important are teams to success. The research in this area is accumulating, but Chandler notes that entrepreneurship would benefit by building off of the work team literature. In particular, the work team literature suggests a framework: forming, storming, norming, performing, and adjourning. This framework provides a lifecycle view for new venture teams. For instance, we can examine team composition within this framework. While it is intuitive that stronger teams have complimentary skills, research suggests that complimentary benefits can be offset if the team is not cohesive. This research cuts across all stages of the new venture team process.

The model also facilitates discussion of adding or firing (or losing) team members and the impact on performance. While the chapter offers a thorough review of the literature and a number of directions in which to further research the phenomenon, the punchline is that ventures founded by teams (which are two-thirds of all new ventures) outperform those founded by individuals.

The successive two chapters continue to dig into elements of the Timmons model, in particular, resources. Chapter 5 reviews what we know about angel financing and chapter 6 looks at VC. The two sources of equity capital are complementary, especially for high-potential ventures. Angels typically fund earlier-stage deals than VCs and as the venture progresses, angels work with the entrepreneurs to obtain follow-on VC financing. Since the goal of this volume is to investigate the new venture process, we do not review debt sources of capital as these typically become available after a firm is operational. Moreover, debt financing has received less attention in the academic literature than either angel or VC financing. Perhaps the area that we should have devoted space and time—but did not—is friend and family financing. Friends and family financing is the most available source during the start-up process and we expect that the motivation for these investors differs dramatically from that of angels and venture capitalists (VCs), yet this area is mostly neglected in the entrepreneurship research literature. Therefore, we did not commission a chapter on friends and family financing, but we hope that academics will find direction for researching this important component by reading the chapters on angels and VCs.

Chapter 5 provides an excellent overview of angel financing. This area is one of the most neglected in the entrepreneurship literature due to the difficulty of identifying and collecting data from angel investors. The chapter, nonetheless, proceeds to review relevant research according to the stage of the investment process (roughly divided into pre- and postinvestment). Next, Amatucci and Sohl highlight that the nature of the angel industry is changing. Although traditional individual angels (who are often former entrepreneurs) still represent the largest segment in terms of investment dollars, there is a rise in informal angel groups and more formalized angel groups. Amatucci and Sohl suggest that due in part to the emergence of these new segments, angel investors are becoming more formal in their process (although they question whether this is good for the overall health of the marketplace). They also suggest that as VCs continue to move to later-stage deals, angels are following and now entering second-stage follow-on financing (while still retaining a large involvement in seed and start-up financing). They suggest that this trend is a function of opportunism, necessity, and protection. It is opportunistic in that there is an investment gap created by VCs looking at later-stage deals. It is a necessity because without angel participation at this stage, many of the companies would fold and endanger earlier round angel investments. Finally, it is protectionist in that when VCs do offer financing, they are cramming down the value of earlier investments by angels, meaning that VC forces angels to revise their initial investment terms, thereby damaging the angel's potential returns. Amatucci and Sohl speculate that the angel market will be self-correcting in that if there develops a large seed/start-up capital gap, angels will return and increase their involvement there. This presumption suggests that VCs would then back in and fill the gap they are creating in second-stage financing. However, considering the ever larger funds that VCs are raising, it is not clear that they will come back to this sector.

Chapter 6 continues the examination of equity financing by looking at VC. VC is disproportionately researched considering the number of new firms that receive VC financing, yet from the overview it appears there is much that we still do not know about it. Zacharakis and Eckermann systematically step through the VC process from raising a fund through to a liquidity event and find many areas that are underresearched. In particular, they look at the many dyads that are involved in the investment process. There is the limited partner and VC dyad to consider when raising a fund. VCs often syndicate financing deals, creating a VC/VC dyad. Additionally, VCs interact with other investors (both earlier-stage and later-stage investors) creating dyads between VCs/angels, earlier- and later-round VCs, and so forth. Of course, the most important dyad and the one receiving the most attention is the VC/entrepreneur dyad. Success in VC is directly a function of how well VCs manage these dyads and recognizing that the relative importance of the dyad depends on the stage of the VC investment process. Zacharakis and Eckermann suggest several research questions surrounding these dyads. Considering the VC boom and bust of the late 1990s and early 2000s, many of these questions need to be reevaluated in light of contextual factors such as the irrational exuberance of a bubble period.

Wiklund in chapter 7 highlights the importance of growth for entrepreneurial survival and success. Wiklund conducted a large-scale study of small business in Sweden and found that entrepreneurs who enact a strategy can achieve growth. Successful growth is more a function of taking action than what type of action the firm takes. Specifically, Wiklund stresses the importance of personal attributes such as the entrepreneur's motivation to grow and asserts that this may be more important than the entrepreneur's skill when it comes to long-term entrepreneurial success. The chapter concludes with a typology of motivation and resources/capabilities. Firms within all quadrants can survive and Wiklund offers some suggestions for these varying firm types based upon where they fall. The chapter concludes with some policy implications for government.

While many might not consider international expansion as part of the new venture process, chapter 8 reviews research that shows just how prevalent it is. For instance, 80 percent of all small and medium-sized enterprises (SMEs) are affected by or involved with international trade.[7] Dickson cites several other studies that also indicate the growing importance of international efforts by entrepreneurial companies. Thus, the chapter builds nicely from chapter 7 on growth in that going global is one form of a growth strategy (although many firms start global from their first day of operation—"born globals"). Dickson notes the increasing literature on this topic and highlights the three competing (complimentary) models of international expansion by entrepreneurial firms. "Gradual globals" stage their international expansion in order to learn and reduce the risk of such moves. This model is similar to the traditional stage model applied to large multinational corporations. However, Oviatt and McDougall changed the nature of international research by identifying "born global" entrepreneurial firms.[8] According to the born-global model, entrepreneurs often think and pursue global expansion at the very earliest stages of their firm's launch. A more recent model is the born-again iteration that suggests that some triggering event causes entrepreneurial domestic-only firms to quickly consider and then expand internationally. While the merit of each of these models continues to be debated, the models do not speak directly to how entrepreneurial firms go international.

Dickson provides a model that ties the strategies employed with enabling and enacting processes (see Figure 8.1). Considering that entrepreneurial firms are resource-constrained during the new venture process, Dickson asserts that the firms seek enabling mechanisms to compensate, such as using intermediaries (via networking or building alliances) or direct means (which have declined in cost dramatically due to new technology such as the Internet). The chapter concludes with an overview of enacting mechanisms such as exporting, foreign direct investment, outsourcing, licensing, franchising, and merger and acquisition activities. This growing field of research is ever more important to entrepreneurs as the world continues to globalize.

Entrepreneurial exit is about realizing the value of the organization that an entrepreneur has built. While the term suggests that entrepreneurs leave the firm at this point, that is often a misnomer. IPOs, for instance, are about bringing in growth capital to take the firm to the next level. In chapter 9, Treichel and Deeds lay out the three most common means of exit (IPOs, acquisitions, and liquidations). IPO research is well developed. It focuses on the antecedents that impact how well the venture does in the IPO process (as most often measured by underpricing and by money raised). While Treichel and Deeds identify dozens of factors that influence IPO performance, it seems that research on which factors have the biggest impact would be valuable. Research on acquisitions and liquidations is less developed. The authors believe two key questions should drive acquisitions research: First, under what conditions do acquisitions allow entrepreneurs and investors to capture the wealth that their new venture has created. Second, how should entrepreneurs and their investors prepare for a successful acquisition? Liquidation is mostly explored in the research on venture failure and thereby receives a cursory glance. It is imperative to directly assess the liquidation process and understand how it can be best managed. Treichel and Deeds call for research into corporate governance as it relates to liquidation.

CONCLUSION

What all these chapters illustrate is the growing breadth and depth of entrepreneurship research. In the ten-plus years that each of us has been an entrepreneurship academic, we have seen an explosion of interest in the field. There have been a number of new entrepreneurship journals introduced such as *Venture Capital: An International Journal of Entrepreneurial Finance* and *The Journal of International Entrepreneurship*. There have been a number of new conferences devoted to entrepreneurship and the existing conferences have seen their submissions grow exponentially. For example, the Babson College Entrepreneurship Research Conference, which is over twenty-five years old, has grown from 200 submissions in 1995 to over 600 submissions today. Likewise, there is growing demand for entrepreneurship professors as more universities create and expand their entrepreneurship offerings.[9] As the field matures, we see our research going deeper into the phenomena under consideration. Likewise, the methods, samples, and data collected are richer and allow for more rigorous tests.

What this means for students and practicing entrepreneurs is a greater knowledge of what works and does not work. In an ever increasingly global and competitive environment, we firmly believe that those students who pursue an entrepreneurial career will achieve greater personal fulfillment and wealth. As our large corporations continue to shed jobs, especially those well-paying factory jobs of past generations, entrepreneurship can be the best means to achieve social mobility. We believe that this book gives the reader a taste of what has been learned in new venture creation, and more importantly what we still need to learn. At the same time, the astute student and entrepreneur will glean best practices that can help them achieve their goals and entrepreneurial success.

NOTES

1. See http://www.gemconsortium.org/.

2. Note that the sum of nascent entrepreneurs (9 percent) plus new business owners (5 percent) plus established business owners (5 percent) is greater than the percentage of people who are involved in at least one of these activities (16 percent) because some individuals are doing more than one activity at a time. In other words, this subset of individuals includes both nascent and new business owners, or nascent and established business owners because they are in the process of starting a second venture.

3. M. Minniti, W. Bygrave, and E. Autio, *Global Entrepreneurship Monitor: 2005 Executive Report* (Babson Park, MA: Babson College and London Business School, 2006).

4. Lawyers, accountants, venture capitalists, advisors, and others.

5. *New Venture Creation for the 21st Century* is in its seventh edition (March 2006). Editions 6 and 7 were written with Stephen Spinelli and published by McGraw-Hill.

6. G. Wallas, *The Art of Thought* (New York: Harcourt-Brace, 1926).

7. Paul D. Reynolds, "New and Small Firms in Expanding Markets," *Small Business Economics* 9, no. 1 (1997): 79–84.

8. Benjamin M. Oviatt and Patricia P. McDougall, "Toward a Theory of International New Ventures," *Journal of International Business Studies* 25, no. 1 (1994): 45–64.

9. T. Finkle, "A Review of Trends in the Market for Entrepreneurship Faculty from 1989–2004," presented at the 2005 Babson Kauffman Entrepreneurship Research Conference, Wellesley, MA, 2005.

1

The Timmons Model of the Entrepreneurial Process

Stephen Spinelli Jr., Heidi M. Neck, and Jeffry A. Timmons

Entrepreneurship is opportunity obsessed, holistic in its approach, resource parsimonious, and leadership driven for the purpose of value creation.[1] As an iterative, business-churning process, entrepreneurship stimulates economic development and generates social wealth through opportunity discovery and exploitation.[2] Fundamental to the research, teaching and practice of entrepreneurship is opportunity exploitation through the enactment of new business models. Briefly described, a business model is an array of resources (inputs) in new ventures or existing organizations, supplying new or better forms of goods and services (outputs) yielding revenue. We take a Shumpeterian view of entrepreneurial pursuits—defined as opportunities with delivery systems and competencies differing significantly from those of existing organizations.[3] The study of entrepreneurship as a phenomenon requires a multidisciplinary lens.[4] Such a holistic and integrated view is well served by frameworks that helps bind content and process and brings some clarity to venture creation. This chapter describes one framework that supports the evolution of the venture creation process from opportunity recognition forward through the decision to exploit the opportunity via start-up.

The framework described herein is the Timmons model that highlights the essential components of the entrepreneurship process: opportunity evaluation, resource marshalling, and entrepreneurial team formation.[5] The Timmons model originally evolved from Jeffry Timmons' doctoral dissertation research at Harvard University about new and growing ventures.[6] It has evolved over nearly three decades and has been enhanced by ongoing research, case study development, teaching and hands-on experience in high-potential ventures and venture capital funds.[7-9] The fundamental components of the model have not changed,

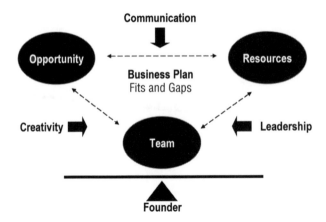

Figure 1.1. The Timmons model.

but their richness and relationships of each to the whole have been steadily enhanced, as they have become better understood.

This chapter seeks to explain the theoretical constructs of the Timmons model (Figure 1.1), yet elevate its use as an applied framework. Teaching entrepreneurship as a rigorous course of study demands the conversion of scholarly research into applied frameworks that can be understood at all levels of education and application. Entrepreneurship education seeks to minimize the risk of venture failure when exploiting new opportunities in the marketplace and the Timmons model reflects the delicate balance of opportunities, resources, and entrepreneurs responsible for execution.

We position the Timmons model as a process that gives fluid boundaries to the entrepreneurship platform that has foundations in opportunity recognition, founding conditions and emergence, resource acquisition and development and human capital and decision making.[10–17] The components of the Timmons model are in constant motion, expanding and contracting as the environment and opportunity change. We begin with an overview of entrepreneurship as process followed by a description of each component in the Timmons model. We conclude with a holistic view of the model and its implications for practice and applications for teaching.

MAPPING THE ENTREPRENEURIAL TERRITORY: A PROCESS ORIENTATION

A process orientation of entrepreneurship necessitates the establishment of boundaries. Entrepreneurship portrayed as the lone entrepreneur starting a small business regardless of growth aspirations is an outdated and underestimated view of a significant business and economic phenomenon. The context in which opportunity is discovered, business models created, and opportunity exploited may occur in many settings and in organizations of all sizes and types including new ventures, corporate new business development, government entities, and nonprofit organizations and the unit of analysis will occur on many levels, such as individual, team, company, industry, and economy.[18–21] However, many core concepts in entrepreneurship are consistent across context and units of analysis.[22] In essence, a framework of entrepreneurial processes describes the nature of economic and psychological opportunity and the patterns of actions and behaviors that create ventures. The motivations for being entrepreneurial are wide ranging, but most research in the field discusses behaviors that foster value creation. Broadly defined, value creation through entrepreneurship is either subjective in nature (from psychology) or financial in nature (from economics).[23, 24] The lessons and principles underlying successful new ventures are embedded in a dynamic process of new venture creation, not a single event or even a series of events. It is the coalescing of dynamic forces, some in the control of the entrepreneur and others not in their control, that we call entrepreneurship. Bygrave and Hofer describe entrepreneurship as a process that is discontinuous, holistic, and unique with outcomes sensitive to a set of antecedent variables.[25] Unlike Garter's view that entrepreneurship is simply the act of creation, we believe entrepreneurship is a continuous cycle of renewal through opportunity identification and exploitation.[26] Thus, growth is central to the process of entrepreneurship.[27, 28]

The entrepreneurship domain provides particularly rich territory for intellectual and practical collisions, between academic theory and the real world of practice. This integrated, holistic balance is at the heart of what we know about the entrepreneurial process.[29, 30] Entrepreneur typologies exist in multitude but the commonality among all entrepreneurial "types" is the act of engagement to create something with the intent to capture value.[31–34] Despite the great variety of businesses, entrepreneurs, geographies, and technologies, central themes dominate this highly dynamic process such as opportunity creation, entrepreneurial teams, resource parsimony and creative resource marshalling, integrated and holistic.[35–39] Furthermore, success is dependent on the fit and balance among these themes. The Timmons model does not intend to capture all nuances in the entrepreneurial process because it is virtually impossible to capture the dynamics of entrepreneurship in one model. However, the Timmons model does describe key areas of disciplinary focus and provides guidelines to assess venture potential. Ultimately, a critical assessment of new venture potential is necessary for bringing the risk-return balance into sharper focus.

COMPONENTS OF THE TIMMONS MODEL

The Timmons model (Figure 1.1) identifies three components of the entrepreneurship process that can be assessed, influenced, shaped, and altered. The entrepreneur is responsible for assessing the opportunity, marshalling resources to capture the opportunity, and developing a team to exploit the opportunity for value creation. An appropriate metaphor for the Timmons model is a juggler bouncing up and down on a trampoline that is moving on a conveyor belt at unpredictable speeds and directions, while trying to keep all three balls in the air. That is the dynamic nature of an early-stage start-up. Few high-growth ventures are started without the assembly of an experienced and skilled team.[40] Creativity, communication, and leadership moderate the strength of the model components and increase the likelihood of venture success. Finally, the business plan provides the language and code for communicating the quality of the three driving forces, of the Timmons model, and of their fit and balance.

The Timmons model aligns with Kirzner's perspective of discovery and alertness to opportunities in the marketplace.[41] Kirzner believed market equilibrium resulted from alert entrepreneurs that capitalize on opportunities waiting to be discovered in the marketplace. Once the opportunity is captured, market gaps diminish and there are movements toward equilibrium. However, the Timmons model argues that a discovery is not sufficient for entrepreneurship. The process of opportunity identification, evaluation, and exploitation must be balanced by resource acquisition and team development. Thus, enactment of the opportunity in creative ways (new business models) is central to the process of entrepreneurship.

Opportunity exploitation is an evolutionary process, though not linear and often stochastic in nature. The venturing process starts with the discovery of an opportunity to the parsimonious use of resources (e.g., capital, labor, and materials) differently than they are currently being used.[42] Again, the creation of a venture is not an event but almost always an evolutionary process, during which entrepreneurs engage in venturing activities such as the acquisition of the requisite competences and resources to realize the venture opportunity's commercial value and the formation of a team.[43] Most genuine opportunities are much bigger than either the talent or capacity of the team or the initial resources available to the team.[44] The role of the lead entrepreneur and the team is to juggle all of these key elements in a changing environment.[45] Organizing these activities is central to the successful creation of a new firm.[46] Successful assemblage and organization is depicted in the Timmons model (Figure 1.1).

We illustrate the entrepreneurial process in the Timmons model as equal size of the circles and therefore assume balance in the model. It is important to understand that perfect balance might never exist for a new venture. And, the striving for balance is a never-ending entrepreneurial behavior. The shape, size, and depth of the opportunity establishes the required shape, size, and depth of both the resources and the team. We have found that many people are a bit uncomfortable viewing the opportunity and resources somewhat precariously balanced by the team. It is especially disconcerting to some because we show the three key elements of the entrepreneurial process as circles, and thus the balance appears tenuous. These reactions are justified, accurate, and realistic. Those who recognize the risks better manage the process and garner more return.

Though the entrepreneurial process is dynamic, it is important to understand each component, or driving force, of the Timmons model. We begin with a discussion of opportunity.

The Opportunity: Identification and Evaluation

At the heart of the entrepreneurial process is the opportunity.[47–52] Generally, entrepreneurs possess distinct cognitive processing skills and capacity that aid opportunity recognition and exploitation.[53] The main theoretical advances regarding opportunity are sourced from Hayek on the dispersed nature of knowledge and Kirzner on entrepreneurial alertness.[54–56] Much of the current theoretical and empirical work on opportunity recognition has focused on the construct of alertness, and in particular its utility in distinguishing entrepreneurs from nonentrepreneurs.[57–60] Kirzner focused on the individual's propensity to recognize opportunity through a process of discovery and posited that entrepreneurs are alert individuals able to identify opportunities when markets are in states of disequilibrium.[61]

Differences in alertness have been attributed to cognitive frameworks developed through possessed knowledge that has come through experience.[62, 63] Shane argues that existing market knowledge, experience in serving markets, and in-depth understanding of customer problems influences both opportunity recognition and opportunity exploitation processes.[64] Existing knowledge relates to mental schemas that allow one individual to have acute observation skills relative to others leading to a level of alertness conducive for opportunity capture.[65] The way different individuals respond to the same innovation stimulus is related to their particular knowledge and understanding of the processes in which they are currently involved. Therefore, it is important to note that separating individuals from the context of their previous and current environment can provide misleading indicators of entrepreneurial propensity. The holistic nature of entrepreneurship is an important qualifier of research, analysis, and execution.

Successful entrepreneurs and investors know that a good idea is not necessarily a good opportunity. In fact, for every 100 ideas presented to venture capitalists in the form of a business plan or proposal of some kind, only one or two ever receive formal funding.[66] Over 80 percent of those rejections occur in the first few hours; another 10 to 15 percent are rejected after investors have read the business plan carefully. Less than 10 percent attract enough interest to merit thorough due diligence and investigation over several weeks, and even months.[67] These are very slim odds. An important skill, whether one is an entrepreneur or an investor, is to be able to quickly evaluate whether serious potential exists, and to decide how much time and effort to invest.

Opportunities have the qualities of being attractive, durable, and timely and are anchored in products or services that create or add value for customers or end users.[68] The most successful entrepreneurs, venture capitalists, and private investors (business angels) are opportunity focused and maintain a keen understanding of the customer and market. Although formal market research may provide useful information and reduce market uncertainties, intuition of "gut feel" based on experience should not be discounted in evaluating market potential.[69] Some researchers have described this intuition in terms of prior knowledge of a particular field that provides individuals the capacity to recognize certain opportunities.[70] For truly innovative products and services, the market may indicate need or acceptance. Customer information and perceived need is of limited use for breakthrough innovation. Similarly, the promise of financial reward triggers an individual's motivated propensity to discover that opportunity.[71]

Beyond motivation and experience-based intuition, developing skill in opportunity analysis adds rigor to the subjective nature of opportunity identification and evaluation. Opportunity evaluation requires analysis at three levels: market demand at the customer level, market size and structure at the industry level, and margin analysis at the organization level.

Assessing market demand requires an understanding of the target market, customer access points, and customer perception of the price-value relationship. In other words, entrepreneurs must exhibit knowledge of market demand in order to provide some confidence to investors regarding the durability of the product or service. Perhaps the most important metric of market demand is the customer perception of value. An early return to the customer, as valued by the customer, enhances the likelihood that an idea will gain traction and prove to be a sustainable opportunity. That is why the customer value proposition is so aptly named. Value to the customer in the earliest period of time supports the notion that the new venture is differentiated from the competition. The longer it takes for a customer to perceive value the more risk inherent in the opportunity.

Initial customer acceptance is not enough to support high potential opportunities. Evidence of market share and growth potential equally underpins the high potential opportunity.[72] A truly valuable product or service gains market share. A low market share projection, sometimes called conservative by the business plan author, is a signal to investors that the entrepreneur is not confident in the customer value proposition. Understanding available channels has significant implications for market share and makes timing and cost assumptions more accurate; it also helps the entrepreneur better understand the value proposition of potential channel partners. Channel partners can be important resource providers.

The size of an opportunity is determined by the depth of its impact. Thus, market structure and size are necessary antecedents of high potential opportunities.[73, 74] An emerging and/or fragmented market is the most fertile territory for the seed of a new opportunity to germinate. An emerging market is one in which there is a foreseeable escalating increase in market demand. New demand can be satisfied by the entering firm and customers can be less difficult to acquire than taking business from an existing competitor. A fragmented market is one in which there are no clear market leaders. As a result, a new entrant to a fragmented market has considerable opportunity for consolidation. Current demand from a fragmented supply base signals need and potential upside value. Additionally, proprietary assets of the new entrant signals differentiation and imply greater durability of the new venture.

Margin analysis exhibits the financial manifestation of an opportunity and is a differentiator between idea and opportunity.[75] The willingness of the marketplace to reward the new firm must eventually surface in the financials and margins. Some researchers support this view, stating that new ventures penalize themselves unless they compete directly with the market leaders, including competing on the basis of price.[76] When vetting ideas the entrepreneur must articulate the manner in which competitive advantages will emerge as margin advantages. Examples of margin advantages include: low-cost provider with robust gross margin; low capital requirement relative to the competition yielding a higher return on invested capital; and shortness of time to cash breakeven correlates with lower risk of venture failure.

In short, the greater the growth, size, durability, and robustness of the gross and net margins and free cash flow, the greater the opportunity. The more imperfect the market, the greater the opportunity. The greater the rate of change, the discontinuities, and chaos, the greater is the opportunity. The greater the inconsistencies in existing service and quality, in lead times and lag times, and the greater the vacuums and gaps in information and knowledge, the greater is the opportunity. Assuming that the opportunity is present, successful opportunity capture depends on the appropriate resource base.

Resources: Creative and Parsimonious

One of the most common misconceptions among untried, nascent entrepreneurs is that all resources must be in place, especially cash, in order to succeed with a venture. The rationale behind such misconceived logic is that an extensive resource base will somehow reduce the perceived risk of starting a new venture. Money follows high potential opportunities conceived of and led by a strong management team. In other words, there is a shortage of quality entrepreneurs and opportunities, not funding. Successful entrepreneurs devise ingeniously creative strategies to marshal and gain control of resources.[77]

The entrepreneur's resource mantra is "minimize and control versus maximize and own" as well as "think cash last."[78] In other words, creative resource marshaling is the art of bootstrapping, which allows entrepreneurs to use resources they may not necessarily own.[79] Leasing rather than buying equipment, working out of a garage before renting space, using credit cards as the sole source of start-up capital, using an advisory board rather than hiring consultants are all examples of bootstrapping. Resource parsimony is a source of competitive advantage for the new venture. Some scholars have argued that too many resources can hinder growth because the firm will lack discipline.[80] The leanness of a new venture encourages creative resource marshalling, a seminal entrepreneurial behavior.[81, 82]

Yet creative resource marshaling is often dependent on the entrepreneur's ability to develop social networks to build a resource base and begin to establish legitimacy for their venturing activities.[83–86] Laumann, Galskeiwicz, and Mardsen defined a social network as "a set of nodes (e.g., persons, organizations) linked by a set of social relationships (e.g., friendship, transfer of funds, overlapping membership) of a specified type."[87] Birley stated that entrepreneurs draw from informal (friends, family, colleagues) and formal (SBA, banks, venture capitalists) networks for resources.[88] Schell developed the notion of "community entrepreneurship" created by formal and informal networks that link the entrepreneurial community to the more powerful organizations in a community.[89] Lipparini and Sobrero argued that entrepreneurs form interfirm linkages to overcome their individual organization's size limitation.[90] Based on network research, it can be concluded that likelihood of venture success is highly correlated to experience and tenure because the more experienced entrepreneurs are likely to have extended networks.

Networks give access to resources but start-up resources are not homogenous. The type of resources needed is determined by the nature of the opportunity as well as the development stage of the business. Resources acquired too early will sit idle; therefore, timing of acquisition is important to ensure timely arrival for competitive posturing. Resource typologies are many. The traditional economic classification of land, labor, and equipment has been expanded by management scholars. Hofer and Schendel classify resources as financial, physical, human, and organizational, which is similar to Barney's classification.[91, 92] Broader classifications include tangible and intangible and general and specific.[93–95]

In sum, the type of resource needed for new venture creation goes far beyond the demand for financial resources; thinking cash first is often to the demise of the new venture. Gathering other, more specific, resources in a creative fashion will often be a source of competitive differentiation. However, the goal is to develop resources that are valuable, inimitable, durable, and value capturing leading to competitive superiority.[96] For the new venture, resources evolve from bootstrapped resources to mature assets as they are developed, leveraged, eventually invested, and continuously upgraded.

The Entrepreneurial Team

Few high-growth ventures are stared without the assembly of an experience and skilled team.[97] Venture capitalist John Doerr reaffirms father of American venture capital General George Doriot's dictum: I prefer a Grade A entrepreneur and team with a Grade B idea, over a Grade B team with a Grade A idea. Doerr stated, "In the world today, there's plenty of technology, plenty of entrepreneurs, plenty of money, plenty of venture capital. What's in short supply is great teams. Your biggest challenge will be building a great team."[98] Famous investor Arthur Rock articulated the importance of the team over a decade ago.[99] He put it this way: "If you can find good people, they can always change the product. Nearly every mistake I've made has been because I picked the wrong people, not the wrong idea."[100] At the apex of new ventures is not a single entrepreneur; rather, there is an entrepreneurial team that drives the start-up and growth of the new venture.[101] Rapid growth can place great pressures on an entrepreneurial firm. A team of multitalented people is often necessary to manage such pressures and overcome obstacles to continued, rapid growth.

The mode of team formation, like resources previously discussed, must be mapped to the opportunity. Different modes of entrepreneurial team formation exist.[102] First, the lead entrepreneur has the business idea and then builds a team to develop the new venture. Second, a team of entrepreneurs recognize an opportunity and develops the idea to fruition. Finally, the team is developed over a period of time. For example, the lead entrepreneur recruits a CFO but waits until product development is complete to recruit a marketing executive to lead commercialization efforts.

As with our discussion on resources, the ability to develop a high performing entrepreneurial team is often dependent on the lead entrepreneur's social network. Dubini and Aldrich distinguished between weak ties and strong ties in an entrepreneur's network.[103] They argued that the diversity of an entrepreneur's network is correlated to the scope of perceived opportunities available.[104] Strong ties are considered to be direct relationships such as family, friends, and colleagues. Conversely, weak ties are indirect relationships such as venture capitalists, trade associations, and banks. It has been argued that too many strong ties and not enough weak ties can limit the entrepreneur and his potential for resource acquisition because strong ties are often with like-minded individuals.[105]

THE HOLISTIC AND INTEGRATED APPROACH OF THE TIMMONS MODEL

The Timmons model depicts a holistic entrepreneurial process. By that we mean it connects opportunity, team, and resources. An impact on any one of the driving forces necessarily affects the other dimensions of the process. The connections among the key drivers is shown as a dotted line, not a solid line because the driving forces will never connect perfectly and create impenetrable barriers to exogenous forces. Uncertainty will, to some extent, influence every new venture and increase the risk of the deal. But the entrepreneur can tighten the bonds among the driving forces through leadership, creativity, and communications.

Importance of Fit and Balance

The concept of fit and balance between and among opportunity, resources, and team is key to understanding the entrepreneurial process. The literature tends to an analysis of the individual entrepreneur's ability to balance the requirements necessary for opportunity recognition and exploitation.[106] It alludes to a systematic balancing of the myriad of variables but tends to focus on the array of variables associated with individual characteristics or behaviors in search of opportunity in a state of disequilibrium. Market equilibrium adjustments via new venture opportunities have a long history of research focus, but equilibrium within a venture is scantly reviewed.[107–109] Venkataraman discusses the equilibration of stakeholder value in the entrepreneurial process.[110] All new ventures require a diverse set of stakeholders to succeed: founders, investors, suppliers, customers, and so on. These stakeholders have vested interests in the entrepreneurial equation. The entrepreneur and founding team must find the balance among the venture variables that generally satisfy the universe of venture stakeholders, which implies a constant balance challenge in the entrepreneurial process.

The Timmons model is explicit. Where there is imbalance there is risk. The model provides a broad framework within which key driving forces can be reviewed and researched. It is the balancing of the key drivers that is at the heart of the model. The positioning of circles on the model is not random. The entrepreneurial team is positioned at the bottom of the triangle in the Timmons model (Figure 1.1). Imagine the founder, entrepreneurial leader of the venture, standing on a large ball, grasping the triangle over her head. The challenge is to balance the balls above her head, without toppling. This imagery is helpful in appreciating the constant balancing act since opportunity, team, and resources rarely match. When envisioning a company's future using this imagery, the entrepreneur can ask herself; what pitfalls will I encounter to get to the next boundary of success? Will my current team be large enough, or will we be over our heads if the company grows 30 percent over the next two years? Are my resources sufficient (or too abundant)? The list of questions is infinite with very few correct answers.

The potential for attracting outside funding for a proposed venture depends on this overall fit, and how the investor believes he or she can add value to this fit, and improve the fit, risk–reward ratio, and odds for success.

Importance of Timing

Equally important is the timing of the entrepreneurial process. Each of these unique combinations occurs in real time, where the hourglass drains continually, and may be friend, foe, or both. However, the literature supports the importance of prior knowledge to opportunity capture. As a result the opportunity presented to an inexperienced entrepreneur can look very different from a skilled and experienced entrepreneur. Stephenson and Roberts urge researchers to connect with the realities of practice by (in part) understanding the specific temporal issues facing entrepreneurs.[111] Seminal work on venture capital returns in the semiconductor industry noted timing variances' important impact on initial public offering and overall return.[112] Decisiveness in recognizing and seizing the opportunity can make all the difference, particularly when the sand disappearing from the hourglass is cash. In fact, there is no such thing as the perfect time to take advantage of an opportunity. Most new businesses run out of money before they can find a sufficient customer-based and experienced team to make it to the next level. Time and place are consumer marketplace and capital marketplace phenomena. Opportunity is a moving target.

The Impact of Leadership, Creativity, and Communication

Despite the fact that the popular press has turned entrepreneurs into rock stars, individual leadership in the creation of business is an essential ingredient of the entrepreneurial process. The entrepreneurial leader is one who focuses the new organization on the nature of the opportunity and takes action to move the venture forward.[113] The entrepreneurial leader sets the work climate as one of urgency. But entrepreneurial leaders also recognize that while the biggest opportunities are found in space that is most uncertain, teams can be paralyzed by ambiguity. Doig and Hargrove researched the use of social networks and rhetoric in entrepreneurial leadership.[114] Simply stated, entrepreneurs inspire their teams to believe in the opportunity. Therefore, we show the greatest influence of leadership on the connection between the opportunity and the team.

Founders bring certainty to their efforts through real options mentality.[115] They make small investments of resources in a number of areas, keeping as many options open as possible. Experimentation and improvisation are commonplace. Most people understand that creativity is necessary for entrepreneurs to generate innovative concepts. But it is equally logical that entrepreneurs be creative to convince a varied set of stakeholders that value can be created and to marshal the resources necessary to exploit the opportunity. Novel approaches to problem-solving can often emerge when previously separate phenomena are combined, sometimes yielding a new set of stimuli.[116] The entrepreneurial process is a particularly rich environment for the combination of divergent forces. Indeed, our argument of a holistic perspective of the entrepreneurship process requires the combination or potential combination of ideas and events. What we have found is that this dynamic and sometimes hectic pace results in a unique perspective on resource marshaling. Some of the most creative thinking in a new venture involves the marshaling of resources to foster parsimony. Multiple stimuli collide with stark necessity and the result is a closer bond between the opportunity and the resources necessary for exploitation.

The entrepreneur has a unique responsibility in mediating the information flow within the team and among new venture stakeholders. Often this role is connected to the governance function of the organization. The requirement of sophisticated communications might be well exampled in the venture capital-backed new firm.[117] Venture capital funds represent other financial intermediaries and supply financial investment to the emergent company. They evaluate hundreds of business plans (a primary form of entrepreneurial communication), interact with the new firm (a second order of entrepreneurial communications), negotiate the supply of capital (a third order of entrepreneurial communications), and then typically serve as an active participant in the governance of the firm (the fourth level of entrepreneurial communications). A similar, albeit somewhat less intense, process occurs between the entrepreneur and suppliers, regulator customers, and host of other stakeholders. Communicating the value-creating nature of the opportunity is at the heart of all of these relationships.

SUMMARY WITH IMPLICATIONS
FOR PRACTICE AND TEACHING

John Doerr is a senior partner at one of the most famous and successful venture capital funds ever, Kleiner, Perkins, Caulfield and Byers, and by all accounts is the most influential venture capitalist of his generation. During his career he has been a highly disciplined student (and teacher) of the entrepreneurial process, investing in entrepreneurs who have created new industries such as Sun Microsystems, Compaq Computer, Lotus Development Corporation, Intuit, Genentech, Millennium, Netscape, and Amazon.com. He describes the understanding of the entrepreneurial process as the key to a vibrant economy. "In the past, entrepreneurs started businesses. Today they invent new business models. That's a big difference, and it creates huge opportunities."[118]

The Timmons model of the entrepreneurship process provides a framework for identifying and evaluating venture potential. It helps determine the viability of new business models and emphasizes rigor in opportunity assessment. The process is driven by opportunity but requires matched balance by the available resources and a highly evolved entrepreneurial team. Moderating the strengths of the relationships between opportunity, resources, and team is creativity, communication, and leadership. The business planning exercise is an analysis of fit and gaps between and among all components.

Any depiction of an entrepreneurial process has controllable components that can be assessed, influenced, and altered. Founders and investors focus on these forces during their careful due diligence process to analyze the risks and determine what changes can be made to improve a venture's chances of success. A common entrepreneurial trap is failing to move forward because of a perceived lack of resources. Too much attention is given to the entrepreneur's quest for funding, yet more attention needs to be given to opportunity identification and shaping as well as developing the Grade A team to further refine the opportunity and move forward as a high potential venture. Funding will find the big opportunity with an effective team.

At first glance, the Timmons model is purposefully simple yet the theoretical foundations of the model are highly complex and illustrate the dynamic nature of the entrepreneurship process. Remember the metaphor of the entrepreneur juggling three balls, each representing opportunity, resources, and team. Rarely are the balls the same size in practice; therefore, successful juggling is not easily achieved without constant shifts in order to maintain rhythm and balance. Furthermore, the components are time- and place-sensitive creating an inherent assumption regarding new ventures: no two ventures are alike and each requires significant analysis, due diligence, and thoughtful decision making. Simplicity in frameworks is needed to explore the territory of new opportunities for venture creation. It helps practicing and nascent entrepreneurs ask the very important questions related to opportunity evaluation and guides an internal discussion on the fits and gaps of the opportunity with the resources available and the current team in place. Course changes are inevitable in entrepreneurial pursuits and it is the wise entrepreneur that can recognize the need for change and alter the course as necessary.

Entrepreneurship research integrates multiple academic disciplines in an attempt to understand the dynamic process of new venture creation. It is well served by frameworks. While we present the Timmons model, by no means do we propose it is the only framework. But the key components of the model—opportunity, team, and resources—are essentially included in most perspectives of the entrepreneurial process. The temporal nature of the model requires researching and understanding entrepreneurship as a dynamic perspective.

The Timmons model is a constructive framework for teaching courses in entrepreneurship and new venture creation. Illustrating the Timmons model in practice through case study discussions, business plan writing projects, feasibility analyses, and other entrepreneurial problem-based exercises is very powerful in a course that requires disciplinary integration. Furthermore, the research literature that exists supporting the opportunity-resource-team framework is rich and extensive, which allows educators to teach at the intersection of theory and practice.

NOTES

1. Jeffry A. Timmons and Stephen Spinelli, *New Venture Creation for the 21st Century*, 7th ed. (New York: McGraw Hill, 2006).

2. S. Venkataraman, "The Distinctive Domain of Entrepreneurship Research," in *Advances in Entrepreneurship, Firm Emergence, and Growth*, eds. J. Katz and R. Brockhaus 3 (1997), 119–138.

3. Joseph Schumpeter, *Theory of Economic Development* (Cambridge, MA: Harvard University Press, 1934).

4. Ian MacMillan and Jerome Katz, "Idiosyncratic Milieus of Entrepreneurship Research: The Need for Comprehensive Theories," *Journal of Business Venturing* 7 (1992): 1–8.

5. Timmons and Spinelli, *New Venture Creation for the 21st Century.*

6. Jeffry A. Timmons, *Entrepreneurial and Leadership Developments in an Inner City Ghetto and a Rural Depressed Area*, unpublished doctoral dissertation, Graduate School of Business Administration, Harvard University, 1971.

7. Jeffry A. Timmons, *The Entrepreneurial Mind* (Andover, MA: Brickhouse, 1989).

8. Jeffry A. Timmons and William Bygrave, *Venture Capital at the Crossroads* (Cambridge, MA: Harvard Business School Press, 1992).

9. Timmons and Spinelli, *New Venture Creation for the 21st Century.*

10. Dimo P. Dimov, "The Nexus of Individual and Opportunity: Opportunity Recognition as a Learning Process," in *Frontiers of Entrepreneurship Research* (Wellesley, MA: Babson College, 2003).

11. Jerome Katz, "The Dynamics of Organizational Emergence: A Contemporary Group Formation Perspective," *Entrepreneurship Theory and Practice* 17, no. 3 (1993): 97–101.

12. Howard Aldrich, *Organizations Evolving* (London: Sage Publications, 1999).

13. James Chrisman, Alan Bauerschmidt, and Charles Hofer, "The Determinants of New Venture Performance," *Entrepreneurship Theory and Practice* 23, no. 1 (1998): 5–29.

14. Robert A. Baron, "Cognitive Mechanisms in Entrepreneurship: Why and When Entrepreneurs Think Differently Than Other People," *Journal of Business Venturing* 13, no. 4 (1998): 275–294.

15. Lowell W. Busenitz and Jay B. Barney, "Differences between Entrepreneurs and Managers in Large Organizations: Biases and Heuristics in Strategic Decision-Making," *Journal of Business Venturing* 12, no. 1 (1997): 9–30.

16. Judith B. Kamm and Aaron J. Nurick, "The Stages of Team Venture Formation: A Decision-Making Model," *Entrepreneurship Theory and Practice* 17, no. 2 (1993): 17–28.

17. Ronald K. Mitchell et al., "Toward a Theory of Entrepreneurial Cognition: Rethinking the People Side of Entrepreneurship Research," *Entrepreneurship Theory and Practice* 27, no. 2 (2002): 93–104.

18. Richard. T. Harrison and Claire. M. Leitch, "Entrepreneurship and Leadership: The Implications for Education and Development," *Entrepreneurship and Regional Development* 6 (1994): 111–125.

19. Howard Aldrich and Ted Baker, "Blinded by the Cites? Has There Been Progress in Entrepreneurship Research," in *Entrepreneurship 2000*, eds. Donald Sexton and Raymond Smilor (Chicago: Upstart, 1997), 377–400.

20. Per Davidsson and Johan Wiklund, "Levels of Analysis in Entrepreneurship Research: Current Research Practice and Suggestions for the Future," *Entrepreneurship Theory and Practice* 25, no. 4 (2001): 81–99.

21. William B. Gartner, "Is There an Elephant in Entrepreneurship? Blind Assumptions in Theory Development," *Entrepreneurship Theory and Practice* 25, no. 4 (2001): 27–40.

22. Timmons and Bygrave, *Venture Capital at the Crossroads.*

23. Ibid.

24. Scott Shane and S. Venkataraman, "The Promise of Entrepreneurship as a Field of Research," *Academy of Management Review* 25, no. 1 (2000): 217–226.

25. William D. Bygrave and Charles W. Hofer, "Theorizing about Entrepreneurship," *Entrepreneurship Theory and Practice* 16, no. 2 (1991): 13–22.

26. William B. Gartner, "Who Is an Entrepreneur? Is the Wrong Question," *Entrepreneurship Theory and Practice* 13, no. 4 (1988): 47–68.

27. Donald L. Sexton and Raymond W. Smilor, eds., *Entrepreneurship 2000* (Chicago: Upstart Publishing, 1997).

28. James W. Carland et al., "Differentiating Entrepreneurs from Small Business Owners: A Conceptualization," *Academy of Management Review* 9, no. 2 (1984): 354–359.

29. Timmons and Bygrave, *Venture Capital at the Crossroads.*

30. Venkataraman, "The Dinstinctive Domain of Entrepreneurship Research."

31. John B. Miner, *The Four Routes to Entrepreneurial Success* (San Francisco: Berrett-Koehler, 1996).

32. E. Holly Buttner and Nur Gryskiewicz, "Entrepreneurs' Problem-Solving Styles: An Empirical Study Using the Kirton Adaption/Innovation Theory," *Journal of Small Business Management* 31, no. 1 (1993): 22–31.

33. Rita McGrath, Ian MacMillan, and Sari Scheinberg, "Elitists, Risk-Takers, and Rugged Individualists? An Exploratory Analysis of Cultural Differences between Entrepreneurs and Non-Entrepreneurs," *Journal of Business Venturing* 7, no. 2 (1992): 115–135.

34. Candida Brush et al., "Doctoral Education in the Field of Entrepreneurship," *Journal of Management* 29, no. 3 (2003): 309–331.

35. Marc J. Dollinger, *Entrepreneurship: Strategies and Resources* (Burr Ridge, IL: Irwin, 1995).

36. Mitchell et al., "Toward a Theory of Entrepreneurial Cognition."

37. David J. Collis and Cynthia A. Montgomery, "Competing on Resources: Strategy in the 1990s," *Harvard Business Review* 73, no. 4 (1995): 118–128.

38. Bygrave and Hofer, "Theorizing about Entrepreneurship."

39. Aldrich, *Organizations Evolving.*

40. Arnold C. Cooper and Catherine M. Daily, "Entrepreneurial Teams," in *Entrepreneurship 2000,* eds. Donald L. Sexton and Ray W. Smilor (Chicago: Upstart, 1997), 127–150.

41. Israel Kirzner, *Competition and Entrepreneurship* (Chicago: University of Chicago Press, 1973).

42. Shane and Venkataraman, "The Promise of Entrepreneurship as a Field of Research."

43. David J. Teece, Gary Pisano, and Amy Shuen, "Dynamic Capabilities and Strategic Management," *Strategic Management Journal* 18, no. 7 (1997): 509–533.

44. Sue Birley, "The Role of Networks in the Entrepreneurial Process," *Journal of Business Venturing* 1 (1985): 107–117.

45. Paola Dubini and Howard Aldrich, "Personal and Extended Networks Are Central to the Entrepreneurial Process," *Journal of Business Venturing* 6, no. 5 (1991): 305–313.

46. Nancy M. Carter, William B. Gartner, and Paul D. Reynolds, "Exploring Start-Up Event Sequences," *Journal of Business Venturing* 11, no. 3 (1996): 151–166.

47. William B. Gartner, Nancy Carter, and Gerald Hills, "The Language of Opportunity," in *New Movements in Entrepreneurship,* eds. Chris Steyaert and Dan Hjorth (2003).

48. Andrew C. Corbett, "Recognizing High-Tech Opportunities: A Learning and Cognitive Approach," in *Frontiers of Entrepreneurship Research* (Wellesley, MA: Babson College, 2002).

49. Justin Craig and Noel Lindsay, "Quantifying 'Gut Feeling' in the Opportunity Recognition Process," in *Frontiers of Entrepreneurship Research* (Wellesley, MA: Babson College, 2001).

50. Dean A. Shepherd and Dawn R. DiTienne, "Prior Knowledge, Financial Reward, and Opportunity Identification," *Entrepreneurship Theory and Practice* 29, no. 1 (2005): 91–112.

51. Dean Shepherd and M. Levesque, "A Search Strategy for Assessing a Business Opportunity," *IEEE Transactions on Engineering Management* 49, no. 2 (2002): 140–154.

52. Mikael Samuelsson, "Modeling the Nascent Venture Opportunity Exploitation Process across Time," in *Frontiers of Entrepreneurship Research* (Wellesley, MA: Babson College, 2001).

53. Dimov, "The Nexus of Individual and Opportunity."

54. Friedrich Hayek, "The Use of Knowledge in Society," *American Economic* Review 35 (1945): 519–530.

55. Israel Kirzner, *Perception, Opportunity, and Profit* (Chicago: University of Chicago Press, 1979).

56. Dimov, "The Nexus of Individual and Opportunity."

57. Maria Minniti, "Entrepreneurial Alertness and Asymmetric Information in a Spin-Glass Model," *Journal of Business Venturing* 19, no. 5 (2004): 637–658.

58. Alexandaer Ardichvili, Richard Cardozo, and Sourav Ray, "A Theory of Entrepreneurial Opportunity Identification and Development," *Journal of Business Venturing* 18, no. 1 (2003): 105–123.

59. Connie Marie Gaglio and Jerome A. Katz, "The Psychological Basis of Opportunity Identification: Entrepreneurial Alertness," *Small Business Economics* 16, no. 2 (2001): 95–111.

60. L. W. Busenitz and J. B. Barney, "Differences between Entrepreneurs and Managers in Large Organizations: Biases and Heuristics in Strategic Decision-Making," *Journal of Business Venturing* 12 (1997): 9–30.

61. Israel Kirzner, *How Markets Work: Disequilibrium, Entrepreneurship, and Discovery,* Hobart Paper No. 133 (London: Institute of Economic Affairs, 1997).

62. Robert A. Baron, "Opportunity Recognition as Pattern Recognition: How Entrepreneurs 'Connect the Dots' to Identify New Business Opportunities," *Academy of Management Perspectives* 20, no. 1 (2006): 104–119.

63. Dimov, "The Nexus of Individual and Opportunity."

64. Scott Shane, "Prior Knowledge and the Discovery of Entrepreneurial Opportunities," *Organization Science* 11, no. 4 (2000): 448–469.

65. Gaglio and Katz, "The Psychological Basis of Opportunity Identification."

66. Timmons and Bygrave, *Venture Capital at the Crossroads.*

67. Ibid.

68. Timmons and Spinelli, *New Venture Creation for the 21st Century.*

69. Gerald E. Hills and Rodney C. Shrader, "Successful Entrepreneurs' Insights into Opportunity Recognition," in *Frontiers of Entrepreneurship Research* (Wellesley, MA: Babson College, 1998).

70. Venkataraman, "The Dinstinctive Domain of Entrepreneurship Research."

71. Kirzner, *Competition and Entrepreneurship*; Kirzner, *Perception, Opportunity, and Profit*; Kirzner, *How Markets Work: Disequilibrium, Entrepreneurship, and Discovery.*

72. Connie Marie Gaglio, "Opportunity Identification: Review, Critique, and Suggested Research Directions," in *Advances in Entrepreneurship, Firm Emergence and Growth,* ed. Jerome A. Katz 3 (1997), 139–202.

73. D. Orr, "The Determinants of Entry: A Study of the Canadian Manufacturing Industries," *Review of Economics and Statistics* 56 (1974): 58–66.

74. Thomas J. Dean and G. Dale Meyer, "Industry Environments and New Venture Formations in U.S. Manufacturing: A Conceptual and Empirical Analysis of Demand Determinants," *Journal of Business Venturing* 11 (1996): 107–132.

75. Arnold C. Cooper, William C. Dunkelberg, and Carolyn Y. Woo, "Optimists and Pessimists: Entrepreneurs and Their Perceived Chances for Success," in *Frontiers of Entrepreneurship Research* (Wellesley, MA: Babson College, 1986).

76. Ian MacMillan and Diana Day, "Corporate Ventures into Industrial Markets: Dynamics of Aggressive Entry," *Journal of Business Venturing* 2, no. 1 (1987): 29–40.

77. Danny Miller and Jamal Shamsie, "The Resource-Based View of the Firm in Two Environments: The Hollywood Film Studios from 1936 to 1965," *Academy of Management Journal* 39, no. 3 (1996): 519–543.

78. Timmons and Spinelli, *New Venture Creation for the 21st Century.*

79. Richard T. Harrison, Collin M. Mason, and Paul Girling, "Financial Bootstrapping and Venture Development in the Software Industry," *Entrepreneurship and Regional Development* 16, no. 4 (2004): 307–333.

80. James Clayton, Bradley Gambill, and Douglass Harned, "The Curse of Too Much Capital: Building New Businesses in Large Corporations," *McKinsey Quarterly* 4 (1999): 48–59.

81. Arthur Stinchombe, "Social Structure and Organizations," in *Handbook of Organizations,* ed. J.G. March (Chicago: Rand-McNally, 1965), 142–193.

82. Jay B. Barney, "Firm Resources and Sustained Competitive Advantage," *Journal of Management* 17, no. 1 (1991): 99–120.

83. Birley, "The Role of Networks in the Entrepreneurial Process."

84. Dubini and Aldrich, "Personal and Extended Networks Are Central to the Entrepreneurial Process."

85. Eric L. Hansen, "Entrepreneurial Networks and New Organization Growth," *Entrepreneurship Theory and Practice* 19, no. 4 (1995): 7–20.

86. Edward J. Malecki, "Entrepreneurs, Networks, and Economic Development: A Review of Recent Research," *Advances in Entrepreneurship, Firm Emergence, and Growth* 3 (1997): 57–118.

87. Edward Laumann, Joseph Galskeiwicz, and Peter Mardsen, "Community Structures as Interorganizational Linkages," *Annual Review of Sociology* 4 (1978): 455–484; 458.

88. Birley, "The Role of Networks in the Entrepreneurial Process."

89. D. W. Schell, "Entrepreneurial Activity: A Comparison of Three North Carolina Communities," in *Frontiers of Entrepreneurship Research* (Wellesley, MA: Babson College, 1983).

90. Andrea Lipparini and Maurizio Sobrero, "The Glue and the Pieces: Entrepreneurship and Innovation in Small-Firm Networks," *Journal of Business Venturing* 9, no. 2 (1994): 125–140.

91. Charles W. Hofer and Dan Schendel, *Strategy Formulation: Analytical Concepts* (St. Paul, MN: West, 1978).

92. Barney, "Firm Resources and Sustained Competitive Advantage."

93. Richard Hall, "A Framework for Linking Intangible Resources and Capabilities to Sustainable Competitive Advantage," *Strategic Management Journal* 14, no. 5 (1993): 607–618.

94. Kathleen R. Conner and C. K. Prahalad, "A Resource-Based Theory of the Firm: Knowledge versus Opportunism," *Organization Science* 7, no. 5 (1996): 477–501.

95. Collis and Montgomery, "Competing on Resources."

96. Barney, "Firm Resources and Sustained Competitive Advantage."

97. Cooper and Daily, "Entrepreneurial Teams."

98. Michael S. Malone, "John Doerr's Startup Manual," *Fast Company* (Feburary 1997): 82.

99. As one of the founding fathers of venture capital—and the man credited with coining the term—Rock has been a major player in the development of the Valley. Working with Thomas J. Davis Jr. in the firm Davis and Rock, as well as on his own (as Arthur Rock and Co.), Rock has backed many of the companies that make the Valley what it is today: Teledyne, Scientific Data Systems, Apple Computer, General Transistor, and Diasonics, to name a few.

100. Arthur Rock, "Strategy vs. Tactics from a Venture Capitalist," *Harvard Business Review* 65, no. 6 (1987): 63–67.

101. Judith B. Kamm et al., "Entrepreneurial Teams in New Venture Creation: A Research Agenda," *Entrepreneurship Theory and Practice* 14, no. 4 (1990): 7–17.

102. Cooper and Daily, "Entrepreneurial Teams."

103. Dubini and Aldrich, "Personal and Extended Networks Are Central to the Entrepreneurial Process."

104. Ibid.

105. Mark S. Granovetter, "The Strength of Weak Ties: A Network Theory Revisited," in *Social Structure and Network Analysis*, eds. G. P. Huber and William H. Glick (Beverly Hills, CA: Sage, 1982).

106. Dimov, "The Nexus of Individual and Opportunity."

107. Frank H. Knight, *Risk, Uncertainty, and Profit* (Boston: Houghton Mifflin, 1921).

108. Hayek, "The Use of Knowledge in Society."

109. Kirzner, *How Markets Work: Disequilibrium, Entrepreneurship, and Discovery.*

110. S. Venkataraman, *Stakeholder Value Equilibration and the Entrepreneurial Process*, Ruffin Lecture Series, University of Virginia, 2000.

111. Howard Stevenson, Michael Roberts, and Irving Grousbeck, *New Business Ventures and the Entrepreneur*, 3rd ed. (Homewood, IL: Irwin, 1989).

112. William Bygrave et al., "Venture Capital High-Tech Investments: Can We Differentiate the Best from the Worst," *Frontiers of Entrepreneurship Research* (Wellesley, MA: Babson College, 1999).

113. Rita McGrath and Ian MacMillan, *The Entrepreneurial Mindset: Strategies for Continuously Creating Opportunity in an Age of Uncertainty* (Boston: Harvard Business School Press, 2000).

114. Jameson Doig and Erwin C. Hargrove, eds., *Leadership and Innovation: A Biographical Perspective on Entrepreneurs and Government* (Baltimore: Johns Hopkins University Press, 1987).

115. McGrath and MacMillan, *The Entrepreneurial Mindset.*

116. Thomas B. Ward, "Cognition, Creativity and Entrepreneurship," *Journal of Business Venturing* 19, no. 2 (2004): 173–188.

117. Sydel Sokuvitz and Stephen Spinelli, "Forming Perceptions of Entrepreneurial Discourse: The Effectiveness of Oral or Transcribed Communication," conference paper, Association for Business Communication, Cambridge, MA, October 2004, http://businesscommunication.org/conventions/Proceedings/2004/PDFs/12ABC04.PDF.

118. Malone, "John Doerr's Startup Manual."

2

Idea Generation from a Creativity Perspective

Dimo Dimov

There is strong agreement that somewhere early in the entrepreneurial process there is an encounter between individuals and opportunities, and this encounter is a distinct and defining feature of the process.[1-6] The accumulating evidence on nascent entrepreneurs (i.e., people committing time and resources to founding new firms) suggests that thinking seriously about a potential business is among the very first events to occur as these individuals enter the entrepreneurial process.[7, 8] Understanding the origin of the business idea (i.e., the recognition and subsequent development of an opportunity) is thus a major milestone in entrepreneurship research. The challenge for researchers, however, is that the original business idea is both ephemeral and fragile in nature, easily distorted by the subsequent unfolding of events and people's post hoc rationalization of them—success turns the idea into a proactive vision, while failure turns it into naivete.

The purpose of this chapter is to review, critique, and direct the research progress on our understanding of the early gestation of business idea (i.e., the idea generation phase of the entrepreneurial process). I start from the assumption that ideas are very important. They are the birth of the entrepreneurial process. Some of them are developed into opportunities while others are abandoned along the way. Ex ante, however, it is close to impossible to discern or foresee the path that a particular idea will take. For this reason, to the extent that we are interested in their emergence, all ideas should be treated equally. I acknowledge, however, that the distinction between idea and opportunity has not been clearly made and accepted. For this reason, I attempt to draw a more formal conceptual separation between the two in the next section.

Entrepreneurship is not the only field interested in the origin of ideas. Neither is it the most advanced. The study of creativity, "the production of novel and useful ideas by an individual or small group of individuals working together," although not accelerated until the 1950s, represents a long and advanced tradition in social and cognitive psychology.[9] In many senses, including intuition, the study of idea generation in the domain of entrepreneurship entails the study of creativity.[10] In addition, creativity further enriches the entrepreneurial process through its role in how ideas, once emerged, are shaped and developed. However, a comprehensive review of this broader literature is beyond the scope of this chapter. (Those interested in this broader literature should review the special issues of journals in this field—*Journal of Creative Behavior* and *Creativity Research Journal.*) I will use some of the more established ideas in it to frame and organize the work in the field of entrepreneurship that has dealt, directly or indirectly, with the topic of idea generation. This will help expose research gaps and thus suggest directions for further research progress.

One of the central ideas in the broader creativity literature is that explaining creativity necessitates an interactionist perspective and thus a constellation of factors: process, product, person, and situation.[11] Woodman and Schoenfeldt suggest that creativity involves a complex interaction between a person and a given situation.[12, 13] While the individual faces the situation with an arsenal of antecedent skills and predispositions—knowledge, cognitive skills, and noncognitive traits—the situation may further facilitate or inhibit the individual's creative accomplishment. What the interactionist perspective suggests, however, is that if we studied the two elements in isolation, there will be a large unexplained component that remains. As I will argue in this chapter, while there has been a growing application of insights from the creativity literature to the field of entrepreneurship, these insights have been limited to only some of the elements mentioned earlier, namely person and process. Therefore, in order to advance entrepreneurship research in this direction, we need to understand the complexities of the creative product and situation as well as their interaction with the creative person and process.

IDEA VERSUS OPPORTUNITY

Are ideas and opportunities distinct? We often teach our students that not every idea is a good opportunity, thereby implying that what is interesting and what has commercial viability are two distinct considerations. Pushing this further, I argue that every opportunity has an initial idea as its progeny (i.e., someone must have thought about it for it to ever become a subject of human discussion). These two arguments suggest that opportunities are nested within the realm of ideas. In other words, ideas are necessary but not sufficient condition for opportunities to emerge. The sufficiency condition is established through accumulating evidence and conviction of commercial viability, existence of potential market, ability to generate profit, and ability to sustain this profit over time in the face of (increasing) competition.

As they become shaped and developed into opportunities, ideas almost never survive in their original form. In fact, in most cases their original form is probably too fuzzy and therefore needs a lot of elaboration and specification. Idea shaping and development require the engagement of other people and, in many cases, parts of an entire organization. The path from idea to opportunity, to the extent that it exists or is found, is therefore an inherently social process of continuous learning. Crossan and colleagues present a formal model, the 4I framework, of the stages and subprocesses that lay between some initial "Aha!" and a venture being launched.[14, 15] This process occurs at three distinct levels: individual, group, and organizational. These levels are linked through four social and psychological processes: intuiting, interpreting, integrating, and institutionalizing (hence the 4I name). At each stage of this process, there is tension between the decision to continue or to abandon the refinement and pursuit of the developing idea. A brief elaboration of this process would help us place the current discussion in the broader entrepreneurial process.

Intuiting is "the preconscious recognition of the pattern and/or possibilities inherent in a personal stream of experience."[16] This is the "cognitive cradle" where ideas are generated. At this stage, individuals simply become aware of what they perceive as holding some potential in meeting current or emerging customer needs.[17] These initial ideas tend to be very basic—simply a sense that something is possible—and there is no way of judging these as right or wrong at this stage. *Interpreting* is "the explaining, through words and/or actions, of an insight or idea to one's self and to others."[18] In this process, potential entrepreneurs engage in explaining, defending, and ultimately shaping the "fuzzy" images of their insights. They thus interact not only with their immediate social network—family, friends, classmates, colleagues, teachers, and so on—but also with some potentially more instrumental stakeholders to the development of the idea: partners, informal and formal investors, consultants, accountants, customers, suppliers, employees, and so on. Through these social interactions, shared understanding of the opportunity idea begins to emerge and thus the overall learning process enters the *integrating* phase. This is the stage at which a nascent entrepreneurial team may be formed as the idea shows continuing merit and induces an even more intensive pursuit. Finally, to the extent that the actions and dialogs associated with integrating become more intentional toward forming a venture in order to exploit the emerging opportunity, there is routinization involved that signifies the process of *institutionalizing*. At this final stage, the well-articulated contours of the idea drive the establishment of decision-making procedures as well as resource planning, acquisition, and organization.

I can summarize my line of thought so far using the following photography metaphor. Idea generation (i.e., intuiting in the model mentioned earlier) pertains to pointing the camera to a fuzzy object that one finds interesting and that one feels could develop into a good picture. Opportunity recognition, capturing the processes of interpreting and integrating, is an unfolding process of zooming, focusing, and adjusting the aperture and shutter speed that may (or may not) reveal that the picture is indeed there and worth making. This chapter is focused on idea generation and thus on the raw input to the entrepreneurial process. While I may use the terms *opportunity* and *opportunity recognition* in ways consistent with the original intentions of the reviewed research, I only draw implications for idea generation (i.e., the early birth of business ideas). As the generation of ideas is the main focus of the creativity literature, understanding creativity in an entrepreneurship context is an important foundation for our field. I have organized the remainder of the paper around the five main areas highlighted by the interactionist perspective on creativity—process, product, person, situation, and the interaction thereof—and conclude with overviews of future research directions and implications for practice.

THE CREATIVITY PROCESS

When pondering how great ideas occur, we intuitively accept, and scholars have duly formalized this intuition, that there is more or less a general process involved. This notion has also been introduced in entrepreneurship research, as evidenced by the continuous effort to identify just how business ideas are born. Because of the significant analogy between opportunity conception and creative insight, there have been several attempts to use a creativity process framework to explain opportunity recognition.

Process Stages

The main influence on the study of creative processes has been Wallas through his five-stage model.[19] The stages involved are preparation, incubation, insight, evaluation, and elaboration. Based on this model, the principal hypothesis guiding entrepreneurship researchers has been that entrepreneurs also follow these steps in conceiving of their business ideas. In their empirical approach, researchers have sought confirmation of this either by searching for common themes in the narratives of entrepreneurs on their early experience with their business ideas or by measuring the degree to which entrepreneurs agreed that they had indeed gone through these stages. In perhaps the earliest study, Long and McMullan, using a small-scale exploratory approach, found support for and proposed a refinement to the original model, consisting of four stages: prevision, point of vision, opportunity elaboration, and decision to proceed.[20] Hills, Shrader, and Lumpkin asked 187 business owners/entrepreneurs about the degree to which they agreed with the thirty-one statements about the opportunity recognition process. Using a factor analysis, they showed that there was good consistency with the model proposed by Wallas.[21, 22] They also extended that model by suggesting that the creative process was a staged one, involving feedback loops between the stages of preparation, incubation, and insight. In their latest elaboration of the model, the five stages are grouped into two main stages—discovery and formation—with a refined elaboration of the feedback loops among the stages.[23] The empirical test of this refined model has met mixed support.[24]

Cognitive Processes

In addition to the general stages describing the process, there has also been interest in the type of thinking employed by entrepreneurs in generating their ideas. Most of the insights here have come from cognitive psychology, a discipline with a long tradition of studying the nature and emergence of insights. I use the term *insight* as representing the process through which a person suddenly moves from a state of not knowing to a state of knowing.[25] Finke further distinguishes between convergent and divergent insight on the basis of the interplay between function and form that they involve: convergent insight is of a form-follows-function type, while divergent insight is of a function-follows-form type.[26] The former involves making sense out of apparently disconnected facts, while the latter is outward flowing, generating possibilities that one might not ordinarily consider.[27, 28] More recent theoretical developments in the entrepreneurship field stress the role of creative cognition, specifically the usage of conceptual combination, analogy, and initial problem formulation in conceiving of opportunities.[29]

Search Processes

While idea generation can certainly be influenced by what goes on in entrepreneurs' heads, it may also be influenced by what entrepreneurs do. In particular, how one goes about searching for information or simply following their gut feeling could plausibly make one more or less likely to spark with ideas. Following in the Carnegie tradition of bounded rationality, attention driven behavior, and problemistic search, entrepreneurship researchers exploring this area have added an important motivation angle to the study of the idea generation process.[30] Since the nature of an insight is greatly dependent on the information available to the individual, how individuals go about searching for information is an important aspect of the process. Notwithstanding the value or personality reasons for seeking entrepreneurial careers, search is driven by the perception that particular aspirations have not been met.[31, 32] The motivated search model, proposed by Heron and Sapienza applies the concept of problemistic search to the context of entrepreneurship by specifying the conditions that propel individuals toward searching for business opportunities.[33] Specifically, they suggest that individuals engage in problemistic search when their current performance is below their aspiration level. In an empirical setting, consistent with the aforementioned predictions, Sine and David showed that environmental jolts shook the institutional logics of incumbent organizations and induced search for new logics, thereby creating an environment of increased ability to discern opportunities.[34]

Motivated search, however, is one of several possible ways for the initiation of the opportunity recognition process. Bhave proposed a model for the venture creation process, which suggested two separate paths leading to opportunity recognition.[35] In the first path, the process initiates with a decision to start a business, while in the second it starts with a recognized need to which a solution is developed. Another distinction made among the search processes is that of directed search and chance occurrences. For example, Long and McMullan found that the path to opportunity vision could lead through either deliberate search or serendipity.[36] The distinction between search and serendipity is also reflected in other early work on this subject.[37]

More recently, there has been active interest in developing more formal classifications of search processes. Chandler, Dahlqvist, and Davidsson developed a taxonomy of opportunity recognition processes by examining the emerging business initiatives of 136 Swedish ventures.[38] They identified three distinct processes: proactive search, reactive search, and fortuitous discovery. Proactive search is exploratory in nature and capitalizes on unique knowledge; reactive search is triggered by poor performance, consistent with Heron and Sapienza's model mentioned earlier; fortuitous discovery pertains to unexpected events involving no search. Similarly, Chandler, DeTienne, and Lyon developed a typology of opportunity detection/development process based on a survey of accomplished entrepreneurs.[39] They also identified three distinct processes: opportunity as a solution to a specific personal problem, opportunity as a solution to a market problem, and opportunity as created, whereby individuals act on their (bold) imagination to disrupt existing market structures and establish new ones. Although all three processes involve active search and fortuitous discovery, they are distinct in the way the process of opportunity recognition is triggered. Overall, where studies have sought to examine the relative prevalence of these search approaches, the empirical results have shown that there is no dominance of one approach over the other.[40–42]

In addition to the type of search employed by entrepreneurs, researchers have also examined the intensity of search, focusing on the amount or type of information sought. Cooper, Folta, and Woo found that the intensity of search was negatively related to prior entrepreneurial experience, domain differences, and confidence.[43] Finally, several studies have looked directly at the sources of opportunity ideas. Almost all sources are, in one way or another, related to the entrepreneurs' prior experience and undertaken action.[44, 45] In a survey of 483 small businesses, Peterson found that spontaneous thoughts had the highest frequency (24 percent), followed by competitor imitation (18 percent) and scanning of business periodicals (11 percent).[46] In a more systematic study, Cooper and colleagues distinguished between professional and personal sources of information and related their usage to the prior experience of entrepreneurs.[47]

They found that the use of professional sources was positively related to domain similarity, while the use of personal sources was negatively related to prior entrepreneurial experience and domain similarity, and positively related to domain differences. Simon and Houghton elaborated further on the entrepreneurs' search processes by providing a theoretical examination of the effects of decision environments, specifically firm age and the introduction of pioneering products.[48] They argue that entrepreneurs in younger firms exhibit more active search and rely more on personal and external sources of information. Further, entrepreneurs striving to introduce pioneering products also exhibit more active search and rely more on personal and external sources of information.

To recapitulate, the process of idea generation has been studied from various angles—from the general stages that the process entails to the more specific cognition and search behaviors that entrepreneurs employ. Perhaps the main deficiency in this area comes from the predominant focus on retroactive accounts of how ideas came about. This poses the well-recognized problems of recollection bias and highlights the need for research that is more contemporaneous with the ideas it studies. In this regard, there is a ripe opportunity to employ the more rigorous research designs that have by now been well established in creativity and cognition research as well as rich qualitative studies.[49] Some of the design possibilities include field observations, field and lab experiments as well as surveys that allow the collection of rich, contextual data.

THE CREATIVITY PERSON

Given the alluded importance of perception, courage, and action for entrepreneurship, one of the oldest research traditions in entrepreneurship has focused on understanding how entrepreneurs differ from the general population in terms of various personal characteristics.[50] In a sense, this mirrors similar developments in the study of great creative persons or great leaders.[51, 52] Similar to these fields, there have been strong criticisms of the trait paradigm, mainly stemming from its failure to account for the diversity among entrepreneurs and the situations they face.[53] As a consequence, there have been suggestions to redirect the study of entrepreneurs toward a focus on behaviors rather than traits.[54] Nevertheless, it has been argued that personality remains an important general predictor of behavior, once specific mediating factors are considered.[55] In the more complex social context of creativity, it is now well accepted that there are three individual factors—cognitive, knowledge, and intrinsic motivation—that are instrumental in accounting for differences in creative outcomes.[56, 57] With the understanding that personality characteristic and specific attitudes affect one's motivation to generate ideas and eventually become an entrepreneur, I will focus in the remainder of this section on the cognitive and knowledge differences among individuals.[58]

Differences in Cognitive Abilities

In the last decade, the emphasis on individuality has staged a strong come-back, through the introduction of a cognitive perspective to entrepreneurship, focusing on the entrepreneurs' unique mental representations of the world.[59–61] Using the conceptual advancement and widening popularity of cognitive psychology, this new paradigm has produced influential studies on the specific and distinguishing characteristics of entrepreneurs that have created some convergence among researchers in regard to the uniqueness of entrepreneurial cognition.[62–64] The cognitive perspective currently represents a powerful theoretical tool in the study of opportunity recognition.[65–68]

In the transition of ideas from cognitive psychology to entrepreneurship, however, there has been a conceptual twist. While cognitive psychology is typically blind to individual differences (i.e., it looks for commonality among people in the mental processes they use), entrepreneurship researchers have, for the most part, assumed that entrepreneurs are somehow better at the processes conducive to idea generation. In keeping with the long and powerful mystique of the entrepreneur, there has been a shifted focus from process to the person.[69] Thus, while many of the perspectives discussed later could easily be perceived as process-focused, their underlying assumption is that the processes discussed apply differently to entrepreneurs versus nonentrepreneurs.

Perhaps the main and most influential idea guiding this research domain has been on the construct of alertness as a distinguishing characteristic of entrepreneurs.[70] Alertness is not a simple possession of knowledge, but rather involves knowing where to obtain and deploy information. Fundamentally, it is the quality (or state of mind) necessary for the discovery of hitherto unknown profit opportunities; it is the "motivated propensity of man to formulate an image of the future."[71] Alertness is considered a personal trait and is assigned a "primordial role" in the Austrian approach.[72, 73] In the subsequent building on Kirzner's work, researchers have tried to establish a more concrete conceptualization of alertness, in terms of distinct cognitive skills or behaviors.

Entrepreneurial cognitions represent "the knowledge structures that people use to make assessments, judgments, or decisions involving opportunity evaluation, venture creation, and growth."[74] Further, it is about "understanding how entrepreneurs use simplifying mental models to piece together previously unconnected information that helps them to identify and invent new products or services, and to assemble the necessary resources to start and grow businesses."[75] In regard to its influence on idea generation, I have discerned three main topics, based on what Ucbasaran and colleagues define as the components of strong entrepreneurial cognition, namely the usage of heuristics, higher-level learning, and off-line evaluation.[76]

With regard to the usage of heuristics, empirical studies have sought to extend the findings from the cognitive psychology literature on heuristics and biases in decision making, pioneered by Kahneman and Tversky, to the context of entrepreneurs.[77] They have thus demonstrated that entrepreneurs use more heuristics than managers and that, cognitive biases are an essential contributor to risk perception and the decision to start a venture.[78–80] In reflecting on this work, Alvarez and Busenitz argue that it is this heuristic-based thinking that gives entrepreneurs the distinct capability to discover opportunities.[81] However, in comparing entrepreneurs and managers in terms of having analytical versus intuitive cognitive styles, Allinson and colleagues found that while entrepreneurs were more intuitive than the general population of managers, they were also no different from senior managers and executives.[82]

Higher-level learning pertains to the achievement of new understanding and interpretations.[83] One conceptualization of this process has focused on the usage of mental schemas, which represent individuals' understanding of how the external world works.[84] In this context, entrepreneurial, alertness is viewed as a particular schema that is of higher complexity and flexibility, and that involves heightened sensitivity to market disequilibrium signals.[85] Finally, offline evaluation is related to the concepts of mental simulations and counterfactual thinking, which pertain to reflection over past and future events and are seen as a distinctive feature of opportunity finders.[86, 87] In an attempt to further focus the application of concepts and findings from cognitive science to the study of opportunity recognition, Baron argues that perception, schemas, and self-regulation of behavior all provide valuable insight into the opportunity recognition process.[88] As most of these presented arguments have been theoretical, one of the main gaps that needs to be filled is the empirical testing and theoretical refinement of this perspective.

While the various aspects of entrepreneurial cognition have greatly enhanced one's theoretical arsenal for studying idea generation, one significant gap remains: explaining why, other than by assumption and definition, entrepreneurs are better able to use or access these particular cognitive processes or possess better cognitive skills.

Differences in Behavior

Again, moving out from inside people's heads to their external behaviors, some work has focused on identifying entrepreneurs' distinct behaviors that could explain their heightened alertness to potential opportunities. The specific behaviors studied include information search, usage, and attention. In a much-cited early study of entrepreneurial alertness, Kaish and Gilad found differences between entrepreneurs and executives in terms of time spent on information search and scanning, sources of information used, and attention to risk cues.[89] However, a wider-scale replication of this study by Busenitz failed to reconfirm these results and suggested that the self-reporting scales used by Kaish and Gilad had low reliability.[90] Subsequent studies within this stream have reported that there are no individual differences in self-perceived alertness as well as in the proportions of sought and triggered opportunities.[91, 92]

These findings essentially add further fuel to the argument that, other than differences related to the motivation to engage in the entrepreneurial process, protruding, stable differences between entrepreneurs and nonentrepreneurs in regard to their opportunity-related behavior may be hard to find.[93–95] With the understanding that this logic runs counter to the general tendency to glorify successful entrepreneurs, perhaps much more rigor and cumulative findings are needed before making such conclusion convincing and informing our teaching and practice.

Differences in Knowledge

One of the central tenets in creativity research is the positive relationship between (domain) knowledge and creativity.[96] In fact, studies of creative people in art have shown that a long period of immersion in a field, often up to ten years, is needed before new, creative paths can be laid out.[97] This notion has also been taken up in entrepreneurship research. In addition to how they think and what they do, people have different ideas because of what they know. Several empirical studies have provided support for a positive relationship between prior knowledge and opportunity recognition. Shane argues that knowledge of markets, of how to serve markets, and of customer problems influences both opportunity recognition and opportunity exploitation processes.[98] His detailed, qualitative analysis of eight different opportunities based on the same MIT technology invention showed that the way different individuals responded to the same innovation stimulus was related to their particular knowledge and understanding of the market processes in which they were involved. Shepherd and DeTienne sought to replicate Shane's findings on the positive effect of prior knowledge of customer problems in an experimental design with seventy-eight MBA students.[99] They manipulated the amount of prior knowledge participants possessed through varying the amount of information provided and affecting the recall of this information. Their results showed that prior knowledge had a positive effect on both the number of opportunities identified and the innovativeness of those opportunities. Ucbasaran, Wright, and Westhead, having surveyed a representative sample of 631 UK entrepreneurs, showed that human capital, in terms of prior business ownership experience, was positively related to the number of identified opportunities within the previous five years.[100]

There have been several studies, however, that have established that the relationship between human capital and opportunity recognition is not a direct one, but is rather moderated by learning or cognitive skills. In a study of 380 technology entrepreneurs, Corbett found that the effect of prior knowledge was moderated by the way individuals learn from experience, as measured by Kolb's Learning Style Inventory.[101, 102] Specifically, for individuals who used more sensory inputs in learning from experience there was no relationship between specific human capital and the number of identified opportunities; conversely, for individuals who used more conceptual abstraction in learning from experience there was a positive relationship between specific human capital and the number of identified opportunities. Similarly, Ko and Butler found that the effect of alertness (prior knowledge) on opportunity recognition was mediated by individuals' bisociative thinking ability.[103] In a sense, this set of studies resonates well with some suggestions in the broader literature on knowledge and creativity that too much domain knowledge may in fact impede one's ability to come up with unusual, outside-the-box solutions.[104] Further understanding the relationship between prior knowledge and idea generation is thus one important area for future research. This also serves to highlight the need for integrating an array of individual and situational factors. In what situations does knowledge enhance idea generation and in what situations does it not?

Differences in Learning

While there is a tendency in the economic literature to treat information in an objective way, assuming that all actors perceive it in the same way, the management cognition literature has pointed to differences in interpretation as an important factor in explaining different behaviors or outcomes.[105] Differences in interpretations are not necessarily due to differences in the perceived quality of the information that individuals receive, but to the different meanings that a given piece of information may contain.[106, 107] An individual's perception and interpretation of a particular action situation is guided by his or her developed cognitive maps or representations of the particular domain.[108] As these maps differ in their structure and complexity across individuals, different individuals are likely to interpret the same stimulus differently.[109] At the basis of such differences in map structures and resulting interpretations lies one's domain-specific knowledge and associated knowledge structures.[110, 111] Experts and novices differ in their cognitive representations of particular problems and such differences imply different abilities to form new knowledge associations and thus achieve novel interpretations. In particular, experts encode and process information in a more abstract way than novices.[112–114]

While this interpretation-based angle is reflected in the social constructivist views of opportunities, attempts to build more precise theories in the entrepreneurship literature are only fledgling at best.[115] This initial work has so far focused only on some of the characteristics that affect information processing. Corbett argues that it is important to account for how knowledge is acquired and processed—cognitive and learning style.[116] He finds evidence that domain knowledge matters only when coupled with a particular learning style. Further expanding his work on experiential learning, Corbett argues that each of the creative process stages requires particular learning skills.[117] Finally, Dimov also uses the construct of learning style as a distinguishing individual characteristic.[118] While certain learning styles are conducive to idea generation in some situations, they may act as a deterrent in others. It interacts with one's specific human capital in responding to particular situations. Beyond individual differences and in further support to the interactionist angle this chapter advocates, there is a rich opportunity for studying how situations differ in the way they present information to individuals and then how different individuals respond to this information.

THE CREATIVE PRODUCT

What do the ideas generated by potential entrepreneurs actually represent? How can we distinguish and conceptually organize the multitude and diversity of ideas that potential entrepreneurs pursue? Are there any differences in how these ideas are conceived, by whom, and in what situations? These are all questions that, I believe few will disagree, are of great importance in entrepreneurship research. Our limited ability to answer them, however, serves to highlight the areas that need work in order to make the field more theoretically sound.

As a beginning in understanding the nature of ideas, there is a tradition, coming mainly from economics, of classification of ideas (opportunities). Shane distinguishes among inventions (ideas) on the basis of their importance, radicalness, and broadness of scope.[119] More recently, Eckhardt and Shane propose a more comprehensive opportunity classification framework that also captures aspects of the change process and has three dimensions: locus of changes, sources of opportunities, and initiator of the change.[120] The locus of change dimensions reflect the elements of the value chain identified by Schumpeter as objects of innovation: products or services, markets, raw materials, methods of production, and ways of organizing.[121] In regard to the sources of opportunities, Eckhardt and Shane identify the following opportunity types: information asymmetries versus exogenous shocks, supply- versus demand-side changes, and productivity-enhancing versus rent-seeking. Finally, opportunities are classified on the basis of the actors initiating the change—noncommercial entities, existing commercial entities, and new commercial entities. While this work is an excellent first step in gaining a richer understanding of the complexity of entrepreneurial ideas, such taxonomies remain disconnected from the other elements of the creative process, namely process, person, and situation.

Another approach to classifying opportunity ideas has been more subjective in nature, based on specific knowledge and beliefs of entrepreneurs. Sarasvathy and colleagues divide human beliefs about the future into three categories: predictable, unpredictable but driven by an independent environment, and unpredictable but driven by human agency.[122] Under the first two beliefs, people are passive observers of how the future unfolds; at best, they can foresee it, yet still without influencing it. Under the last belief, while the future is unpredictable, people play active roles in shaping it. The authors further argue that each of these beliefs would be associated with a pursuit of opportunities associated with more or less clear sources of demand and supply. Under beliefs about the predictability of the future, entrepreneurs would pursue opportunities involving clear sources of supply and demand. Under beliefs in an unpredictable future resulting from an independent environment, entrepreneurs would pursue opportunities involving a clear source of either demand or supply. Finally, under beliefs in an unpredictable future resulting from human agency, entrepreneurs would pursue opportunities with no clear sources of demand and supply. Using a similar logic of demand and supply knowledge, Ardichvili, Cardozo, and Ray present atypology of opportunities based on their origin (value sought) and degree of development (value creation capability).[123] They categorize value sought as unidentified and identified, and value creation capability as undefined and defined. Their main argument in relation to this typology is that the more established the value sought and value creation capability, the higher the likelihood that a venture pursuing this opportunity will succeed.

While the knowledge and beliefs are treated as exogenous factors here, it is quite plausible that their particular configurations may be found only in some situations and not in others. In addition, one's beliefs in the predictability of the future may drive what and how one perceives change.

THE CREATIVE SOLUTION

There is a well-known phenomenon in social psychology—the fundamental attribution error—whereby in judging the behavior and deeds of others, people typically underestimate the power of situations and situational pressures and thus ascribe what they see to individual strengths or weaknesses.[124] When we talk and think about (great) entrepreneurs, the fundamental attribution error is evident in our tendency to praise their individual characteristics or skills and overlook the enabling force of their environment. There are, however, many aspects of one's surrounding that enable or impede one's ability to come up with opportunity ideas. Among these are available information, situational motivation, incentives, social network, and situational pressures. Each of these serves to make ideas accessible to some individuals and not to others.

One of the fundamental characteristics of the economic environment is the dispersed nature of knowledge.[125] In some cases what one needs to know is missing, while in other cases what one knows does not appear immediately needed. This dispersion is further swirled by continuous change in all aspects of society. Drucker argues that change and its perception by various actors is one of the fundamental drivers of the entrepreneurial process.[126] In a very insightful discussion, he proposes a classification of opportunity ideas based on their source or stimulus. He distinguishes between sources within a particular industry or activity setting (the unexpected, the incongruity, process need, changes in industry or market structure) and outside (changes in demographics, perception, and knowledge) of it. While this work does not exactly hone in on how perceptions of change are built and acted upon, it does move us closer toward a person–situation interaction. Only certain people can be found in certain situation and thus able to acknowledge the particular change.

In addition to the information they provide, situations may affect idea generation through the way the information is framed and perceived. McMullen and Shepherd show that different framings may induce an offensive or defensive motivation and thus trigger different behavior.[127] Dimov argues that the way information is structured and presented pushes those willing to come up with idea toward different types of thinking (convergent or divergent).[128] In an experimental setting, he shows that the individual responses in such situations vary depending on how easy it is for individuals to engage in such thinking.

Situations are also instrumental through the incentives or other pressure and stress conditions they create for individuals to think and act. Shepherd and DeTienne show that the promise of financial reward may act as an inducement for idea generation.[129] This also reflects the wider, macroeconomic argument that the incentive structure of the capitalist process is the one that promotes entrepreneurship.[130] Baron argues that differences in opportunity recognition may be due to the different situational pressures that entrepreneurs and nonentrepreneurs face.[131] Such contextual influences create conditions that induce cognitive biases in people. Among the conditions suggested are information overload, uncertainty, novelty, emotions, time pressure, and fatigue.[132] These in turn make people more prone to employ counterfactual thinking, regret, and affect infusion, self-serving bias, planning fallacy, and self-justification. Similarly, Simon and Houghton argue that specific decision environments, particularly those of younger firms and firms introducing pioneering products enhance the cognitive biases of entrepreneurs in regard to the inferences and decisions they make in estimating market demand, competitors' responses, and the need for complementary assets.[133] In developing this perspective further, more focus is needed on the empirical testing and further refinement of these theoretical arguments.

One's social network also influences the generation of ideas.[134] Findings have shown that the number of social network contacts as well as the number of weak ties in a network are positively related to both the number of venture ideas identified and the number of opportunities recognized.[135] The size and diversity of the network have been shown to influence a new venture team's performance prospects, as demonstrated by Vissa in the context of eighty-four high-technology ventures in India.[136] Such network-based advantage stems from the importance of information diversity for the quality and speed of decision making, and so for the refinement of opportunities.[137]

Some of the opportunities for future research in this area come from incorporating change into the situational characteristics. Are people in highly changing environments more likely to generate ideas? What particular personal characteristics make one better able to comprehend and respond to such changes with new ideas? Are there different processes associated with idea generation in slow- versus fast-changing environments?

THE INTERACTION AMONG THE ELEMENTS

Although there has not been, so far, any work in the entrepreneurship field that focuses on more complex interactions among process, product, person, and situation, some of the studies reviewed in the preceding section integrate more than one factor and thus represent building blocks for a more advanced interactionist perspective. I will summarize these briefly.

Baron integrates process and situation by arguing that certain heuristics and biases are more likely to emerge in certain situations.[138] Dimov integrates person and situation by showing that the match between one's learning style and the situation at hand plays an instrumental role in idea generation and further action.[139] In addition, he also argues that these interactions may generate qualitatively different ideas (i.e., products). Corbett presents a person–process interaction by arguing that the various stages of the creative process necessitate specific experiential learning skills (i.e., aspects of one's learning style).[140] Finally, another person–process interaction relates to the findings that one's domain-specific knowledge affects one's search direction and intensity as well as one's opportunity interpretation.[141, 142]

The next step in increasing the order of interaction entails integrating and reconciling existing research findings and theoretical models, thereby allowing the theoretical mechanisms highlighted in some to activate the boundary conditions of others. There are many intuitive questions that help guide such integration. Here is but a small, teasing sample. Is a particular knowledge or skill equally important in all situations? Do they lead to qualitatively different ideas in different situations? Are these different ideas generated through qualitatively different processes?

OVERVIEW OF FUTURE RESEARCH DIRECTIONS

Perhaps the main research challenge facing entrepreneurship scholars in studying idea generation and opportunity development is building upon the respective advances on the topic in the creativity and cognition literatures. There has now been a longstanding recognition that creativity is a complex phenomenon that necessitates study from and integration of many different angles. Such recognition is now due in the entrepreneurship field as the research rigor in it increases. Understanding how ideas emerge and are subsequently developed (into opportunities) entails paying careful attention to the nuances that process, product, person, and situation as well as their interaction bring. There are specific questions that guide the building of more coherent theories within each of these areas, as I have outlined in my review of these areas earlier. In addition to these, we need a collective effort in building a well-balanced picture of how (potential) entrepreneurs generate ideas by integrating each of the process, person, product, and situation aspects. Achieving four-factor integration right away is far from realistic. Rather, research will follow a more disciplined, incremental path, elaborating first the two-factor models and gradually relaxing their boundary conditions by including additional constructs into the models.

OVERVIEW OF PRACTICAL IMPLICATIONS

The practical implications of a better understanding of how ideas are generated are clear. Entrepreneurship is taking a firm ground in many schools and universities. While teaching students how to prepare a business plan is very valuable, no one gets to a business plan without first having an idea. And teaching students how to generate, evaluate, and shape ideas is not a trivial task. We need to harness their personalities, abilities, knowledge, and experiences, and so, understanding the conditions under which these are most conducive to generating novel ideas would make course designs more than a shot in the dark.

Based on the ideas presented in this chapter, there are two main aspects in which the educational experience related to idea generation may be enhanced. The first pertains to having students unleash the generative potential of their minds. There are many creativity modules in business school programs, focused on inducing students to think "outside the box" by putting them in relaxing, mind-freeing situations and teaching them some idea-generation and idea-enhancing techniques. While this approach tends to overemphasize the creative skill component, it downplays the roles of situation, intrinsic motivation, and the students' own knowledge and ways of thinking. Many students find such exercises futile, as they simply do not consider themselves having a creative spark. Such dejection is based on the well-ingrained tendency to glorify the individuality and uniqueness of creative minds, and to make it a question of "either I am or I am not." To make one's motivation really intrinsic, we need to suspend our normative judgment of what is good creativity, and emphasize to and convince students that everyone is creative in their own, unique way. In addition, given the diversity of students' prior knowledge and experience, we need to provide them with a sufficient diversity of situations in order to ensure that each will find their own, exciting domain in which to be creative.

The second aspect of enhancing the educational experience pertains to teaching and encouraging students to suspend their initial judgment of their ideational embryos. Very often, it is our own tendency, based on our own beliefs and experience, to call an idea stupid that prevents us from ever verbalizing it and letting it take a life of its own. Removing this self-imposed hurdle will increase not only the number of ideas floating in the classroom but also their growth and impact as they absorb the input from the other class participants.

Moving away from the classroom, there are also implications for practitioners in regard to improving the gestation and impact of their ideas. Restraining and suspending initial judgment could work equally well in the domain of practice—increased intrinsic motivation and flow of ideas could make the wheel of the social process of opportunity development spin even faster. In addition, through building teams to complement their knowledge and skills, potential entrepreneurs could harness the complexity of idea generation to their own benefit. They could either increase the fit with a current situation by harnessing new knowledge and ways of thinking or expose themselves to better-fitting situations by leveraging their social network.

NOTES

1. W. D. Bygrave and C. W. Hofer, "Theorizing about Entrepreneurship," *Entrepreneurship Theory and Practice* 16, no. 2 (1991): 13–22.

2. S. Shane and S. Venkataraman, "The Promise of Entrepreneurship as a Field of Research," *Academy of Management Review* 25 (2000): 217–226.

3. H. H. Stevenson and J. C. Jarillo, "A Paradigm of Entrepreneurship: Entrepreneurial Management," *Strategic Management Journal* 11, no. Special Issue, Summer (1990): 17–27.

4. J. A. Timmons, D. F. Muzyka, H. H. Stevenson, and W. D. Bygrave, "Opportunity Recognition: The Core of Entrepreneurship," in *Frontiers of Entrepreneurship Research* (Wellesley, MA: Babson College, 1987).

5. S. Venkataraman, "The Distinctive Domain of Entrepreneurship Research," in *Advances in Entrepreneurship, Firm Emergence, and Growth*, ed. J. A. Katz (Greenwich, CT: JAI Press, 1997), 119–138.

6. K. H. Vesper, "New-Venture Ideas: Do Not Overlook the Experience Factor," *Harvard Business Review* (July–August 1979): 164–170.

7. W. B. Gartner and N. M. Carter, "Entrepreneurial Behaviour and Firm Organizing Processes," in *Handbook of Entrepreneurship Research: An Interdisciplinary Survey and Introduction*, eds. Z. J. Acs and D. B. Audretsch (Dodrecht, Netherlands: Kluwer, 2003), 195–221.

8. P. D. Reynolds and S. White, *The Entrepreneurial Process* (Westport, CT: Quorum Books, 1997).

9. T. M. Amabile, *Creativity in Context* (New York: Westview Press, 1996).

10. G. T. Lumpkin, G. E. Hills, and R. C. Shrader, "Opportunity Recognition," in *Entrepreneurship: The Way Ahead*, ed. H. P. Welsch (New York: Routledge, 2003).

11. R. W. Woodman, J. E. Sawyer, and R. W. Griffin, "Toward a Theory of Organizational Creativity," *Academy of Management Review* 18 (1993): 293–321.

12. R. W. Woodman and L. F. Schoenfeldt, "Individual Differences in Creativity: An Interactionist Perspective," in *Handbook of Creativity*, eds. J. A. Glover, R. R. Ronning, and C. R. Reynolds (New York: Plenum Press, 1989), 77–92.

13. R. W. Woodman and L. F. Schoenfeldt, "A Interactionist Model of Creative Behaviour," *Journal of Creative Behavior* 24 (1990): 279–290.

14. M. M. Crossan, H. W. Lane, and R. E. White, "An Organizational Learning Framework: From Intuition to Institution," *Academy of Management Review* 24, no. 3 (1999): 522–537.

15. D. Dutta and M. M. Crossan, "The Nature of Entrepreneurial Opportunities: Understanding the Process Using the '4I' Organizational Learning Framework," *Entrepreneurship Theory and Practice* 29, no. 4 (2005): 425–449.

16. K. E. Weick, *Sensemaking in Organizations* (Thousand Oaks, CA: Sage Publications, 1995).

17. Dutta and Crossan, "The Nature of Entrepreneurial Opportunities."

18. Crossan, Lane, and White, "An Organizational Learning Framework."

19. G. Wallas, *The Art of Thought* (New York: Harcourt-Brace, 1926).

20. W. Long and W. E. McMullan, "Mapping the New Venture Opportunity Identification Process," in *Frontiers of Entrepreneurship Research* (Wellesley, MA: Babson College, 1984).

21. G. E. Hills, R. C. Shrader, and G. T. Lumpkin, "Opportunity Recognition as a Creative Process," in *Frontiers of Entrepreneurship Research* (Wellesley, MA: Babson College, 1999).

22. Wallas, *The Art of Thought.*

23. Lumpkin, Hills, and Shrader, "Opportunity Recognition."

24. D. J. Hansen, G. E. Hills, and G. T. Lumpkin, "Testing the Creativity Model of Opportunity Recognition," presented at Babson-Kauffman Entrepreneurship Research Conference (Babson College, June 9–11, 2005).

25. R. E. Mayer, *Thinking, Problem Solving, Cognition* (New York: Freeman, 1992).

26. R. A. Finke, *Creative Imagery: Discoveries and Inventions in Visualization* (Hillsdale, NJ: Erlbaum, 1990).

27. Ibid.

28. R. A. Finke, "Creative Insight and Preinventive Forms," in *The Nature of Insight,* eds. R. J. Sternberg and J. E. Davidson (Cambridge, MA: MIT Press, 1995), 255–280.

29. T. B. Ward, "Cognition, Creativity, and Entrepreneurship," *Journal of Business Venturing* 19 (2004): 173–188.

30. R. M. Cyert and J. G. March, *A Behavioral Theory of the Firm* (Englewood Cliffs, NJ: Prentice-Hall, 1963).

31. N. M. Carter, W. B. Gartner, K. G. Shaver, and E. J. Gatewood, "The Career Reasons of Nascent Entrepreneurs," *Journal of Business Venturing* 18 (2003): 13–39.

32. A. Rauch and M. Frese, "Psychological Approaches to Entrepreneurial Success: A General Model and an Overview of Findings," in *International Review of Industrial and Organizational Psychology,* eds. C. L. Cooper and I. T. Robertson (Chichester, NY: Wiley, 2000), 101–142.

33. L. Heron and H. J. Sapienza, "The Entrepreneur and the Initiation of New Venture Launch Activities," *Entrepreneurship Theory and Practice* 17, Fall (1992): 49–55.

34. W. D. Sine and R. J. David, "Environmental Jolts, Institutional Change, and the Creation of Entrepreneurial Opportunity in the US Electric Power Industry," *Research Policy* 32 (2003): 185–207.

35. M. P. Bhave, "A Process Model of Entrepreneurial Venture Creation," *Journal of Business Venturing* 9 (1994): 223–242.

36. Long and McMullan, "Mapping the New Venture Opportunity Identification Process."

37. R. H. Koller, "On the Source of Entrepreneurial Ideas," in *Frontiers of Entrepreneurship Research* (Wellesley, MA: Babson College, 1988).

38. G. N. Chandler, J. Dahlqvist, and P. Davidsson, "Opportunity Recognition Processes: A Taxonomy and Outcome Implications," in *Frontiers of Entrepreneurship Research* (Wellesley, MA: Babson College, 2002).

39. G. N. Chandler, D. DeTienne, and D. W. Lyon, "Outcome Implications of Opportunity Creation/Discovery Processes," in *Frontiers of Entrepreneurship Research* (Wellesley, MA: Babson College, 2003).

40. G. E. Hills and R. C. Shrader, "Successful Entrepreneurs' Insights into Opportunity Recognition," in *Frontiers of Entrepreneurship Research* (Wellesley, MA: Babson College, 1998).

41. S. Kaish and B. Gilad, "Characteristics of Opportunities Search of Entrepreneurs versus Executives: Sources, Interests, General Alertness," *Journal of Business Venturing* 6 (1991): 45–61.

42. C. Zietsma, "Opportunity knocks—or Does It Hide? An Examination of the Role of Opportunity Recognition in Entrepreneurship," in *Frontiers of Entrepreneurship Research* (Wellesley, MA: Babson College, 1999).

43. A. C. Cooper, T. B. Folta, and C. Woo, "Entrepreneurial Information Search," *Journal of Business Venturing* 10 (1995): 107–120.

44. W. Long and J. B. Graham, "Opportunity Identification Processes: Revisited," in *Research in the Marketing/Entrepreneurship Interface*, eds. G. E. Hills, R. W. LaForge, and B. J. Parker (Chicago: Office of Entrepreneurial Studies, University of Illinois–Chicago, 1988).

45. Vesper, "New-Venture Ideas."

46. R. T. Peterson, "An Analysis of New Product Ideas in Small Business," *Journal of Small Business Management* 26 (1988): 25–31.

47. Cooper, Folta, and Woo, "Entrepreneurial Information Search."

48. M. Simon and S. M. Houghton, "The Relationship among Biases, Misperceptions, and the Introduction of Pioneering Products: Examining Differences in Venture Decision Contexts," *Entrepreneurship Theory and Practice* 27, no. 2 (2002): 105–124.

49. For example, C. B. Bingham and K. M. Eisenhardt, "Learning from Heterogeneous Experience: The Internationalisation of Entrepreneurial Firms," working paper (Stanford University, Department of Management Science and Engineering, 2005).

50. R. E. Hebert and A. N. Link, *The Entrepreneur: Mainstream Views and Radical Critiques* (New York: Praeger, 1988).

51. For example, D. K. Simonton, "Biographical Typicality, Eminence, and Achievement Styles," *Journal of Creative Behavior* 20 (1986): 14–22.

52. G. Yukl, "Managerial Leadership: A Review of Theory and Research," *Journal of Management* 15, no. 2 (1989): 251–289.

53. W. B. Gartner, " 'Who Is an Entrepreneur?' Is the Wrong Question," *Entrepreneurship Theory and Practice* 13, no. 4 (1989): 47–68.

54. W. B. Gartner, "A Conceptual Framework for Describing the Phenomenon of New Venture Creation," *Academy of Management Review* 10, no. 4 (1985): 696–706.

55. Rauch and Frese, "Psychological Approaches to Entrepreneurial Success."

56. T. M. Amabile, "The 'Atmosphere of Pure Work': Creativity in R&D," in *The Social Psychology of Science*, eds. W. R. Shadish and G. Kaufman (New York: Guilford Press, 1994).

57. Woodman, Sawyer, and Griffin, "Toward a Theory of Organizational Creativity."

58. Rauch and Frese, "Psychological Approaches to Entrepreneurial Success."

59. R. A. Baron, "The Cognitive Perspective: A Valuable Tool for Answering Entrepreneurship's Basic 'Why' Questions," *Journal of Business Venturing* 19 (2004): 221–239.

60. R. K. Mitchell, L. Busenitz, T. Lant, P. P. McDougall, E. A. Morse, and J. B. Smith, "Toward a Theory of Entrepreneurial Cognition: Rethinking the People Side of Entrepreneurship Research," *Entrepreneurship Theory and Practice* 27, no. 2 (2002): 93–104.

61. K. G. Shaver and L. R. Scott, "Person, Process, Choice: The Psychology of New Venture Creation," *Entrepreneurship Theory and Practice* 16, Winter (1991): 23–45.

62. For example, L. W. Busenitz and J. B. Barney, "Differences between Entrepreneurs and Managers in Large Organizations: Biases and Heuristics in Strategic Decision-Making," *Journal of Business Venturing* 12 (1997): 9–30.

63. For example, M. Simon, S. M. Houghton, and K. Aquino, "Cognitive Biases, Risk Perception, and Venture Formation: How Individuals Decide to Start Companies," *Journal of Business Venturing* 15 (2000): 113–134.

64. Mitchell et al., "Toward a Theory of Entrepreneurial Cognition."

65. R. A. Baron, "Cognitive Mechanisms in Entrepreneurship: Why and When Entrepreneurs Think Differently Than Other People," *Journal of Business Venturing* 13 (1998): 275–294.

66. Baron, "The Cognitive Perspective: A Valuable Tool for Answering Entrepreneurship's Basic 'Why' Questions."

67. C. M. Gaglio, "Opportunity Identification: Review, Critique, and Suggested Research," in *Advances in Entrepreneurship, Firm Emergence, and Growth*, ed. J. A. Katz (Greenwich, CT: JAI Press, 1997), 139–202.

68. C. M. Gaglio and J. A. Katz, "The Psychological Basis of Opportunity Identification: Entrepreneurial Alertness," *Journal of Small Business Economics* 16 (2001): 95–111.

69. R. J. Sternberg and T. I. Lubart, "The Concept of Creativity: Prospects and Paradigms," in *Handbook of Creativity*, ed. R. J. Sternberg (Cambridge, UK: Cambridge University Press, 1999).

70. I. M. Kirzner, *Perception, Opportunity, and Profit: Studies in the Theory of Entrepreneurship* (Chicago: University of Chicago Press, 1979).

71. I. M. Kirzner, *Discovery and the Capitalist Process* (Chicago: University of Chicago Press, 1985).

72. Kirzner, *Perception, Opportunity, and Profit: Studies in the Theory of Entrepreneurship.*

73. Kirzner, *Discovery and the Capitalist Process.*

74. Mitchell et al., "Toward a Theory of Entrepreneurial Cognition."

75. Ibid.

76. D. Ucbasaran, M. Wright, P. Westhead, and L. W. Busenitz, "Using Cognitive Processes and Knowledge Structures to Distinguish between Novice and Habitual Entrepreneurs," working paper (University of Nottingham, 2002).

77. See D. Kahneman, P. Slovic, and A. Tversky, *Judgment under Uncertainty: Heuristics and Biases* (Cambridge, MA: Cambridge University Press, 1982).

78. Busenitz and Barney, "Differences between Entrepreneurs and Managers in Large Organizations."

79. H. T. Keh, M. D. Foo, and B. C. Lim, "Opportunity Evaluation under Risky Conditions: The Cognitive Processes of Entrepreneurs," *Entrepreneurship Theory and Practice* 27, no. 2 (2002): 125–148.

80. Simon, Houghton, and Aquino, "Cognitive Biases, Risk Perception, and Venture Formation: How Individuals Decide to Start Companies."

81. S. A. Alvarez and L. W. Busenitz, "The Entrepreneurship of Resource-Based Theory," *Journal of Management* 27 (2001): 755–775.

82. C. W. Allinson, E. Chell, and J. Hayes, "Intuition and Entrepreneurial Behaviour," *European Journal of Work and Organizational Psychology* 9 (2000): 31–43.

83. Ucbasaran, Wright, Westhead, and Busenitz, "Using Cognitive Processes and Knowledge Structures to Distinguish between Novice and Habitual Entrepreneurs."

84. Gaglio, "Opportunity Identification: Review, Critique, and Suggested Research."

85. Gaglio and Katz, "The Psychological Basis of Opportunity Identification: Entrepreneurial Alertness."

86. R. A. Baron, "Counterfactual Thinking and Venture Formation: The Potential Effects of Thinking about 'What Might Have Been,'" *Journal of Business Venturing* 15 (1999): 79–91.

87. C. M. Gaglio, "The Role of Mental Simulations and Counterfactual Thinking in the Opportunity Identification Process," *Entrepreneurship Theory and Practice* (in press).

88. Baron, "The Cognitive Perspective: A Valuable Tool for Answering Entrepreneurship's Basic 'Why' Questions."

89. Kaish and Gilad, "Characteristics of Opportunities Search of Entrepreneurs versus Executives."

90. L. W. Busenitz, "Research on Entrepreneurial Alertness," *Journal of Small Business Management* 34 (October 1996): 35–44.

91. Hills and Shrader, "Successful Entrepreneurs' Insights into Opportunity Recognition."

92. Zietsma, "Opportunity Knocks—or Does It Hide?"

93. Carter, Gartner, Shaver, and Gatewood, "The Career Reasons of Nascent Entrepreneurs."

94. A. Utsch, A. Rauch, R. Rothfuss, and M. Frese, "Who Becomes a Small Scale Entrepreneur in a Post-Socialist Environment: On the Differences between Entrepreneurs and Managers in East Germany," *Journal of Small Business Management* 37, no. 3 (1999): 31–42.

95. Rauch and Frese, "Psychological Approaches to Entrepreneurial Success."

96. T. M. Amabile, "A Model of Creativity and Innovations in Organizations," in *Research in Organizational Behavior*, eds. B. M. Staw and L. L. Cummings (Greenwich, CT: JAI Press, 1988), 123–167.

97. R. W. Weisberg, "Creativity and Knowledge: A Challenge to Theories," in *Handbook of Creativity*, ed. R. J. Sternberg (Cambridge: Cambridge University Press, 1999), 226–250.

98. S. Shane, "Prior Knowledge and the Discovery of Entrepreneurial Opportunities," *Organization Science* 11 (2000): 448–469.

99. D. A. Shepherd and D. DeTienne, "Prior Knowledge, Potential Financial Reward, and Opportunity Identification," *Entrepreneurship Theory and Practice* 29, no. 1 (2005): 91–112.

100. D. Ucbasaran, M. Wright, and P. Westhead, "Human Capital Based Determinants of Opportunity Identification," presented at Babson-Kauffman Entrepreneurship Research Conference, 2003.

101. A. C. Corbett, "Recognizing High-Tech Opportunities: A Learning and Cognitive Approach," in *Frontiers of Entrepreneurship Research* (Wellesley, MA: Babson College, 2002).

102. D. A. Kolb, *Experiential Learning: Experience as the Source of Learning and Development* (Englewood Cliffs, NJ: Prentice Hall, 1984).

103. S. Ko and J. Butler, "Alertness, Bisociative Thinking Ability, and Discovery of Entrepreneurial Opportunities in Asian Hi-tech Firms," in *Frontiers of Entrepreneurship Research* (Wellesley, MA: Babson College, 2003).

104. P. A. Frensch and R. J. Sternberg, "Expertise and Intelligent Thinking: When Is It Worse to Know Better?," in *Advances in the Psychology of Human Intelligence*, ed. R. J. Sternberg (Hillsdale, NJ: Erlbaum, 1989), 157–188.

105. For example, J. E. Dutton and S. E. Jackson, "Categorizing Strategic Issues: Links to Organizational Action," *Academy of Management Review* 12 (1987): 76–90.

106. Crossan, Lane, and White, "An Organizational Learning Framework."

107. R. L. Daft and G. Huber, "Making Sense of Improvisation," in *Advances in Strategic Management*, eds. A. Huff and J. Walsh (Greenwich, CT: JAI Press, 1987), 14.

108. A. S. Huff, *Mapping Strategic Thought* (New York: Wiley, 1990).

109. J. P. Walsh, "Selectivity and Selective Perception: An Investigation of Managers' Belief Structures and Information Processing," *Academy of Management Journal* 31 (1988): 873–896.

110. W. G. Chase and H. A. Simon, "Perception in Chess," *Cognitive Psychology* 4 (1973): 55–81.

111. J. P. Walsh, "Managerial and Organizational Cognition: Notes from a Trip Down Memory Lane," *Organization Science* 6, no. 3 (1995): 280–321.

112. R. Glaser and M. T. H. Chi, "Overview," in *The Nature of Expertise*, eds. M. T. H. Chi, R. Glaser, and M. J. Farr (Hillsdale, NJ: Erlbaum, 1988).

113. M. Chi, R. Glaser, and E. Rees, "Expertise in Problem Solving," in *Advances in the Psychology of Human Intelligence*, ed. R. J. Sternberg (Hillsdale, NJ: Erlbaum, 1982), 7–75.

114. D. H. Gitomer, "Individual Differences in Technical Troubleshooting," *Human Performance* 1 (1988): 111–131.

115. W. B. Gartner, N. M. Carter, and G. E. Hills, "The Language of Opportunity," in *New Movements in Entrepreneurship*, eds. C. Steyaert and D. Hjorth (London: Edward Elgar, 2003).

116. Corbett, "Recognizing High-Tech Opportunities."

117. A. C. Corbett, "Experiential Learning within the Process of Opportunity Identification and Exploitation," *Entrepreneurship Theory and Practice* 29, no. 4 (2005): 473–491.

118. D. P. Dimov, "The Glasses of Experience: Opportunity Enactment, Experiential Learning, and Human Capital," PhD thesis (University of London, 2004).

119. S. Shane, "Technological Opportunities and New Firm Creation," *Management Science* 47 (2001): 205–220.

120. J. T. Eckhardt and S. A. Shane, "Opportunities and Entrepreneurship," *Journal of Management* 29 (2003): 333–349.

121. J. Schumpeter, *Theory of Economic Development* (Cambridge, MA: Harvard University Press, 1934).

122. S. D. Sarasvathy, N. Dew, S. R. Velamuri, and S. Venkataraman, "A Testable Typology of Entrepreneurial Opportunity: Extensions of Shane and Venkataraman," working paper (University of Maryland, 2002).

123. A. Ardichvili, R. Cardozo, and S. Ray, "A Theory of Entrepreneurial Opportunity Identification and Development," *Journal of Business Venturing* 18 (2003): 105–123.

124. L. Ross, "The Intuitive Psychologist and His Shortcomings: Distortions in the Attribution Process," in *Advances in Experimental Social Psychology*, ed. L. Berkowitz (New York: Academic Press, 1977), 173–220.

125. F. A. Hayek, "The Use of Knowledge in Society," *The American Economic Review* 35 (1945): 519–530.

126. P. F. Drucker, *Innovation and Entrepreneurship* (Oxford: Butterworth-Heinemann, 1985).

127. J. S. McMullen and D. A. Shepherd, "Regulatory Focus and Entrepreneurial Intention: Action Bias in the Recognition and Evaluation of Opportunities," in *Frontiers of Entrepreneurship Research* (Wellesley, MA: Babson College, 2002).

128. Dimov, "The Glasses of Experience."

129. Shepherd and DeTienne, "Prior Knowledge, Potential Financial Reward, and Opportunity Identification."

130. W. J. Baumol, "Entrepreneurial Cultures and Countercultures," *Academy of Management Learning and Education* 3 (2004): 316–326.

131. Baron, "Cognitive Mechanisms in Entrepreneurship."

132. Ibid.

133. Simon and Houghton, "The Relationship among Biases, Misperceptions, and the Introduction of Pioneering Products."

134. R. P. Singh, "A Comment on Developing the Field of Entrepreneurship Through the Study of Opportunity Recognition and Exploitation," *Academy of Management Review* 26 (2001): 10–12.

135. R. P. Singh, G. E. Hills, R. C. Hybels, and G. T. Lumpkin, *Opportunity Recognition through Social Network Characteristics of Entrepreneurs*," in *Frontiers of Entrepreneurship Research* (Wellesley, MA: Babson College, 1999).

136. B. Vissa, "Top Management Teams' External Ties and New Venture Success: Empirical Evidence from India and the UK," PhD thesis (University of London, 2003).

137. R. S. Burt, *Structural Holes: The Social Structure of Competition* (Cambridge, MA: Harvard University Press, 1992).

138. Baron, "Cognitive Mechanisms in Entrepreneurship."

139. Dimov, "The Glasses of Experience."

140. Corbett, "Experiential Learning within the Process of Opportunity Identification and Exploitation."

141. Cooper, Folta, and Woo, "Entrepreneurial Information Search."

142. Shane, "Prior Knowledge and the Discovery of Entrepreneurial Opportunities."

3

Perceiving and Shaping New Venture Opportunities through Mindful Practice

Andrew C. Corbett and Jeffery S. McMullen

"How do I find a good opportunity? I would really like to start my own business, but I just don't know where to begin." This question is familiar to anyone who has ever consulted with nascent entrepreneurs or taught a class on entrepreneurship. More often than not, the question is inadequately answered. Instead of instructing nascent entrepreneurs on how to identify opportunities, we discuss what entrepreneurship is, drawing on a number of descriptive theories from economics, or we offer instruction in industry and organizational analysis by using theoretical frameworks from strategic management.[1–7] However, if you stop and listen carefully, the question is rarely, "How do I gain and sustain competitive advantage?" and it is almost never, "What do entrepreneurs do?" No, what most aspiring entrepreneurs want to know is, "How do I perceive new venture opportunities?"

Given this question, very few theoretical explanations exist. One can either create opportunities through new combinations of resources or discover them through either entrepreneurial alertness or formal search.[8–10] The logic of the first approach appears to be responsible for the creativity exercises that many consultants and professors use. Though fun, these exercises tend to generate impractical possibilities that ignore market demands. In contrast, subscribing to the logic of discovery leads to the unhelpful advice "keep your eyes open" or to exercises designed to search for inefficiencies resulting from exogenous shocks to the economy caused by changes in technology, consumer tastes, regulation, or demographics.[11, 12] Like creativity exercises, the formal search of industry analysis tends to be so generic that it produces a slew of impersonal and often impractical possibilities, which ignore the idiosyncrasies that define every individual, including who and what they are (i.e., passion, knowledge, roles filled in their family and community, and so on) and who and what they would like to be (i.e., dreams, duties, desired contribution or legacy, and so on).

Filling some of this gap is the theory of effectuation which takes an inside-out approach to entrepreneurship.[13] Effectuation begins with the effects that individuals wish to create and then focuses on how entrepreneurs achieve these effects by asking and answering questions, such as who am I, what do I know, and whom do I know? At the firm level, resource-based theory (RBT) and dynamic capabilities theory (DCT) operate in a similar manner, suggesting that firms should seek competitive advantage by developing core competences around the resources and capabilities in their control.[14-17]

Although these theories are exceptionally helpful in transforming ideas into profitable realities, they tend to assume that actors have a clear understanding of what they want. With effectuation, the actor is deliberately attempting to enact some desired effect, whereas the firm of RBT or DCT is clearly striving for competitive advantage and the above-average profits it promises. The frustration experienced by would-be entrepreneurs, however, is often attributed to the fact that they do not know what they want. Therefore, what these individuals seem to want to know, is what to do, then and in some cases only then are they interested in learning how to do it.

Thus, there are a significant number of nascent entrepreneurs who are asking a question that is not answered by effectuation, RBT, industrial organization, or even entrepreneurial alertness. This is by no means an indictment of the utility of these theories which have proven to be extremely powerful tools for describing what entrepreneurs do and how people may best bring their ideas to fruition to create value for both themselves and their stakeholders. However, there is a process that precedes them, a process that speaks to these nascent entrepreneurs' frustration. This process concerns the interface between individuals and the ever-changing environment in which they live. It is a process that goes beyond factors of production and beyond the means of human action to strike at its motive and opportunity for realization.

We define an opportunity as a situation that allows advancement toward the fulfillment of some desire. With this definition in mind, we recognize the importance of two often-neglected variables: motivation (as captured by "fulfillment of some desire") and environment (as captured by "situation that allows advancement"). Although there is no reason to believe that the theoretical approach we are proposing is limited to new venture opportunities, we have limited our analysis in this respect because it is this subclass of opportunities which is of interest to most aspiring entrepreneurs. Therefore, we define a *new venture* opportunity as a situation that allows advancement toward the fulfillment of some desire through the creation of a new venture, which, in turn, presumably meets customers' needs through the introduction of either a new good or service or a new and improved way of providing existing goods and services.

Because the creation of a new good, service, or firm, involves novelty, we argue that this creation is better conceived as a process than an act, which begins and ends in a moment's time. Therefore, we equate new venture opportunities with projects, which can vary in duration and complexity.[18] As a result, we view the acts of perceiving and shaping opportunities as inextricably linked and evolving over time. However, we also recognize that entrepreneurial action, like all human action, is hierarchical in meaning. Therefore, what constitutes a new venture opportunity for a prospective entrepreneur depends upon the motive that an individual is seeking to fulfill. Accordingly, we limit our discussion to the opportunity perception and shaping process that transpires between the decision to become an entrepreneur and completion of the business plan that one writes to specify how one intends to achieve this goal.

We argue that teaching people to become better at perceiving and shaping new venture opportunities does not require knowledge of the particularities of an individual's motivation and environment. For example, detectives are taught that motive, means, and opportunity are required before an individual can be considered a viable suspect in a crime, but that is not the same thing as applying the process to solve a particular crime. Therefore, it is the structure of the entrepreneurial process that we emphasize in this chapter, and perhaps more importantly, how to use it to become more intentional in developing one's ability to perceive and shape new venture opportunities.

To this effect, we introduce the concept of mindfulness from psychology. Like the crime analogy mentioned earlier, we suggest that opportunity is only one of three pillars that individuals must consider if they hope to ever initiate the entrepreneurial action of new venture creation. By acknowledging each of these elements (the others being means and motive), we argue that individuals can take steps to enhance the mindfulness that they experience and that this mindfulness will contribute significantly to an individual's entrepreneurial alertness, which enables the recognition and exploitation of opportunities. Unlike entrepreneurial alertness, however, mindfulness can be developed. This potential for development allows entrepreneurial alertness to be transformed from a trait that someone either does or does not have to a skill that can be learned. In turn, this transformation allows economic theory to be used at the individual as well as the system level.[19]

AN INTRODUCTION TO MINDFULNESS

> You can't think and hit at the same time.
> Yogi Berra

When some people think about the concept of mindfulness, they think about focus and tend to misinterpret that to mean proceeding with tunnel vision. This understanding, however, is contradictory to the concept of mindfulness as it is discussed in the psychology literature. Although attention and awareness are important related factors, mindfulness is slightly different, emphasizing the importance of being truly cognizant of one's present situation.

Consider the following story of Kirk Gibson's dramatic home run in game one of baseball's 1988 World Series. The moment proved to be a rallying point that propelled the Los Angeles Dodgers to a five-game victory over the heavily favored Oakland Athletics in the series. You may recall pictures or video footage of a gimpy and limping Gibson rounding the bases and pumping his fists after hitting a game-winning two-out two-run home run in the bottom of the ninth inning. Gibson's hit is part of baseball's fabled lore because of its timing, the stage, and Gibson's ability to get beyond his physical pain. However, as is often the case in feats of unusual athletic wonder, the mind plays as big a part as the body.

The 1988 World Series began with experts expecting the Athletics to stomp the Dodgers. In the first game, the Dodgers were hanging tough, trailing by only 4–3, but were now down to their last out in the bottom of the ninth. Unfortunately for Gibson and the Dodgers, All-Star pitcher and future Hall of Famer Dennis Eckersley was now on the mound for Oakland. Eckersley, the dominant relief pitcher of the time, had saved forty-five games that year and had just saved all four Oakland victories in the previous series. He was as un-hittable as a pitcher gets. With two outs, Eckersley walked a batter and now faced Gibson who was sent in to pinch hit.

Gibson played baseball with the mentality of a football player. Over his career, he had the bruises, breaks, sprains, strains, and pulled muscles to show for it. Unable to swing a bat the day before the game, Gibson was nursing two bad legs that had left him unable to even jog. He was so certain he would not be able to play that he did not even arrive at the stadium in time to be introduced during pregame ceremonies.[20]

During the game, Gibson spent considerable time in the clubhouse getting treatment for his legs and thinking about what might happen if he was able to try to hit. Gibson remarked, "Throughout the game, while you're working on your leg, you just kind of visualize and create this moment in your mind. You say things to yourself like, 'When I walk out of the dugout, the fans are going to go nuts and then I won't hurt anymore.' And you visualize certain pitches that you're going to see. And you visualize yourself running around the bases, celebrating."[21]

Before the game Gibson was practicing visualization, a very popular technique used by athletes and others in an attempt to prepare one's mind for an upcoming action. During the game, however, he also practiced mindfulness. Visualization occurs before the action, and mindfulness occurs during the moment. Eckersley immediately fired two strikes, but Gibson battled back to get the count to three balls and two strikes. It was at that time that Gibson recalled that his hitting coach had told him that Eckersley would always use a backdoor slider as his out pitch.[22] In baseball *out pitch* refers to each pitcher's favorite pitch—the one that he believes is most likely to produce a strikeout or a bad swing by a batter. Knowing that Eckersley was in a bind and that the backdoor slider was coming, Gibson was ready.

Eckersley had thrown Gibson seven pitches. The crowd was going crazy, but Gibson was able to block out the noise, stay alert to the current environment, and remain attentive and aware of what was to come. This was Gibson's time to make something happen. Now, in the present, as it turns out, injuries would not allow him to play in the final four games of the series. Remembering what his coach had told him, Gibson now had his mindful moment. He called timeout and stepped out of the batter's box. "I looked at Eckersley and I said to myself, 'Partner, as sure as I'm standing here breathing, you're going to throw me that 3-and-2 backdoor slider.' And I got it. He threw it. And I did it."[23]

As we progress through this chapter it will become apparent how Gibson's actions have the telltale signs of someone acting mindfully. He was alert to the distinctive circumstances and was prepared for this exact context. Most important, while focusing on the task at hand (hitting the ball) and with all the excitement and craziness surrounding him, he was able to stay mindfully in the present—pause, gather his thoughts—and recognize the opportunity that was about to come to him (a backdoor slider). Admittedly, hitting a home run in a baseball game and identifying new venture opportunities may have little in common. However, we see mindfulness as the one common denominator between Gibson's actions and those of prospective entrepreneurs seeking opportunities to create new companies or create value within existing organizations.

Shortly, we detail the construct of mindfulness, and together with its other dimensions, highlight the importance of staying in the present. But before we do, a second example of mindfulness involving the Gibson home run may be beneficial. When initially preparing to write this chapter, the authors discussed the need for an example of mindfulness that could help readers identify with the process. Just after our phone conversation, one of us was listening to the radio on the way home from work and heard the Gibson story. Like Gibson, he was prepared and mindful of the present and therefore was able to find an example to satisfy our need.

What Mindfulness Is Not

Mindfulness is not simply about being aware, paying better attention to the object at hand, or focusing exclusively on it. Mindfulness certainly is related to attention and awareness because together the three concepts form the construct of consciousness.[24] However, compared to awareness and attention, mindfulness remains relatively underresearched and misunderstood.[25] For example, scholars find that—contrary to popular perception—being mindful is not about holding an image still as if focusing a camera.[26] This type of unwavering focus is more descriptive of attention. In contrast, mindfulness is about noticing new insights by varying your stimulus (i.e., seeing something common in an uncommon way).

Another way to understand mindfulness is to look at its antithesis: mindlessness. Researchers explain that mindlessness comes from the routinization of tasks and standardization of processes, which leaves humans with little apparent need to engage in active thought.[27] These authors warn that because of standardization, mindlessness has crept into many professions. Although some might argue that automating mundane processes allows individuals more free time to think, discover, and perceive new opportunities, research suggests that it tends to lead to human error, prejudice, and stereotyping.[28] In fact, authors Ellen Langer and Mihnea Moldoveanu argue that disastrous consequences could be in store for many complex tasks that have become increasingly mechanized, such as flying planes and performing surgery. Previous research found mindlessness to be the root cause of most American military casualties, more than actual military conflict.[29] Thus, it appears that mindlessness numbs individuals into accepting conditions and situations as absolute.

Because the entrepreneurial action of new venture creation is inherently novel to the actor, it is inconsistent with the mindlessness that characterizes standards, routines, and stereotyping. Instead, identification of a new venture opportunity would appear to require mindfulness, at least to the degree of the novelty inherent in the project. Therefore, we believe an examination of mindfulness and its usefulness for enhancing the perception of new venture opportunities and, consequently, the likelihood of entrepreneurial action is needed.

Mindfulness and Related Constructs

Many Eastern philosophies and spiritual traditions speak about the connections between consciousness and well-being.[30] Consciousness is comprised of three primary capacities: attention, awareness, and mindfulness. Because they operate together, it is difficult to dissect awareness and attention. For example, awareness can be seen as the background radar of consciousness that continually monitors a person's environment. Attention is the process through which one focuses this awareness to produce an increased sensitivity to a particular experience.[31] Therefore, attention is contingent upon awareness as it "pulls figures out of the 'ground' of awareness, holding them focally for varying lengths of time."[32]

In relation to awareness and attention, mindfulness has been described as open or receptive awareness and attention.[33, 34] For example, Nyanaponika Thera defines mindfulness as "the clear and single-minded awareness of what actually happens to us and in us at the successive moments of perception."[35] Similarly, mindfulness has been described as "keeping one's consciousness alive to the present reality."[36] In this sense, it stands in direct contrast to the "autopilot" many of us use as we drive home or perform more routine activities.

Whereas attention and awareness are relatively constant features of normal functioning, mindfulness has begun to grow in popularity not only because of its more discriminatory nature, but also because of its demonstrated efficacy within the domains of psychology, business, education, and general health.[37, 38] For instance, within the field of health, mindfulness has been shown to lead to increased longevity and to reduce adverse ills, such as arthritis and alcoholism.[39, 40] In education, researchers have demonstrated that mindfulness can be used to heighten creativity simply by using conditional rather than absolute language.[41] Other researchers have found that varying stimuli evokes mindfulness and the noticing of new things.[42] Within business, mindfulness has been linked to increased creativity and decreased burnout as well as productivity.[43, 44]

What Mindfulness Is

Mindfulness can be seen as a state of psychological freedom without an attachment to any point of view or being attentive to and aware of what is occurring in the present.[45, 46] It has also been referred to as a process of drawing novel distinctions.[47] Langer and Moldoveanu explain that instead of relying upon categorizations and distinctions made in the past, we can find novelty by being more mindful of our current context and actions. These authors explain that if individuals rely on past categorizations "rules and routines" will supersede our ability to view the current situation and its potential novel distinctions. Behaving in this manner leads to mindless behavior. Conversely, if individuals are mindful they will be more open to their environment, more open to new information, and more likely to find new ways to structure problems by developing new perspectives.

Langer defines mindfulness as having five components, all of which have been empirically tested.[48] The five dimensions include:

- *Openness to novelty*—the ability to reason with relatively novel kinds of stimuli
- *Alertness to distinction*—the ability to distinguish minute differences in the details of an object, list, action, or environment
- *Sensitivity to different contexts*—tasks and abilities will differ depending on context
- *Awareness of multiple perspectives*—the ability to think dialectically
- *Orientation in the present*—paying attention to current surroundings

We believe that placing these dimensions in an entrepreneurial context provides prima facie support for exploring the possibility that mindfulness may enhance the ability to perceive and shape new venture opportunities. For example, consider the following sentence: By being open to novelty and aware of multiple perspectives, a prospective entrepreneur is able to discern opportunities by seeing possible distinctions in everyday experiences and applying them in different contexts.

MINDFULNESS AS ENABLER OF ENTREPRENEURIAL ALERTNESS

Even though opportunity identification research has advanced greatly in the past decade, there remains a need for more empirical studies, and perhaps even more importantly, a theoretical approach which might ultimately lead to useful prescriptions for practicing professionals.[49] Foremost among the handful of theories that have discussed entrepreneurial action as a process of opportunity recognition is Israel Kirzner's theory of entrepreneurial alertness. Entrepreneurial alertness has been defined as a set of perceptual and processing skills that help aid the opportunity identification process.[50–52] Much of the research on entrepreneurial alertness has sought answers to the questions: How do entrepreneurs represent and interpret the market environment to discover opportunity? And do these representations and interpretations differ from those of nonentrepreneurs?[53]

Kirzner's theory of entrepreneurial alertness has proven to be an important step forward in the theoretical understanding of opportunity perception. Arguing that the economy's health depends on the pursuit of opportunities by individuals who are alert to market imperfections, Kirzner's theory discusses opportunity recognition as a means to an end but not an end in itself. Therefore, owing to its economic tradition, this perspective does not easily lend itself to application in individual practice. This is because Kirzner's theory is based at a system level where the focus is on some individual within the marketplace perceiving an opportunity and converting it to a new product or business. As a result, "[w]ho acts is inconsequential as long as someone does."[54] Thus, Kirzner's theory does an exemplary job in explaining what alertness is and what it does for the economy. However, it leaves individual practitioners still asking the question "How do I find a good opportunity?"

Recognizing the psychological implications of Kirzner's theory, Connie Marie Gaglio and Jerry Katz develop a detailed model of entrepreneurial alertness in an attempt to describe how entrepreneurs identify opportunities.[55] Using social cognition as a foundation, these authors build a number of interesting propositions regarding the alertness skills of entrepreneurs. The authors state that their work is built around a proposition that "there is a chronic schema that heightens the individual entrepreneur's awareness to the possibility of innovations that have commercial potential" (p. 98).

Schemas are mental models based on each individual's knowledge and beliefs about how the world works. Generally enacted unconsciously, a chronic schema is the habitual activation of a schema regardless of its appropriateness to the current moment or situation.[56, 57] Therefore, with respect to delineating mindfulness from alertness, there are a couple of important implications of the work of Gaglio and Katz. First, the use of a chronic schema suggests that the ability to identify opportunities is contingent upon a chronic mental model that one either does or does not possess. This is useful for discovering differences between entrepreneurs and nonentrepreneurs as these authors state. However, it suggests that you either have it or you don't and implies that entrepreneurs are born, not made. Although Gaglio and Katz's work provides an eloquent model for alertness and for uncovering distinctions between entrepreneurs and others, its dependence on a chronic schema prevents it from helping to equip those who are not alert to opportunities.

Gaglio and Katz theorize that entrepreneurs use their alertness schema to filter information from the market in an effort to determine whether it affects their current interpretations of the market, industry, and society. They suggest that this process will lead to opportunity identification. Our intention here is, not to argue against Gaglio and Katz, but to augment their perspective. We believe that mindfulness allows an individual to become alert and is therefore its enabler. Gaglio and Katz demonstrate *how* alertness affects opportunity identification. In contrast, we believe mindfulness explains *why* individuals are alert to opportunities, and perhaps more importantly, how anyone can become more perceptive of new venture opportunities. That is, unlike alertness, which is descriptively rooted in chronic schema, mindfulness can be developed through practice regardless of one's innate ability or natural endowments.

Thus, we believe that mindfulness acts as the bridge that moves alertness from the system level of the economy to the individual level of the practitioner. By moving beyond what entrepreneurial alertness is and does for the economy, mindfulness demonstrates how one can heighten his or her entrepreneurial alertness. As a result, a mindful approach to opportunity perception allows us not only to view alertness from a psychological lens, but it enables individuals to develop their alertness intentionally. Our perspective, therefore, builds upon the work of Gaglio and Katz's by using mindfulness to engage and disrupt our chronic schemas in an effort to perceive opportunities.

Figure 3.1 shows the mindfulness construct as a precursor to Gaglio and Katz's model of alertness schema. Gaglio and Katz theorize that entrepreneurs use their alertness schema to filter information, which affects their current interpretations of the market, industry, and society. Here we augment their model to show how mindfulness enables alertness.

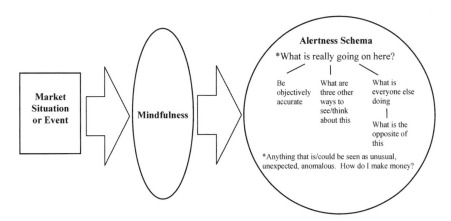

Figure 3.1. Mindfulness and alertness.

We believe that by practicing mindfulness, individuals can heighten their awareness and increase their ability to perceive opportunities. This distinction is important because it directly addresses the needs of practitioners who are looking for tactics to become alert to more opportunities. If an individual wants to become an entrepreneur, mindfulness is a technique that allows him to activate a need that stimulates alertness to opportunities. Following this reasoning, we posit a number of propositions that connect mindfulness to alertness.

Gaglio and Katz theorize that alert individuals are more sensitive to market disequilibrium. They argue that alert individuals have radar that lets them detect a "herd mentality" and that they also can develop contrarian positions, which can often be useful in seeing alternatives. We see mindfulness as a precursor to this sensitivity. Therefore, we propose that mindfulness will heighten the perception of new venture opportunities by allowing individuals to activate their alertness schema, which subsequently increases sensitivity to market disequilibrium.

When an event in the marketplace does not fit with the schema of an alert individual, he will change his schema to make more sense of the occurrences in the market. In contrast, nonalert individuals will attempt to change the information.[58] We see mindfulness as the trigger that allows individuals to change or contradict their chronic schemas. Thus, mindfulness will also heighten the perception of new venture opportunities by allowing individuals to disengage from their chronic schema.

Research indicates that nonalert individuals are likely to accept information in its original form which makes them susceptible to relying upon a base of knowledge built from inaccurate information.[59, 60] In this case nonalert individuals have a frame of reference that is potentially flawed due to inaccurate framing effects. Alert individuals tend to "be impervious to framing effects."[61] The psychological freedom from any point of view that defines mindfulness supports our last proposition: mindfulness heightens perception of new venture opportunities by allowing individuals to resist framing effects.[62]

By explicating the relationship of mindfulness to entrepreneurial alertness and ultimately to the perception of opportunities, these propositions offer scholars a base for future research. For practitioners, however, the question becomes, "How can mindfulness enhance my ability to perceive new venture opportunities?"

DEVELOPING ENTREPRENEURIAL MINDFULNESS: A PRESCRIPTIVE MODEL

In this section, we rely on research that examines mindfulness in other domains to develop an approach for enhancing one's ability to perceive new venture opportunities.[63–65] Our goal is to prescribe a set of action steps that prospective entrepreneurs can take to improve their ability to perceive and shape new venture opportunities.

How Mindful Are You?

Mindfulness has attributes of being a cognitive ability, personality trait, and a cognitive style.[66] Regardless of precise delineation, viewing the construct of mindfulness as a state rather than a trait may be most beneficial for entrepreneurs and for the practice of perceiving and shaping new venture opportunities. "People may differ in their average levels of mindfulness, but perhaps the standard deviation in a person's mindfulness is a more interesting construct than the mean."[67] Highlighting the fact that a person's ability to be mindful varies implies that it can be purposefully enacted, trained, or enhanced. This contention is supported by previous empirical research that suggests that mindfulness is a naturally occurring characteristic and that mindfulness can be trained.[68, 69]

Before seeking to develop one's mindfulness, it may be beneficial to determine your base-rate (i.e., the degree to which you experience mindfulness on a day-to-day basis as compared to a normal population of individuals). Research shows that mindfulness varies from person to person, so please take a moment to complete the Mindful Attention Awareness Scale (MAAS, Figure 3.2), an instrument designed to measure mindfulness in day-to-day experiences by examining variations in awareness and attention to actions, interpersonal communication, thoughts, emotions, and physical states.[70]

To give you some idea of how you measure up against the sample ($N = 313$) employed by Brown and Ryan, we have included the means and standard deviations of each item (Table 3.1). Remember that 64 percent of the population falls within one standard deviation of the mean. Therefore, if your score is outside this range, you are either extraordinarily high or low in mindfulness.

Perhaps you are within one standard deviation of the mean, suggesting that your mindfulness is fairly normal for that particular item. What does this imply about your level of entrepreneurial alertness, and consequently your ability to perceive new venture opportunities? Obviously, it depends. Perhaps you are high in mindfulness but have no interest in identifying new venture opportunities. Or, vice versa, you may be low in mindfulness but heavily interested in identifying new venture opportunities. In the first case, mindfulness is likely to contribute to heightened perception of opportunities, but not entrepreneurial opportunities, such as possibilities for new ventures, goods, or services. In the second case, a lack of mindfulness is unlikely to stop you from engaging in deliberate search for opportunities in a manner that resembles industry analysis.[71] However, this will put you at a comparative disadvantage with someone who possesses similar knowledge and motivation but who is more mindful of his environment—we return to this point later.

Thus, mindfulness is not the only determinant of new venture opportunity identification and entrepreneurial action. However, we would argue that more mindfulness leads to better perception of opportunities, which means that a larger opportunity set is generated, thereby increasing the likelihood of discovering one

Below is a collection of statements about your everyday experience. Using the 1-6 scale below, please indicate how frequently or infrequently you currently have each experience. Please answer according to what really reflects your experience rather than what you think experience should be.

1. I could be experiencing some emotion and not be conscious of it until some time later.

1	2	3	4	5	6
almost always	very frequently	somewhat frequently	somewhat infrequently	very infrequently	almost never

2. I break or spill things because of carelessness, not paying attention, or thinking of something else.

1	2	3	4	5	6
almost always	very frequently	somewhat frequently	somewhat infrequently	very infrequently	almost never

3. I find it difficult to stay focused on what's happening in the present.

1	2	3	4	5	6
almost always	very frequently	somewhat frequently	somewhat infrequently	very infrequently	almost never

4. I tend to walk quickly to get where I'm going without paying attention to what I experience along the way.

1	2	3	4	5	6
almost always	very frequently	somewhat frequently	somewhat infrequently	very infrequently	almost never

5. I tend not to notice feelings of physical tension or discomfort until they really grab my attention.

1	2	3	4	5	6
almost always	very frequently	somewhat frequently	somewhat infrequently	very infrequently	almost never

6. I forget a person's name almost as soon as I've been told it for the first time.

1	2	3	4	5	6
almost always	very frequently	somewhat frequently	somewhat infrequently	very infrequently	almost never

7. It seems I am "running on automatic" without much awareness of what I'm doing.

1	2	3	4	5	6
almost always	very frequently	somewhat frequently	somewhat infrequently	very infrequently	almost never

8. I rush through activities without being really attentive to them.

1	2	3	4	5	6
almost always	very frequently	somewhat frequently	somewhat infrequently	very infrequently	almost never

9. I get so focused on the goal I want to achieve that I lose touch with what I am doing right now to get there.

1	2	3	4	5	6
almost always	very frequently	somewhat frequently	somewhat infrequently	very infrequently	almost never

10. I do jobs or tasks automatically, without being aware of what I'm doing.

1	2	3	4	5	6
almost always	very frequently	somewhat frequently	somewhat infrequently	very infrequently	almost never

11. I find myself listening to someone with one ear, doing something else at the same time.

1	2	3	4	5	6
almost always	very frequently	somewhat frequently	somewhat infrequently	very infrequently	almost never

Figure 3.2. Brown and Ryan's mindful attention awareness scale (MAAS).

12. I drive places on "automatic pilot" and then wonder why I went there.

1	2	3	4	5	6
almost always	very frequently	somewhat frequently	somewhat infrequently	very infrequently	almost never

13. I find myself preoccupied with the future or the past.

1	2	3	4	5	6
almost always	very frequently	somewhat frequently	somewhat infrequently	very infrequently	almost never

14. I find myself doing things without paying attention.

1	2	3	4	5	6
almost always	very frequently	somewhat frequently	somewhat infrequently	very infrequently	almost never

15. I snack without being aware that I'm eating.

1	2	3	4	5	6
almost always	very frequently	somewhat frequently	somewhat infrequently	very infrequently	almost never

Figure 3.2. (*continued*)

that is highly feasible (i.e., exploitable with the means at one's disposal) and desirable (i.e., profitable in terms of the actor's motive).

Although empirical evidence is necessary to formulate more specific expectations, the reasoning presented in this chapter suggests that someone of average mindfulness would be likely to perceive an average number of opportunities. Given that entrepreneurship is a break with the norm, and therefore somewhat

Table 3.1. Means and Standard Deviations of the Mindful Attention Awareness Scale (MAAS)

Item	Mean	Standard Deviation
1	4.02	1.12
2	4.13	1.47
3	3.80	1.23
4	3.41	1.27
5	3.83	1.22
6	3.40	1.54
7	3.72	1.24
8	3.81	1.11
9	3.74	1.15
10	3.70	1.20
11	3.52	1.16
12	4.36	1.42
13	2.66	1.03
14	3.66	1.14
15	4.11	1.42

anomalous in nature, an average amount of mindfulness would suggest that entrepreneurial action would remain less likely, and in the off-chance that it did take place, would probably involve a suboptimal goal. Therefore, the question becomes, is there some way in which mindfulness can be developed?

Can Mindfulness Be Developed?

Over the past three decades, Robert Boice has applied mindfulness to the process of scholarship.[72] Like entrepreneurship, scholarship is a process that involves discovery, novelty, uncertainty, and experimentation. Although important distinctions exist, the parallels between the two processes suggest that research establishing how mindfulness has been cultivated to enhance scholarly performance may prove exceptionally useful to individuals wanting to perceive and shape new venture opportunities. For example, in the prolog to Hébert and Link's survey of economic theories of the entrepreneur, economist George Shackle observes:

> [R]egarding the creative process of discovery, the basic entrepreneurial act, there is little difference between the scientist and the businessman/entrepreneur. Apparent differences may exist in the motivation and/or the milieu of each class of actors. But consider the process of discovery alone for the moment. Those geniuses who have been responsible for the major innovation in the history of thought or in the world of affairs seem to have certain characteristics in common. One shared characteristic is skepticism, sometimes carried to the point of iconoclasm, in their attitudes to traditional ideas or ways of doing things. The other is an open-mindedness, often verging on naïve credulity, toward new concepts and techniques. Out of the combination comes the capacity to perceive a familiar situation or problem in a new light.[73]

In studying highly effective scholars, Boice observed general themes that represented seven simple practices of mindfulness and from them derived ten rules that he has used successfully to train others in how to become more mindful in their own writing. Although we would love to discuss each practice and rule in detail, space precludes us from doing so. Instead, what we offer is a simple three-step model that combines the dimensions of experimentally derived MAAS scale of mindfulness with the lessons learned from Boice's field studies of successful writers.[74, 75]

Three Steps to Becoming More Mindful

Using a medical analogy, we organize our examination of the role of mindfulness in the perceiving and shaping of new venture opportunities around three steps: (1) stop to recognize symptoms; (2) wait actively to derive a clear diagnosis; and (3) moderate emotions when prescribing treatment.

Step 1: Stop to Recognize Symptoms

Because mindfulness "offer[s] a bare display of what is taking place," it enhances sensitivity to one's external and internal environment.[76] It asks the questions, "What's happening around me and within me?" As a result, it is highly attuned to the emergence of new needs or the recognition of existing but unmet needs, especially when these needs are perceived as anomalies or violations of the normal order or functioning of the world.

Unlike many forms of self-awareness, which examine one's own cognitive processes through "reflexive consciousness," mindfulness is "prereflexive" operating on, rather than within, thought, feeling, and other contents of consciousness.[77, 78] Therefore, mindfulness concerns the quality of consciousness itself. For example, in asking yourself, "How conscious am I of what I am experiencing at this very moment," you become more mindful. Boice notes:

> The experience of awakeness begins with the elementary act of stopping to notice our customary reactions to ongoing experience. Awakeness alerts us when we are caught in blind thinking or impulsive action, unaware of why we are doing what we are doing. Once awakened, we become more aware and involved.[79]

The simple act of breathing provides a clear illustration of this phenomenon. In periods of stress people often hold their breath without realizing it, but if they stop to pay attention to their breathing, they find that it returns almost instantly to deeply drawn breaths that provide immediate relaxation and beneficial change in both their mental and physical condition. The transformation involves little more than a shift of attention, but the effect is dramatic. Therefore, learning to stop and wake up to one's ongoing reactions to real or imaginary stimuli enhances mindfulness and one's awareness of symptoms. Often indicative of abnormalities, these symptoms tend to signal a change in external conditions, which are likely to leave customer needs unmet, thereby justifying or even mandating the emergence of new ventures in situations where existing organizations leave these changes, and the needs they represent, unattended.

Step 2: Wait Actively to Derive a Clear Diagnosis

Upon recognizing symptoms, many people leap to treatment without an adequate diagnosis. Thus, questions, such as "What am I currently experiencing, and why do I feel this way?" are often left unexamined in favor of jumping to action. Mindless behavior prevents the diagnosis of symptoms addressed by these questions, but just as importantly it precludes one from sufficiently contemplating what if anything should be done about them. This prevents mindfulness from revealing the novel distinctions of a condition or event, which would occur under a more thorough examination. Therefore, to encourage the necessary reflection, mindfulness scholars recommend a combination of active waiting and beginning early.

Active waiting is a process in which individuals intentionally hold back from impetuously diving into making irreversible commitments of resources. This, however, takes patience. It is often hard for writers (or entrepreneurship students) to believe that they will get more done by starting out slowly, patiently, planfully (i.e., by waiting around), but the patience of active waiting is essential for slowing and preparing the mind, which otherwise races on to the next crisis. Thus, "active waiting is less a matter of time management than of emotional management."[80] For instance, Jon Kabat-Zinn notes,

> To find our way, we will need to pay more attention to this moment. It is the only time that we have in which to live, grow, feel, and change.... There is nothing passive about it. And when you decide to go [after waiting and attending to the moment], it's a different kind of going because you stopped. The stopping actually makes the going more vivid, richer, more textured.[81]

By pausing reflectively, you enhance the likelihood that your actions will seek to answer the right question, and you diminish the tendency to rebuke yourself for making inevitable missteps. Thus, active waiting occurs in the space between stopping to recognize symptoms and prescribing a treatment. It involves considering *and* reconsidering what we might do until eventually arriving at a clear understanding of what we are going to do and how we are going to do it. In the process, active waiting takes advantage of the numerous environmental stimuli that often go unnoticed in our surrounding environment. That is, unlike passive waiting, which is the child of mindlessness and the parent of procrastination, active waiting is purposeful. As a result, awareness is activated to bring environmental cues to our attention, making us more mindful of relevant information and making us the beneficiaries of seemingly costless gifts of relevant information extracted from our environment as we engage in other activities.

Although this process occurs regularly, its development can be encouraged by looking forward enough to set goals and imagining what means would provide opportunities and threats to attaining this goal. For example, the professor who has a lecture in a couple of weeks may decide that she would like to discuss mission statements that day and determine that what she needs to bring her class to life is a hook (i.e., a good illustration that her audience finds relevant and interesting). Going about her normal business, she runs across some relevant articles from the *Wall Street Journal* only to "luckily" catch, as she is relaxing in front of the television, the opening scene of the movie, *Jerry Maguire*, which is all about a compelling mission statement. She thinks to herself, "Perfect! And I didn't even have to search for it." Had she searched for the illustration, she may have only uncovered a *WSJ* article. Not only would she have had to invest time and energy for that exclusive purpose, but the result would have been suboptimal in comparison to the movie clip that she costlessly discovered by a combination of active waiting and beginning early.

Following these first two steps, we suggest that individuals who want to improve their ability to perceive opportunities first stop and ask themselves,

"Why do I want to be an entrepreneur? What's my motivation? How is starting a new venture going to serve this purpose?" By actively waiting and mindfully attending to one's thoughts and feelings, one increases the saliency of the need producing them. As a result, one's awareness, which is perpetually monitoring the environment, is tasked with the goal of finding a possible means of filling this need, often leading to what appears to be a serendipitous discovery, but is in reality a search process occurring outside of one's focal awareness (i.e., attention). To set this process in motion, however, one must take a moment to wake up from routine, especially when this routine is characterized by intense feelings of stress. Whereas unexamined stress, anxiety, or worry has a tendency to stifle creativity and constrict awareness, it seems that these same feelings can also be the clues to people's most salient needs. Consequently, stopping to examine them activates them such that mindfulness is allowed to task awareness with the job of finding relevant information encountered in the environment.

The process of diagnosing needs may produce benefits well beyond the enhancement of our conscious understanding. That is, if articulating a need activates it, and if activating a need triggers our awareness to be on the lookout for relevant stimuli, then the very process of diagnosis can prime our perception, thereby enhancing the likelihood of seemingly serendipitous discoveries. This possibility explains why it is crucial to begin the search for new venture opportunities early and to refrain from premature commitments to a particular course of action in favor of an approach grounded in active waiting. This can be highly counterintuitive and frustrating to the proactive individuals so often drawn to entrepreneurship. This frustration, however, is often grounded in the need to learn (a) how to manage excessive emotion and (b) how to channel one's proactive tendency primarily into thought rather than behavior. Doing so enhances the quality of the "treatment" prescribed while lowering its costs.

Step 3: Moderate Emotions When Prescribing Treatment

We argue that recognition of symptoms, and diagnosis of the needs they represent, leads to the contemplation of what treatment, if any, to prescribe. For the prospective entrepreneur this often takes shape as a feasibility or business plan. Despite the belief of many nascent entrepreneurs, rarely does a business plan resemble the initial idea that stimulated its creation. Therefore, it is likely to benefit greatly from the informational discoveries made through the practices of active waiting and beginning early. Additionally, a mindful approach requires that you moderate your emotions to avoid getting too attached to a flawed idea or impulsively rejecting a potentially successful idea. Our experience and that of the numerous colleagues with whom we have spoken, suggests that few creative processes are momentary acts as Kirzner's theory of entrepreneurial alertness suggests. Instead, they are a process of converting chaos to coherence. And as such, individuals would benefit greatly by moderating their emotions. From a less emotionally charged state, individuals can then play a seemingly endless game of "what if" until arriving at the cleanest, clearest storyline before committing what will become sunk costs.

This mindful moderation of emotion is achieved in a number of ways.[82] First, prospective entrepreneurs must learn to work with constancy and moderation. This is done by recognizing the power of brief daily sessions, which are devoted to ideation and the clarification of the initial business concepts that one generates. Second, and perhaps more difficult, prospective entrepreneurs must learn to stop in a timely fashion. That is, one should not proceed to turning to the prose of a feasibility plan, or worse yet contractual commitments, until she can create a clear conceptual outline, which Donald Murray suggests requires answers to the following questions (note: we offer an equivalent business concept in parentheses to aid the reader in transferring the concept from writing to entrepreneurship):[83]

- You see possibilities for writing on something you have studied, noted, and filed. (You have identified what you believe may be an opportunity for someone.)
- You have a definite, perhaps distinctive, point of view on the writing topic. (You have a clear value proposition.)
- You have listened to yourself prepare until you sense a "voice" in how you might present it; the writing will sound distinctively like you. (You have a distinctive competence regarding this value proposition.)
- What you have to say is news—for example, somewhat novel information or a novel way of presenting it. (The good or service is new or a new improvement to existing goods or services.)
- You have a single line to begin the manuscript, one that informs and entices readers while giving you more sense of control as the writer. (You have an elevator pitch and your venture has a clear identity.)
- You see a pattern in the subject, one that begins to suggest a shape for the entire piece of writing. (You have a strategy and/or business model.)
- You begin to see and hear images that will help guide that whole. (You continually notice relevant environmental cues, such as examples in the media.)
- You know, with some clarity, what problem you are going to solve in your manuscript and you are confident you can get it said in prose. You are, at last, ready to stop conceptual outlining and to start prose writing. (You know who your intended customers are and what need your venture will contribute to filling in their lives.)

Through these brief daily sessions and timely stopping, individuals establish conditions that allow them to enjoy flow, which is often described as a state of behavioral fluency in which one is lost in consideration of how best to implement a task and unlikely to revisit expectancy-value issues, such as whether the goal of becoming an entrepreneur is still likely to produce the desired effect.[84]

As one decides to commit to a course of action and initiate "treatment," the entrepreneurial function becomes increasingly managerial in nature. Given that resources must be irreversibly committed at that point and that sunk costs will therefore play a greater role in decision making, it would seem that the entrepreneurial manager may be well served by developing mindfulness during the planning process, as this ability is likely to become more, rather than less, in demand. After all, commitment requires investments of physical resources and reputation in addition to the emotional attachment to ideas experienced in the planning phase. This makes it all the more difficult to work mindfully with the reflective contemplation necessary to keep immediate concerns in a broader perspective. Thus, researchers interested in mindfulness may find the construct particularly helpful for managers engaged in the early stages of organizational emergence or the difficult transitions that accompany strategic renewal.

CONCLUSION

"How do I find new venture opportunities? Can I improve my ability to perceive opportunities?" These are questions that professors of entrepreneurship have faced from many students. Typically, the response has been grounded in economic theories that describe what entrepreneurs do, but provide little advice in how to do it. Or, the professor is left recommending fairly generic content-driven models of industrial organization in which opportunity is thought to arise from exogenous shocks to the economy as the result of a change in consumer tastes, technology, demographics, or regulation.

What we offer in this chapter is a prescriptive process-oriented model of enhancing one's perception of new venture opportunities. In so doing, we show how individuals can enhance their perception of new venture opportunities, thereby contributing to the amount of entrepreneurial alertness that they experience. This should not only provide them with a larger opportunity set from which to choose, but also help to prevent settling on the pursuit of a suboptimal goal.

However, the mindfulness that acts as the engine of our model is not limited to identifying entrepreneurial opportunities. For example, mindfulness has been shown to be positively related to a person being perceived as more genuine by others.[85] We believe this finding has important implications for entrepreneurs' "postopportunity perception" because this perceived sincerity may be of great assistance as an entrepreneur attempts to recruit individuals, build a team, and close sales. Therefore, future work may benefit from investigating the role that mindfulness plays throughout the entrepreneurial action process.

Finally, because entrepreneurial alertness is only one possible area in which mindfulness pays dividends, investment in developing it is likely to enrich an individual's life in many other ways as well, whether it is putting your kids to bed, enjoying the landscape as you walk from your car to work, or doing dishes, life takes on new meaning when one is truly present and experiencing it with a childlike curiosity, playfulness, awareness, and passion.

NOTES

The authors of this chapter are listed in alphabetical order and have contributed equally to this chapter.

1. J. A. Schumpeter, *The Theory of Economic Development* (New Brunswick, NJ: Transaction Publishers, 1934).

2. I. Kirzner, *Competition and Entrepreneurship* (Chicago: University of Chicago Press, 1973).

3. M. E. Porter, *Competitive Strategy: Techniques for Analyzing Industries and Competitors* (New York: Free Press, 1980).

4. B. Wernerfelt, "A Resource-Based View of the Firm," *Strategic Management Journal* 5 (1984): 171–180.

5. J. Barney, "Firm Resources and Sustained Competitive Advantage," *Journal of Management* 17, no. 1 (1991): 99–120.

6. C. K. Prahalad and G. Hamel, "The Core Competence of the Corporation," *Harvard Business Review* 66 (May/June, 1990).

7. D. J. Teece, G. Pisano, and A. Shuen, "Dynamic Capabilities and Strategic Management," *Strategic Management Journal* 18, no. 7 (1997): 509–533.

8. Schumpeter, *The Theory of Economic Development.*

9. Kirzner, *Competition and Entrepreneurship.*

10. Porter, *Competitive Strategy.*

11. Kirzner, *Competition and Entrepreneurship.*

12. Porter, *Competitive Strategy.*

13. S. D. Sarasavathy, "Causation and Effectuation: Toward a Theoretical Shift from Economic Inevitability to Entrepreneurial Contingency," *Academy of Management Review* 26, no. 2 (2001): 243–263.

14. Wernerfelt, "A Resource-Based View of the Firm."

15. Barney, "Firm Resources and Sustained Competitive Advantage."

16. Teece, Pisano, and Shuen, "Dynamic Capabilities and Strategic Management."

17. Prahalad and Hamel, "The Core Competence of the Corporation."

18. M. Casson, "The Discovery of Opportunities: Extending the Economic Theory of the Entrepreneur," conference presentation, Neo-Schumpeterian Economics, Trest, Czech Republic, June 2006.

19. Kirzner, *Competition and Entrepreneurship.*

20. R. Smith, *Baseball's 25 Greatest Moments* (St. Louis, MO: Sporting News Publishing, 1999).

21. "Gibson Delivers in a Pinch." http://tsn.sportingnews.com/baseball/25moments/6 .html#.

22. K. Gibson, Radio interview, Mike & Mike in the Morning, ESPN Radio, 2005.

23. "Gibson Delivers in a Pinch."

24. K.W. Brown and R. M. Ryan, "The Benefits of Being Present: Mindfulness and Its Role in Psychological Well-Being," *Journal of Personality and Social Psychology* 84, no. 4 (2003): 822–848.

25. Ibid.

26. E. J. Langer, *The Power of Mindful Learning* (Reading, MA: Addison Wesley, 1997).

27. E. J. Langer and M. Moldoveanu, "The Construct of Mindfulness," *Journal of Social Issues* 56, no. 1 (2000): 1–9.

28. Ibid.

29. S. Snook, "The Friendly Fire Shootdown over Northern Iraq" (doctoral dissertation, Harvard University, 1996).

30. K. Wilber, *Integral Psychology: Consciousness, Spirit, Psychology Therapy* (Boston: Shambhala, 2000).

31. Sarasavathy, "Causation and Effectuation"; D. Westen, *Psychology: Mind, Brain, and Culture* (New York: Wiley, 1999).

32. Brown and Ryan, "The Benefits of Being Present."

33. A. J. Deikman, *The Observing Self* (Boston: Beacon Press, 1982).

34. J. R. Martin, "Mindfulness: A Proposed Common Factor," *Journal of Psychotherapy Integration* 7 (1997): 291–312.

35. Nyanaponika Thera, *The Power of Mindfulness* (San Francisco, CA: Unity Press, 1972).

36. T. N. Hanh, *Miracle of Mindfulness* (Boston: Beacon, 1976).

37. Brown and Ryan, "The Benefits of Being Present."

38. Langer and Moldoveanu, "The Construct of Mindfulness."

39. C. Alexander, E. J. Langer, R. Newman, H. Chandler, and J. Davies, "Aging, Mindfulness, and Meditation," *Journal of Personality and Social Psychology* 57 (1989): 950–964.

40. E. J. Langer, P. Beck, R. Janoff-Bulman, and C. Timko, "The Relationship between Cognitive Deprivation and Longevity in Senile and Non-Senile Elderly Populations," *Academic Psychology Bulletin* 6 (1984): 211–226.

41. E. J. Langer and A. Piper, "The Prevention of Mindlessness," *Journal of Personality and Social Psychology* 53 (1987): 280–287.

42. E. J. Langer and T. Bodner, "Mindfulness and Attention" (unpublished manuscript, Harvard University, 1995).

43. E. J. Langer, D. Heffernan, and M. Kiester, "Reducing Burnout in an Institutional Setting: An Experimental Investigation" (unpublished manuscript, Harvard University, 1988).

44. K. Park, "An Experimental Study of Theory-Based Team Building Intervention: A Case of Korean Work Groups" (doctoral dissertation, Harvard University, 1996).

45. Martin, "Mindfulness."

46. Brown and Ryan, "The Benefits of Being Present."

47. Langer and Moldveanu, "The Construct of Mindfulness."

48. Langer, *The Power of Mindful Learning*.

49. C. M. Gaglio, "Opportunity Identification: Review, Critique, and Suggested Research Directions," in *Advances in Entrepreneurship, Firm, Emergence, and Growth*, ed. J. Katz (Greenwich, CT: JAI Press, 1997), 139–202.

50. Kirzner, *Competition and Entrepreneurship*.

51. I. Kirzner, *Perception, Opportunity, and Profit* (Chicago: University of Chicago Press, 1979).

52. I. Kirzner, *Discovery and the Capitalist Process* (Chicago: University of Chicago Press, 1985).

53. K. G. Shaver and L. R. Scott, "Person, Process, Choice: The Psychology of New Venture Creation," *Entrepreneurship: Theory and Practice* 16, no. 2 (1991): 23–45.

PROCESS

54. J. S. McMullen and D. A. Shepherd, "Entrepreneurial Action and the Role of Uncertainty in the Theory of the Entrepreneur," *Academy of Management Review* 31, no. 1 (2006.): 1–21.

55. C. M. Gaglio and J. A. Katz, "The Psychological Basis of Opportunity Identification: Entrepreneurial Alertness," *Small Business Economics* 16 (2001): 95–111.

56. Gaglio and Katz, "The Psychological Basis of Opportunity Identification."

57. S. T. Fiske and S. E. Taylor, *Social Cognition*, 2nd ed. (New York: McGraw-Hill, 1991).

58. Ibid.

59. Ibid.

60. P. Slovic, "From Shakespeare to Simon: Speculations and Some Evidence about Man's Ability to Process Information," *Oregon Research Institute Bulletin* 12 (1972).

61. Gaglio and Katz, "The Psychological Basis of Opportunity Identification," 101; D. Kahneman and A. Tversky, "Choices, Values, and Frame," *American Psychologist* 39, no. 4 (1986): 341–350.

62. Martin, "Mindfulness."

63. Brown and Ryan, "The Benefits of Being Present."

64. R. Boice, *Advice for New Faculty Members* (Boston: Allyn and Bacon, 2000).

65. D. N. Stull, "Strategy as Waiting," *Harvard Business Review* (September 2005): 121–129.

66. R. J. Sternberg, "Images of Mindfulness," *Journal of Social Issues* 56, no. 1 (2000): 11–26.

67. Ibid.

68. Brown and Ryan, "The Benefits of Being Present."

69. J. Kabat-Zinn, *Full Catastrophe Living: Using the Wisdom of Your Body and Mind to Face Stress, Pain and Illness* (New York: Delacourt, 1990).

70. Brown and Ryan, "The Benefits of Being Present."

71. Porter, *Competitive Strategy.*

72. Boice, *Advice for New Faculty Members.*

73. R. F. Hébert and A. N. Link, *The Entrepreneur: Mainstream Views and Radical Critiques* (New York: Praeger Publishers, 1988), 6.

74. Brown and Ryan, "The Benefits of Being Present."

75. Boice, *Advice for New Faculty Members.*

76. J. Shear and R. Jevning, "Pure Consciousness: Scientific Exploration of Meditation Techniques," in *The View from Within*, eds. F. J. Varela and J. Shear (Thorverton, England: Imprint Academics, 1999), 189–209.

77. R. F. Baumeister, "The Nature and Structure of Self: An Overview," in *The Self in Social Psychology*, ed. R. F. Baumeister (Philadelphia: Psychology Press, 1999), 1–20.

78. J. L. Bermudez, *The Paradox of Self-Consciousness* (Cambridge, MA: MIT Press, 1998).

79. Boice, *Advice for New Faculty Members,* 108.

80. Kabat-Zinn, *Full Catastrophe Living.*

81. Boice, *Advice for New Faculty Members.*

82. D. Murray, *The Craft of Revision* (New York: Harcourt Brace, 1995).

83. M. Csikszentmihalyi, *Flow: The Psychology of Optimal Experience* (New York: Harper and Row, 1990).

84. C. Kawakami and J. White, "Mindful and Masculine: Freeing Women Leaders from the Constraints of Gender Roles," *Journal of Social Issues* 56, no. 1 (2000): 49–63.

4

New Venture Teams

Gaylen N. Chandler

The focus of this chapter is new venture teams. It is intended for a broad audience that includes both practitioners and academic researchers. It presents a comprehensive review of the new venture team literature and discusses recent advances in knowledge. The compiled findings are intended to provide very practical prescriptions for practitioners and direction for researchers with respect to the formation, composition, and team development processes employed by new venture teams.

In spite of the fact that empirical research regarding new venture teams has been somewhat slow to emerge, there is agreement among experienced entrepreneurs, investors, and researchers that the success of an emerging business is strongly influenced by the venture start-up team. In a 1990 review article the authors concluded that our lack of knowledge regarding new venture teams represents a fundamental gap in the literature.[1] They went on to state that many businesses are started by teams and that new venture teams seem to importantly impact the venture's performance; yet, these teams are difficult to assemble and keep together, and neither practitioners nor academics know much about them and how to avoid or overcome the associated problems. In 1997 another review of the literature discussed the definition of entrepreneurial teams, concluded that the research on new venture team formation processes is scarce, and discussed team composition issues.[2] In 2000 a third review discussed the definition of new venture teams, their composition, and the impact of differential team size.[3] These review articles captured the state of knowledge at the time they were written, however, in the past four or five years a number of articles have appeared that substantially increase our knowledge of new venture teams, how they are composed, and how they function. These articles begin to explore a number of interesting issues with respect to new venture teams. Thus, after a significant time-lag following a call to study new venture teams, our knowledge of new venture teams is beginning to develop.

This chapter materially augments the review articles that have been written previously and presents the state of the art with respect to knowledge about new venture teams. Because a number of articles have been published during the last five years the current review moves substantially beyond previous reviews.

I will address the following questions with respect to what is known and disseminated. Each of these questions deals with some aspect of new venture teams for which new information is available since the last review articles were published:

1. What is a new venture team?
2. How and when do new venture teams form?
   a. How do teams develop team processes as the firm evolves?
   b. What happens when members are added or subtracted from the team?
   c. If venture capitalists are involved, what influence do they have on the team?
3. How important are teams with respect to successful launch and future performance?
   a. What guidelines should be followed as new venture teams are composed?
   b. How do teams learn and develop?

The answers to these questions, along with the acknowledgment of gaps in knowledge regarding these questions will provide a good benchmark against which to measure progress in our understanding of new venture teams.

WHAT IS A NEW VENTURE TEAM?

The term *new venture team* implies that two criteria must exist in order for a group of individuals to be considered a new venture team. First is the term *new venture*. There has been little discussion of what constitutes a new venture in the literature. For example, if a team of individuals purchases an already-existing business, do they become a new venture team? Is it a new venture team if it is an owner-managed second-generation family business? Some researchers consider the team an entrepreneurial team if it is associated with a recent independent start-up while others include privately held firms up to fifty years old.[4, 5] Because firm dynamics change as organizations develop, it is of vital importance to clearly consider what is meant by a "new venture."[6] One study justified using a period of the first five years of a venture's existence, because in retrospective interviews it appeared that team membership tended to stabilize within a five-year period.[7] However, there is no commonly shared opinion of what this time period should be. Amidst the ambiguity, I propose that the term "new venture" refers to an independent start-up going through the process of establishing and initial growth of a business organization.

This leads to the second important question. Who should be counted as a member of the team? In discussions with entrepreneurs and a review of the literature it is obvious that there is not a universally accepted definition of who should be considered as a member of the new venture team. Some restrict their view of team membership to individuals who have financial membership and decision-making responsibility, as I have done here. However, while I was interviewing entrepreneurs as part of an earlier project, it became obvious that some entrepreneurs are fairly restrictive in their use of the word *team*, applying it to the small group of individuals with financial ownership and decision-making responsibility, while others consider all employees and advisors to be a part of the team. There is one principle reason why it is important to clearly define who should be counted as part of the new venture team. For researchers if a uniform definition is not applied, findings may not be generalizable beyond a specific study. For practitioners, it is difficult to follow prescriptive recommendations if the concept of team is not clearly specified and mutually understood. For example, adding an employee is likely to be very different from adding a management team member who has financial ownership and executive-level decision-making responsibility.

In the existing literature there have been varying definitions of who should be counted as part of the entrepreneurial team. The research agenda proposed in 1990 by Kamm, Shuman, Seeger, and Nurick did not clearly define who should be counted and considered to be a member of the new venture team.[8] However, subsequent researchers have grappled with the issue as they have sought to operationalize the new venture team construct. Some researchers have defined the entrepreneurial team as the group of people holding full-time executive positions at the time of founding.[9] Cooper and Daily stated that membership in an entrepreneurial team involves a shared commitment to the new venture, but did not clearly define shared commitment.[10] They concluded that at the time of their review that there was no consensual definition in the literature. Birley and Stockley pointed out that various researchers have used different definitions including equity ownership and managerial involvement, which might include a responsible position within the hierarchy or several other measures of commitment or involvement.[11]

Schoedt suggested that an entrepreneurial team consists of two or more persons who have an interest, financial and otherwise to the venture's future and success, and that they are considered to be at the executive level in the early phases of the venture.[12] As criteria for inclusion in the new venture team, Ensley, Pearson, and Amason required that two of the following conditions were met: being a founder, having equity ownership, and exercising significant decision-making responsibility.[13] They, however, did not clearly define what it meant to be a founder. Indeed, as the area of study has evolved, the field has evolved toward a position that requires both financial ownership and decision-making responsibility as criteria for inclusion in the new venture team.[14-17]

This definition incorporates both ownership and control, and is relatively easy to operationalize. It clearly defines the construct. Viewed from a practical perspective, managers without financial ownership usually do not have the same decision-making authority as those with ownership.[18] However, the ownership requirement ignores the role of key employees or individuals affiliated in other ways that may have a substantial influence in the team and on the development of an emerging venture. In spite of this drawback, it is necessary to draw a definitional line and even though it may be prudent to not include employees and advisors as part of the formal definition of the new venture team, this does not imply that the contributions of such individuals should be ignored.

HOW AND WHEN DO NEW VENTURE TEAMS FORM?

It has been pointed out that nothing in the venture creation process is less understood than the dynamics of organizing and building effective entrepreneurial teams.[19] Kamm et al. stated that there was a gap in the literature with respect to how and why individuals seek venture partners, where they look, what criteria they use for selection, and methods used to recruit and induce partners to join them.[20]

Although there are recent efforts to better understand these issues, in general the new venture team literature has not relied very heavily on the long and rich literature discussing the formation, development, and functioning of work teams. Forty years ago, after reviewing the existing literature, Tuckman proposed a four-stage model of team development describing a "forming, storming, norming, and performing" sequence.[21] A subsequent review concluded that the literature generally supported the original model, to which a fifth stage ("adjourning") was added.[22] In the current team literature, the stages are considered to have some face validity as a general sequence.[23] That is to say, the stages may have considerable face validity as a general sequence, yet empirical observations of specific teams expose complexities that do not cleanly fit the model. For example, teams may never attain a norm of performance, or may regress to an earlier stage of development. The basic model starts with an initial orientation process (forming), which continues until key interpersonal conflicts are uncovered and resolved (storming). The resolution of conflict establishes group expectations (norming). Then, team efforts are directed toward task accomplishment (performing). In the concluding part of the model, the team terminates either because the task is completed or membership is disrupted (adjourning). The implication of the model is that teams must go through several stages of development. It is assumed that individual needs and concerns must be resolved in order to establish behavioral norms and achieve task effectiveness.

Other researchers have also discussed team-building issues in substantial detail. For example, Dyer discusses several different approaches to team building, as does Golembiewski.[24, 25] My intention here is not to do a thorough review of the general team-building literature, but rather to indicate that the new venture teams literature has not relied heavily on the already existing body of team-building literature. I suggest that more focus should be placed on determining exactly how new venture teams differ from work teams, and then determining how and when existing models might apply to our understanding of new venture teams.

As I mentioned earlier, the processes by which new venture teams form has only recently been addressed. The available information suggests that new venture team formation is not a systematic process. In the scant documentation available, the process starts with an idea that someone champions.[26] One person may have the idea and recruit potential partners, or alternatively that the team may form from the outset on the basis of a shared idea.[27] The latter type of team may be subject to jockeying for position.[28] It would be useful to study these processes and provide better evidence of the interpersonal dynamics associated with these potential different types of team-formation processes. Tuckman's stage model may provide a framework for this investigation.[29]

Research suggests that teams can be composed based either on a demographic composition model or alternatively on a social network model.[30] The demography approach, consistent with that frequently prescribed in the new venture teams literature, proposes that it is necessary to ensure that new venture teams are well balanced in terms of functional expertise.[31, 32] However, research findings suggest that demographic characteristics are rarely considered, and there have been mixed results with respect to the relationship between functional completeness of the new venture team and performance.[33] Some studies have found no evidence that functional completeness is a significant predictor of team performance.[34, 35] In contrast, others have found that team functional heterogeneity was significantly and positively correlated with small firm growth.[36] The studies finding a relationship measured functional heterogeneity at a point of time several years after start-up and not at start-up. One explanation for the discrepancy between the studies is that new venture teams may evolve toward functional heterogeneity as the organization grows and develops. Indeed, the evidence suggests that sales growth is usually accompanied by increasing specialization and formalization, providing some support for that explanation.[37] Taken together there is little evidence that functional heterogeneity is important at start-up, but there is evidence that as the organization grows and specializes, the management team must develop functional heterogeneity.

On the other hand, there is some evidence that demographic heterogeneity (differences in age, job tenure, race, sex, and religion) in new venture teams has a positive influence on venture performance. Using a composite measure of new venture team heterogeneity, Chandler and Lyon provided evidence of relationships between demographic heterogeneity and sales levels in four out of five years.[38]

The second major rationale that has been discussed with regard to the formation of new venture teams is the social networks model. Consistent with this model, most new venture teams are comprised of friends, relatives, and associates from work.[39, 40] The social network explanation focuses more on the interpersonal characteristics of the relationships rather than the functional completeness of the team. Kamm and Nurick stated that when they asked entrepreneurs how they decided who would make a good team member, the entrepreneurs responded that it is like a marriage and the appropriateness is based on interpersonal attraction and chemistry.[41] This is consistent with the observation by Chandler and Lyon that little emphasis appears to be given to functional area expertise as a criterion for selecting team members.[42] Rather, mutual interest in the technology of the business, the excitement of a start-up, or independence and growth opportunities tend to be the driving factors.

Kamm and Nurick point out that interpersonal attraction theory suggests that we are attracted to individuals who are associated with rewarding situations.[43] In addition, research suggests that individuals are more likely to be attracted to those they have more exposure and proximity to and those who are perceived to be similar in a variety of ways.[44, 45] Thus, the evidence suggests that theories focusing on factors related to interpersonal attraction may be more useful than theories focusing on functional heterogeneity to explain why individuals are motivated to join a new venture team. Even though the research is currently very limited in scope, interpersonal attraction theory may provide a reasonable starting place for the study of how partners in entrepreneurial ventures are selected.

These combined findings have practical implications for those who may be considering putting together a new venture team. Being able to work with and get along with team members seems to be an important part of new venture team composition process. In addition, it is important to recognize that teams must resolve individual needs and concerns in order to establish behavioral norms and achieve task effectiveness. It appears to be useful to have some diversity in the team. However, it appears that functional differentiation can be developed, as the development of the venture requires. Thus, team members must be willing to learn and specialize as the venture grows.

HOW DO NEW VENTURE TEAMS DEVELOP EFFECTIVE TEAM PROCESSES?

There is a small body of research that focuses on the development of effective team processes. In the general field of organization development, the process of intervening in organizations to improve productivity has been called team building. Before a group of people can begin to improve their performance, group members must be able to work together effectively and collaboratively. The group process model predicts that process will be directly related to organizational performance with process accounting for variation in performance that demography leaves unexplained.[46] Bettenhausen reviewed 250 articles that referenced team and group research.[47] In his summary discussion he included group cohesion, commitment, conflict, and goal setting as key topic areas in team-process research. Subsequent researchers have added group innovation processes to the mix, while others have focused on interpersonal processes, which would include cohesion and conflict, group norms, and individual roles as part of the team process.[48, 49] Although there is a large volume of research focusing on team and group processes, there is very limited research regarding the team processes of new venture teams. The research has focused on three major areas: (1) cohesion and conflict, (2) decision making, and (3) team interpersonal processes. This research is summarized in the following.

Team researchers have long discussed the benefits of team cohesiveness.[50, 51] Ensley and Pearce examine the implications of shared strategic cognition and develop theoretical underpinnings supporting the importance of shared cognition regarding organizational strategies.[52] Cohesion and conflict in new venture teams have been shown to be related to performance. Ventures with cohesive teams experience higher levels of sales growth.[53] Utilizing similar measures, Ensley and Pearson added a dimension of potency, or the belief by the team that they can be effective, and studied differences between family and nonfamily firms on these group process characteristics.[54] They showed that there are significant differences in group potency, group cohesion, shared strategic cognition, idea conflict, and relationship conflict between two types of family firm top management teams and the top management teams of nonfamily firms. The first type of family top management team is referred to as a parental team, in which a small number of closely related family members control decision making. The second type is a familial team, in which a larger group of extended family members control decision making. This type of management team has been referred to as a *cousin consortium*.[55] Parental teams had higher levels of group potency and cohesion. Familial teams had higher levels of shared strategic cognition, but also higher levels of idea conflict and relationship conflict. Nonfamily teams were between the two types of family teams on all five dimensions.[56] Thus, different types of family relationships impact the interpersonal dynamics associated with team processes. However, neither parental teams, familial teams, nor nonfamily teams were universally superior.

In a related vein, Talaulicar, Grundei, and Werder investigated differences between the CEO model and the departmental model of top management team organization in a sample of fifty-six German start-up companies.[57] In the CEO model, a single CEO is given decision-making authority for the organization. In the departmental model, each top management team member has decision-making authority for her or his individual area of responsibility. The findings suggest that the departmental model led to greater decision comprehensiveness, defined as the degree to which a decision is based on thorough problem analysis. In addition, the departmental model is linked with greater speed of decision making.

Watson, Ponthieu, and Critelli studied the interpersonal effectiveness of new venture team dyads.[58] Building on the team literature and grounded theory development, they identified four dimensions of new venture team interpersonal process: leadership, interpersonal flexibility, team commitment, and helpfulness. Teams that regarded themselves as more effective on team interpersonal processes also regarded themselves as more successful business ventures. Leadership and team commitment were stronger predictors than flexibility and helpfulness.

In summary, new venture team process issues have not been studied extensively, yet there is information that if applied could strengthen team performance. As pointed out earlier, there is some recent research on cohesion and conflict, decision-making processes, and team interpersonal processes. However, there remains much about team process issues in the specialized context of new venture teams that we do not understand. In addition, there are issues discussed in the general team literature that have not been studied extensively enough in the new venture team literature to appear in journals or scholarly books. For example, the team-building process has not been extensively analyzed. Individual roles in new venture teams have not been analyzed or discussed. Likewise, the establishment of group norms and involvement in goal-setting activities in new venture teams has received very little attention.

WHAT HAPPENS WHEN TEAMS GAIN AND LOSE MEMBERS?

Recent research suggests that membership in new venture teams often changes during the early stages of development, yet research focusing on new venture teams has usually focused on conditions at start-up or at a single point in time.[59] Only recently have entrepreneurship researchers started to look at what happens when new venture teams gain and lose members. If Tuckman's stage model were applied, the team adjourns when members exit.[60] Thus, the team-development process would start over when team composition changes. However, because the venture is an ongoing entity, it is important to study how the organization reacts to team changes. Such changes have been shown to have an impact on the development of firms, which suggests that more complex modeling may need to be used. In the top-management team literature, changes in the management team are viewed as an adaptation mechanism that is frequently associated with strategic changes.[61, 62] Yet most of the studies with new venture teams have treated start-up team composition as a static variable and have not accounted for changing team membership.[63, 64] A related issue is that the demands on a team may differ at different developmental stages.[65] Possible differences in requisite team characteristics at different developmental stages have been noted in the evolutionary literature; but such speculations have not been verified empirically in the literature on entrepreneurial teams.[66, 67]

A study in the United Kingdom analyzed team characteristics with respect to their impact on member entry and exit.[68] The researchers found that the size of the team was negatively associated with subsequent team member entry. Functional heterogeneity was positively associated with entry. Heterogeneity of prior entrepreneurial experience was positively related with member exit, and family firm teams were less likely to experience exits. The study did not investigate the impact of entries and exits on subsequent performance.

In contrast, in a study in Sweden and the western United States initial team size was found to be positively related to entry in the Swedish sample and positively related to exit in the U.S. sample.[69] In addition, heterogeneity of industry experience was positively related to both entries and exits. In contrast religious heterogeneity was related only to exits, and heterogeneity of educational backgrounds was positively related to entries. Although the results are partially conflicting, in general, they seem to indicate that more heterogeneous teams are likely to experience more entries as well as exits, and entries and exits may be somewhat correlated.

Entries and exits of team members have been shown to influence new venture performance.[70] A common prescription in the entrepreneurship literature is that emerging firms can gain access to expertise by adding team members. Huber refers to the addition of members to the team as *grafting*.[71] Organization learning theorists specify that teams can gain knowledge by adding new members who have knowledge that the organization previously did not possess.[72, 73] Grafting team members appears to be somewhat successful in rapidly changing environments; however, there is evidence that adding team members in stable environments is detrimental. One study showed that perceived environmental dynamism was a positive moderator of the relationship between adding team members and sales growth. In other words, adding team members was positively associated with sales growth when respondents perceived that their environments were changing rapidly, but negatively related to sales growth when there was little perceived dynamism.[74] It has been proposed that these negative results occur because new team members disrupt the social flow of the team and the disruption of team processes translates into negative performance outcomes for the emerging venture.[75]

The research regarding changing membership in new venture teams consists of only a few articles. The overall results conflict with respect to the impact of team size on entry and exit. The conflicting results suggest that initial team size influences turnover, differentially based on undefined contextual differences. The studies converge with respect to heterogeneity in that heterogeneous teams are more likely to have both entries and exits. It has been suggested that new team members may disrupt the social flow of the team.[76] However, there is little empirical research to substantiate that view. Additional research needs to focus on explaining why adding team members is frequently associated with negative performance results. In addition, the direction of causality needs to be investigated. Do teams perform poorly because they have added members, or do poorly performing teams add members in hopes that the new team member will make a dramatic enough difference to save the company?

HOW ARE NEW VENTURE TEAMS IMPACTED
BY VENTURE CAPITALISTS?

When venture capitalists are involved in an emerging venture it appears to influence team processes. Although a small minority of new ventures is funded by venture capital, such firms are usually in industries with substantial growth potential. Venture capital has been a driving force in the development of many of the most vibrant economies.[77] As a result, venture capitalists and the firms they finance are often the targets of research.[78, 79] This is true also with respect to the relationship between venture capitalists and new venture teams.

The relationship between venture capitalists and new venture teams occurs at two levels: (1) the selection of venture opportunities by venture capitalists, and (2) ongoing control and guidance of the team during the time period covered by the particular round of financing. Shepherd provides evidence that venture capitalists assess the probability of success to be higher when founding teams have higher educational capability and greater industry-related competence.[80] Indeed, the quality of the new venture team is often viewed to be more important than the product or service, industry structure, and perceived competitive intensity in the industry.[81]

A few recent articles address the impact of the venture capitalists in the ongoing management of the firm. In contrast to most other forms of investment, venture capitalists frequently play a role in helping to manage the ventures in which they have invested.[82] The objective of venture capitalists is to increase the perceived value of the organization for the next round of financing or to groom the organization for a buyout or an initial public offering (IPO). In order to do so, venture capitalists often play a key role in recomposing the management team in cases of conflict and as a signal to potential investors further down the stream that the venture is well poised for the next stage of development.[83]

Busenitz, Moesel, Fiet, and Barney point out that the venture capitalist–new venture team relationship is a two-way exchange of information and value.[84] However, in an empirical study, Busenitz, Fiet, and Moesel could find no evidence to support the proposition that venture capitalists provide value by adding strategic information.[85] In addition, they proposed that according to agency theory, dismissing new venture team members would decrease the amount of conflict inherent in the relationship, and have a long-term positive benefit. However, their findings indicate that dismissing venture team members has a negative impact on long-term venture performance. This finding is in direct opposition to what Chandler, Honig, and Wiklund found in their sample of firms that were not venture capital funded.[86] It appears that exits initiated by the venture capitalists do not have the same effect as voluntary departures or departures initiated by team members. Although there are a variety of potential explanations, the simplest appears to be that the presence of venture capitalists changes the dynamics of the relationship between the exit of team members and venture performance.

Busenitz and his coauthors introduce the concept of procedural justice to the relationship between the new venture team and venture capitalists.[87] Their initial study suggests some inherent conflict in the relationship because venture capitalists often prefer to invest in companies with team members who have experience working with each other and in the industry. However, the evidence suggests that such teams are less receptive to input from the venture capitalists. In spite of those conflicts, the evidence suggests that perceived procedural justice is positively associated with long-term venture performance.[88] In a later study, Busenitz, Fiet, and Moesel proposed that the proportion of ownership retained by the new venture team would signal their expectations for the performance of the venture, but they found no support for their proposition.[89]

In summary, the research provides some insights into the relationship between venture capitalists and new venture teams. However, there is much that we do not know about how the presence of venture capitalists impacts the new venture team. The special case of new venture teams and venture capitalists represents an area where substantial additional research could be conducted. For example, do internal team dynamics change because of the presence of venture capitalists? Busenitz et al. propose that dismissals may have a negative impact because suitable replacements are hard to find.[90] However, an alternative explanation may be found by examining the internal dynamics of the new venture team. When dismissals of existing team members are initiated by venture capitalists it may result in a negative effect, which changes team processes in a negative way. Clearly, more fine-grained research needs to be conducted to explain the anomaly. Additionally, it is unclear how lack of procedural justice between the new venture team and the venture capitalists may impact the internal functioning and performance of the team.

HOW IMPORTANT ARE TEAMS WITH RESPECT TO SUCCESSFUL LAUNCH AND SUBSEQUENT PERFORMANCE?

Researchers have provided evidence that a significant proportion of new ventures are started by more than one individual.[91–94] Even though the topic of new venture teams has become increasingly researched over the past decade, relatively few studies report the number or proportion of team-founded ventures. This occurs because a significant number of studies select only team-founded ventures.[95] Alternatively, a number of studies report mean number of founders, but do not differentiate between team-founded and individual-founded ventures.[96] Although the sample size does not allow the findings to be conclusive, evidence from eight samples in which the proportion of team versus individually founded ventures is reported indicates that approximately two-thirds of ventures in the industries covered by these studies were team founded.[97–101] Cooper and Daily make the point that the proportion of team-founded ventures is likely to vary by industry, yet there is little empirical evidence to verify this speculation.[102] The fact that a large proportion of new ventures are started by teams is important from the perspective that it highlights the importance of new venture teams in general, and also suggests that it is important for researchers to continue to study the effects that teams have on the new venture creation process and subsequent outcomes.

HOW DO TEAM CHARACTERISTICS INFLUENCE THE DEVELOPMENT AND PERFORMANCE OF EMERGING FIRMS?

This section summarizes what is known about how team characteristics and processes influence the performance of new businesses. There is substantial support for the proposition that team-founded ventures achieve better performance than individually founded ventures.[103–105] Research has extended this finding to show that larger teams tend to achieve better venture results.[106] The logic used to support this finding is typically a resource-based explanation. Larger teams have greater pooled human resources (knowledge, skills, and abilities) and also greater social resources. As a result, they have larger contact networks. This finding has been verified over more studies and a longer time period than any other knowledge we have about how teams impact performance.

Initial team size is significantly and positively related to performance. Yet there is evidence that change in team membership is fairly common during the emerging phases of new businesses. One study found that 37 percent of teams added members, and 45 percent dropped members during the first five years of the venture.[107] The results show that adding team members was negatively related to performance (except in highly dynamic environments), and dropping team members was positively related to performance. In contrast, Busenitz and coauthors found a negative relationship with performance when venture capitalists dismiss team members.[108] Even though there is no complete agreement about the direction of the relationship, the combined evidence suggests a significant link between the addition and departure of team members and the performance of the firm. It should be noted, however, that performance might be a factor that leads to change in the top management team. As a field we are only beginning to scratch the surface as we seek to better understand the relationship between changes to the venture team and new venture performance.

There is also some evidence that team processes make a performance difference. Ensley and Pearce provided evidence that involvement in processes that lead to shared cognitive models was significantly linked to new venture performance.[109] They developed a theoretical frame that ties shared strategic cognition to group process and new venture performance. The results indicate that the group processes leading to the development of shared strategic cognition are more important than the outcome of shared strategic cognition in terms of predicting organizational performance. In a related study, Ensley et al. provide evidence that ventures with cohesive teams experience higher levels of sales growth.[110] Watson et al. found that teams that regarded themselves as more effective on team interpersonal processes also regarded themselves as more successful business ventures.[111] Leadership and team commitment were stronger predictors than flexibility and helpfulness. The success of these initial studies in linking team interpersonal processes with performance provides some indication that this may lead to a fruitful stream of research.

HOW DO NEW VENTURE TEAMS LEARN AND DEVELOP?

When new venture teams are composed, the individuals involved usually pay little attention to the functional completeness of the team. When a new venture is formed, it has access only to the knowledge of environments and processes that founders already possessed prior to the birth of the organization. Thus, new ventures tend to start without a full measure of knowledge, skills, and abilities. Yet if the complementarity of skills is not a significant criterion when selecting team members, how do new ventures acquire or develop the necessary competencies after start-up?

This question can be partially addressed by the organizational learning literature and some recent studies that focus on organizational learning in new ventures.[112–117] The knowledge possessed by team members when the team is composed is referred to as congenital learning.[118] The founding team is the heart of the company and individual knowledge is transformed into organizational competencies.[119–122]

However, the concept of congenital learning does not explain how new venture teams are able to gain knowledge and competencies that they do not possess at venture start-up. The literature on organizational learning provides some insights into how new venture teams acquire the necessary competencies. Teams can gain knowledge by adding new members who have the knowledge the organization previously did not possess.[123, 124] Huber refers to the addition of members to the team as grafting.[125] The evidence suggests that grafting team members occurs somewhat frequently. In two studies reporting the addition of team members, one (in a sample from the western United States) reported that 37 percent of teams in their study added one or more members during the preceding six years and another (in a sample from the United Kingdom) reported that 42 percent of their teams added members during the first five years of the business.[126, 127] Grafting team members appears to be somewhat successful in rapidly changing environments; however, there is evidence that adding team members in other circumstances is detrimental because new team members disrupt the social flow of the team and the disruption of team processes often translates into negative performance outcomes for the emerging venture.[128]

Although many teams attempt to graft knowledge by adding members, virtually all teams gain knowledge as a part of the venture-development process.[129] In other words, the evidence seems to indicate that much of the knowledge necessary to successfully start and grow a company is developed as the organization itself grows and develops. This appears to happen in a variety of different ways. An expanding body of research focuses on experimental learning in new ventures.[130–134] Organizations change as they accumulate experiences, adjusting reactions to problems while absorbing feedback and developing routines of various types to capture positive outcomes for the future.[135] The basic premise of experimental learning is that organizations learn by the outcomes of past decisions, and that present decisions are informed by that knowledge.[136]

Thus, new venture teams acquire knowledge by grafting team members, and by experimental learning—learning by doing. In addition, Huber discusses vicarious learning and search and notice learning as additional processes.[137] Building on these concepts, involvement by team members in informal learning activities (talking to people familiar with the particular industry, benchmarking activities, gathering information about competitors and competitive practices, reading trade journals and publications), nonformal education (attendance at seminars, workshops, and other structured educational experiences) and formal education (involvement in formal trade school or university-based training) has been shown to be positively related to sales growth.[138]

Combined, the evidence suggests that functional completeness is typically not a primary consideration when new venture teams are composed. However, as the venture develops, team members are likely to engage in a variety of different learning activities in order to gain the necessary competencies. Certainly, involvement in these different forms of knowledge acquisition activities is not mutually exclusive. Emerging organizations can graft team members, be involved in experimental learning, and gather information from a variety of vicarious sources. However, in general, involvement in knowledge acquisition activities appears to be more effective than grafting team members into the organization.

SUMMARY

This section presents a very practical summary of what we know about new venture teams. There is much we still do not know about new venture teams, but knowledge has expanded significantly since the last published review. First of all, new venture teams are important. There is evidence suggesting that about two-thirds of all businesses are founded by teams of two or more individuals.

The field is converging on a definition of the new venture team, which requires individuals to have financial ownership and decision-making responsibility in order to be considered as part of the team. This is useful from a research perspective and also useful to help interpret and apply results. However, it is not meant to imply that employees, advisors, or other individuals not formally recognized as a team member cannot have a substantial impact on the development of an emerging venture.

Individuals are attracted to new venture teams because of interpersonal connections and shared interest. For the most part, there seems to be very little emphasis on putting together a team that has the necessary competencies to grow a firm beyond start-up. Although it is frequently prescribed that the functional composition of the new venture team is important, there is little empirical evidence supporting this position. However, there is substantial evidence suggesting that teams must gain the competencies necessary to support change and growth more effectively by learning through experimentation and participation in activities, such as searching out and reading relevant articles and books, talking to knowledgeable people, attending seminars and workshops, and enrollment in formal educational programs.

There is still very little information to suggest how venture teams develop effective team processes. I believe there is much to be gained by linking more closely to the existing teams literature, and recommend that researchers do so. From a practical perspective, effective team processes are associated with decision-making effectiveness and performance. The initial evidence suggests that leadership, interpersonal flexibility, team commitment, and helpfulness of individuals are associated with better team performance. In addition, collaborative decision-making processes lead to greater decision comprehensiveness. The evidence strongly suggests that team cohesiveness is more important than the initial functional composition in predicting performance.

Adding team members appears to be effective in highly dynamic environments. However, in more stable environments, adding team members is negatively associated with performance. It appears that the disruption caused by adding a team member upsets the social fabric of the team, making it difficult to integrate the individual's knowledge, skills, and abilities. When team members leave the organization, the impact is significantly beneficial with the exception of when venture capitalist firms are involved. Venture performance is affected negatively when the venture capitalist firm removes team members.

This work represents a comprehensive review of the published research on new venture teams. Our knowledge has advanced significantly within the past five years. The accumulated knowledge provides evidence to support four very practical prescriptions. First, there is strong support for the belief that team-founded ventures outperform those founded by individuals. In general, it appears to be more functional to start with a larger team and allow members to drop out as they choose. However, the involvement of venture capitalists changes the dynamics of the team in such a way that dismissals from the team become dysfunctional. Second, extensive involvement in a variety of knowledge acquisition activities by existing team members is generally more efficacious than trying to graft new members into an already existing team. Third, team cohesiveness appears to be an important ingredient in developing and growing a business effectively. Therefore, new venture teams should seek cohesiveness. Fourth, participative decision styles are more efficacious than styles in which a lead entrepreneur makes decisions with little consultation with other team members.

NOTES

1. Judith B. Kamm, Jeffrey C. Shuman, John A. Seeger, and Aaron J. Nurick, "Entrepreneurial Teams in New Venture Creation: A Research Agenda," *Entrepreneurship Theory and Practice* 14, no. 4 (1990): 7.

2. Arnold C. Cooper and Catherine M. Daily, "Entrepreneurial Teams," in *Entrepreneurship 2000,* eds. D. L. Sexton and R. W. Smilor (Chicago: Upstart Publishing, 1997), 127.

3. Sue Birley and Simon Stockley, "Entrepreneurial Teams and Venture Growth," in *Blackwell Handbook of Entrepreneurship*, eds. D. L. Sexton and H. Landstrom (Malden, MA: Blackwell Publishers, 2000), 287.

4. Gaylen N. Chandler, Benson Honig, and Johan Wiklund, "Antecedents, Moderators, and Performance Consequences of Membership Change in New Venture Teams," *Journal of Business Venturing* 20, no. 5 (2005): 705.

5. Deniz Ucbasaran, Andy Lockett, Mike Wright, and Paul Westhead, "Entrepreneurial Founder Teams: Factors Associated with Member Entry and Exit," *Entrepreneurship Theory and Practice* 27, no. 2 (2003): 107.

6. Steven H. Hanks, Collin J. Watson, Erik Jansen, and Gaylen N Chandler, "Tightening the Life-Cycle Construct: A Taxonomic Study of Growth Stage Configurations in High-Technology Organizations," *Entrepreneurship Theory and Practice* 18, no. 2 (1993): 5.

7. Chandler, Honig, and Wiklund, "Antecedents, Moderators, and Performance Consequences."

8. Kamm, Shuman, Seeger, and Nurick, "Entrepreneurial Teams in New Venture Creation."

9. Kathleen M. Eisenhardt and Claudia Bird Schoonhoven, "Organizational Growth: Linking Founding Team, Strategy, Environment, and Growth among U.S. Semiconductor Ventures, 1978–1988," *Administrative Science Quarterly* 41 (1990): 659.

10. Cooper and Daily, "Entrepreneurial Teams."

11. Birley and Stockley, "Entrepreneurial Teams and Venture Growth."

12. Leon Schoedt, "Entrepreneurial Teams: Definition and Determinants," Proceedings of the USASBE 2002 Annual National Conference (2002).

13. Michael D. Ensley, Allison W. Pearson, and Allen Amason, "Understanding the Dynamics of New Venture Top Management Teams: Cohesion, Conflict, and New Venture Performance," *Journal of Business Venturing* 17 (2002): 365.

14. Chandler, Honig, and Wiklund, "Antecedents, Moderators, and Performance Consequences."

15. Judith B. Kamm and Aaron J. Nurick, "The Stages of Team Venture Formation: A Decision-Making Model," *Entrepreneurship Theory and Practice* 17 (1993): 17.

16. Ucbasaran, Lockett, Wright, and Westhead, "Entrepreneurial Founder Teams."

17. Warren E. Watson, Louis D. Ponthieu, and Joseph W. Critelli, "Team Interpersonal Process Effectiveness in Venture Partnerships and Its Connection to Perceived Success," *Journal of Business Venturing* 10, no. 5 (1995): 393.

18. Oliver Hart, *Firms, Contracts, and Financial Structure* (Oxford, UK: Clarendon Press, 1995).

19. Jeffry A. Timmons, "The Entrepreneurial Team: An American Dream or Nightmare?" *Journal of Small Business Management* 13 (1975): 33.

20. Kamm, Shuman, Seeger, and Nurick, "Entrepreneurial Teams in New Venture Creation."

21. Bruce W. Tuckman, "Development Sequence in Small Groups," *Psychological Bulletin* 63, no. 6 (1965): 384.

22. Bruce W. Tuckman and Michael C. Jensen, "Stages of Small Group Development Revisited," *Group and Organizational Studies* 2 (1977): 419.

23. David Buchanan and Andrzej Huczynski, *Organizational Behaviour: An Introductory Text,* 3rd ed. (London: Prentice-Hall, 1997).

24. William G. Dyer, *Team Building: Issues and Alternatives* (Reading, MA: Addison Wesley, 1977).

25. Robert T. Golembiewski, *The Small Group* (Chicago: University of Chicago Press, 1962).

26. Bart Clarysse and Nathalie Moray, "A Process Study of Entrepreneurial Team Formation: The Case of a Research-Based Spin-off," *Journal of Business Venturing* 19, no. 1 (2004): 55.

27. Timmons, "The Entrepreneurial Team."

28. Cooper and Daily, "Entrepreneurial Teams."

29. Tuckman, "Development Sequence in Small Groups."

30. Ray Reagans, Ezra Zuckerman, and Bill McEvily, "How to Make the Team: Social Networks vs. Demography as Criteria for Designing Effective Teams," *Administrative Science Quarterly* 49 (2004): 101.

31. Gaylen N. Chandler and Douglas W. Lyon, "Entrepreneurial Teams in New Ventures: Composition, Turnover and Performance," in *Best Paper Proceedings of the Academy of Management Conference,* ed. Dennis Nagao (August 3–8, 2001)

32. Ian C. MacMillan, Robert Siegel, and P. N. Subba Narasimha, "Criteria Used by Venture Capitalists to Evaluate New Venture Proposals," *Journal of Business Venturing* 1 (1985): 119.

33. Chandler and Lyon, "Entrepreneurial Teams in New Ventures."

34. Reagans, Zuckerman, and McEvily, "How to Make the Team."

35. Chandler and Lyon, "Entrepreneurial Teams in New Ventures."

36. Laurence G. Weinzimmer, "Top Management Team Correlates of Organizational Growth in a Small Business Context," *Journal of Small Business Management* 14, 35, no. 3 (1997): 1.

37. Hanks, Watson, Jansen, and Chandler, "Tightening the Life-Cycle Construct."

38. Chandler and Lyon, "Entrepreneurial Teams in New Ventures."

39. Kamm and Nurick, "The Stages of Team Venture Formation."

40. Chandler and Lyon, "Entrepreneurial Teams in New Ventures."

41. Kamm and Nurick, "The Stages of Team Venture Formation."

42. Chandler and Lyon, "Entrepreneurial Teams in New Ventures."

43. Kamm and Nurick, "The Stages of Team Venture Formation."

44. Ted L. Huston and George Levinger, "Interpersonal Attraction and Relationships," *Annual Review of Psychology* 29, no. 1 (1978): 15.

45. R. Matthew Montoya and Robert S. Hoya, "On the Importance of Cognitive Evaluation as a Determinant of Interpersonal Attraction," *Journal of Personality and Social Psychology* 86, no. 5 (2004): 696.

46. Shailendra Vyakarnam and Jari Handelberg, "Four Themes of the Impact of Management Teams on Organizational Performance: Implication for Future Research of Entrepreneurial Teams," *International Small Business Journal* 23, no. 3 (2005): 236.

47. Kenneth L. Bettenhausen, "Five Years of Groups Research: What We Have Learned and What Needs to Be Addressed," *Journal of Management* 17, no. 2 (1991): 345.

48. Susan G. Cohen, Gerald E. Ledford Jr., and Gretchen M. Spreitzer, "A Predictive Model of Self-Managing Work Team Effectiveness," *Human Relations* 49, no. 5 (1996): 643.

49. Eric Sundstrom, Kenneth P. De Meuse, and David Futrell, "Work Teams: Applications and Effectiveness," *American Psychologist* 45, no. 2 (1990): 120.

50. Daniel Katz and Robert L. Kahn, *The Social Psychology of Organizations* (New York: Wiley, 1978).

51. Joseph E. McGrath, *Groups: Interaction and Performance* (Englewood Cliffs, NJ: Prentice Hall, 1984).

52. Michael D. Ensley and Craig L. Pearce, "Shared Cognition in Top Management Teams: Implications for New Venture Performance," *Journal of Organizational Behavior* 22, no. 2 (2001): 145.

53. Ensley, Pearson, and Amason, "Understanding the Dynamics of New Venture Top Management Teams."

54. Michael D. Ensley and Allison W. Pearson, "An Exploratory Comparison of the Behavioral Dynamics of Top Management Teams in Family and Non-Family New Ventures: Cohesion, Conflict, Potency, and Consensus," *Entrepreneurship Theory and Practice* 29, no. 3 (2005): 267.

55. Kelin E. Gersick, John A. Davis, Marion M. Hampton, and Ivan Lansberg, *Generation to Generation: Lifecycles of Family Business* (Boston: Harvard Business School Press, 1997).

56. Ensley and Pearson, "An Exploratory Comparison of the Behavioral Dynamics of Top Management Teams."

57. Till Talaulicar, Jens Grundei, and Axel V. Werder, "Strategic Decision Making in Start-ups: The Effect of Top Management Team Organization and Processes on Speed and Comprehensiveness," *Journal of Business Venturing* 20, no. 4 (2005): 519.

58. Watson, Ponthieu, and Critelli, "Team Interpersonal Process Effectiveness."

59. Chandler, Honig, and Wiklund, "Antecedents, Moderators, and Performance Consequences."

60. Tuckman, "Development Sequence in Small Groups."

61. Warren Boeker, "Executive Migration and Strategic Change: The Effect of Top Manager Movement on Product-Market Entry," *Administrative Science Quarterly* 42 (1997): 213.

62. Margarethe F. Wiersema and Karen A. Bantel, "Top Management Team Turnover as an Adaptation Mechanism: The Role of the Environment," *Strategic Management Journal* 14 (1993): 485.

63. Weinzimmer, "Top Management Team Correlates of Organizational Growth."

64. Ensley, Pearson, and Amason, "Understanding the Dynamics of New Venture Top Management Teams."

65. Birley and Stockley, "Entrepreneurial Teams and Venture Growth," 287.

66. Howard Aldrich, *Organizations Evolving* (Thousand Oaks, CA: Sage Publications, 1999).

67. Hanks, Watson, Jansen, and Chandler, "Tightening the Life-Cycle Construct."

68. Ucbasaran, Lockett, Wright, and Westhead, "Entrepreneurial Founder Teams."

69. Chandler, Honig, and Wiklund, "Antecedents, Moderators, and Performance Consequences."

70. Ibid.

71. George P. Huber, "Organizational Learning: The Contributing Processes and the Literatures," *Organization Science* 2, no. 1 (1991): 88.

72. Herbert A. Simon, "Bounded Rationality and Organizational Learning," *Organization Science* 2 (1991): 125.

73. Wiersema and Bantel, "Top Management Team Turnover as an Adaptation Mechanism."

74. Chandler, Honig, and Wiklund, "Antecedents, Moderators, and Performance Consequences."

75. Ibid.

76. Ibid.

77. Leslie A. Jeng and Philippe C. Wells, "The Determinants of Venture Capital Funding: Evidence across Countries," *Journal of Corporate Finance* 6 (2000): 241.

78. Harry J. Sapienza and Anil Gupta, "Impact of Agency Risks and Task Uncertainty on Venture Capitalists—CEO Interaction," *Academy of Management Journal* 37, no. 6 (1994): 1618.

79. Sanford Ehrlich, Tracy Moore, Alex DeNoble, and Richard Weaver, "After the Cash Arrives: A Comparative Study of Venture Capital and Private Investor Involvement in Entrepreneurial Firms," *Journal of Business Venturing* 9, no. 1 (1994): 67.

80. Dean Shepherd, "Venture Capitalists Assessment of New Venture Survival," *Management Science* 45, no. 5 (1999): 621.

81. Ian C. MacMillan, Lauriann Zemann, and P. N. SubbaNarasimha, "Criteria Distinguishing Successful from Unsuccessful Ventures in the Venture Screening Process," *Journal of Business Venturing* 2, no. 1 (1987): 23.

82. Lloyd Steier and Royston Greenwood, "Venture Capitalist Relationships in the Deal Structuring and Post-Investment," *Journal of Management Studies* 32, no. 3 (1995): 337.

83. Garry Bruton, Vance Fried, and Robert D. Hisrich, "Venture Capitalist and CEO Dismissal," *Entrepreneurship Theory and Practice* 21, no. 3 (1997): 41.

84. Lowell W. Busenitz, Douglas D. Moesel, James O. Fiet, and Jay B. Barney, "The Framing of Perceptions of Fairness in the Relationship between Venture Capitalists and New Venture Teams," *Entrepreneurship Theory and Practice* 21, no. 3 (1997): 5.

85. Lowell W. Busenitz, James O. Fiet, and Douglas D. Moesel, "Reconsidering the Venture Capitalists' 'Value Added' Proposition: An Interorganizational Learning Perspective," *Journal of Business Venturing* 19, no. 6 (2004): 787.

86. Chandler, Honig, and Wiklund, "Antecedents, Moderators, and Performance Consequences."

87. Busenitz, Moesel, Fiet, and Barney, "The Framing of Perceptions of Fairness in the Relationship between Venture Capitalists and New Venture Teams."

88. Busenitz, Fiet, and Moesel, "Reconsidering the Venture Capitalists' 'Value Added' Proposition."

89. Lowell W. Busenitz, James O. Fiet, and Douglas D. Moesel, "Signaling in Venture Capitalist–New Venture Team Funding Decisions: Does It Indicate Long-Term Venture Outcomes?" *Entrepreneurship Theory and Practice* 29, no. 1 (2005): 1.

90. Busenitz, Fiet, and Moesel, "Reconsidering the Venture Capitalists' 'Value Added' Proposition."

91. Arnold C. Cooper, "Technical Entrepreneurship: What Do We Know?" *R&D Management* 3, no. 2 (1973): 59.

92. Kathleen M. Eisenhardt and Claudia Bird Schoonhoven, "Resource-Based View of Strategic Alliance Formation: Strategic and Social Effects in Entrepreneurial Firms," *Organization Science* 7, no. 2 (1996): 136.

93. Kamm, Shuman, Seeger, and Nurick, "Entrepreneurial Teams in New Venture Creation."

94. Robert Kazanjian and Hayagreeva Rao, "Research Note: The Creation of Capabilities in New Ventures—A Longitudinal Study," *Organization Studies* 20, no. 1 (1999): 125.

95. Ensley, Pearson, and Amason, "Understanding the Dynamics of New Venture Top Management Teams."

96. Weinzimmer, "Top Management Team Correlates of Organizational Growth."

97. Cooper, "Technical Entrepreneurship."

98. Richard D. Teach, Fred A. Tarpley Jr., and Robert G. Schwartz, "Software Venture Teams," in *Frontiers of Entrepreneurship Research,* eds. R. Ronstadt, J. Hornaday, R. Peterson, and K. Vesper (Wellesley, MA: Babson College, 1986).

99. Ucbasaran, Lockett, Wright, and Westhead, "Entrepreneurial Founder Teams."

100. Talaulicar, Grundei, and Werder, "Strategic Decision Making in Start-ups."

101. Chandler, Honig, and Wiklund, "Antecedents, Moderators, and Performance Consequences."

102. Cooper and Daily, "Entrepreneurial Teams."

103. Arnold C. Cooper and Albert V. Bruno, "Success among High-Technology Firms," *Business Horizons* 20, no. 2 (1977): 16.

104. Teach, Tarpley Jr., and Schwartz, "Software Venture Teams."

105. Chandler, Honig, and Wiklund, "Antecedents, Moderators, and Performance Consequences."

106. Ibid.

107. Ibid.

108. Busenitz, Fiet, and Moesel, "Reconsidering the Venture Capitalists' 'Value Added' Proposition."

109. Ensley and Pearce, "Shared Cognition in Top Management Teams."

110. Ensley, Pearson, and Amason, "Understanding the Dynamics of New Venture Top Management Teams."

111. Watson, Ponthieu, and Critelli, "Team Interpersonal Process Effectiveness."

112. Christopher A. Bartlett and Sumantra Ghoshal, "The Myth of the Generic Manager: New Personal Competencies for New Management Roles," *California Management Review* 40, no. 1 (1997): 92.

113. Robert J. Baum, "The Relationship of Traits, Competencies, Motivation, Strategy and Structure to Venture Growth," PhD dissertation (University of Maryland, 1994).

114. Gaylen N. Chandler and Erik Jansen, "The Founder's Self-Assessed Competence and Venture Performance," *Journal of Business Venturing* 7, no. 3 (1992): 223.

115. Robert J. Baum, Edwin A. Locke, and Ken G. Smith, "A Multidimensional Model of Venture Growth," *Academy of Management Journal* 44, no. 2 (2001): 292.

116. Gaylen N. Chandler and Steven H. Hanks, "Market Attractiveness, Resource-Based Capabilities, Venture Strategies, and Venture Performance," *Journal of Business Venturing* 9, no. 4 (1994): 331.

117. Gregory G. Dess, G. T. Lumpkin, and Jeffrey G. Covin, "Entrepreneurial Strategy Making and Firm Performance: Tests of Contingency and Configurational Models," *Strategic Management Journal* 18, no. 9 (1997): 677.

118. Huber, "Organizational Learning."

119. Chandler and Jansen, "The Founder's Self-Assessed Competence and Venture Performance."

120. Baum, Locke, and Smith, "A Multidimensional Model of Venture Growth."

121. Per Davidsson and Benson Honig, "The Role of Social and Human Capital Among Nascent Entrepreneurs," *Journal of Business Venturing* 18, no. 3 (2003): 301.

122. Rebecca A. Reuber and Eileen M Fischer, "Entrepreneurs' Experience, Expertise, and the Performance of Technology-Based Firms," *IEEE Transactions on Engineering Management* 41, no. 4 (1994): 1.

123. Simon, "Bounded Rationality and Organizational Learning."

124. Wiersema and Bantel, "Top Management Team Turnover as an Adaptation Mechanism."

125. Huber, "Organizational Learning."

126. Chandler, Honig, and Wiklund, "Antecedents, Moderators, and Performance Consequences."

127. Ucbasaran, Lockett, Wright, and Westhead, "Entrepreneurial Founder Teams."

128. Chandler, Honig, and Wiklund, "Antecedents, Moderators, and Performance Consequences."

129. Ibid.

130. Africa Ariño and Jose de la Torre, "Learning from Failure: Towards an Evolutionary Model of Collaborative Ventures," *Organization Science* 9, no. 3 (1998): 306.

131. Benson Honig, "Learning Strategies and Resources for Entrepreneurs and Intrapreneurs," *Entrepreneurship Theory and Practice* 26, no. 1 (2001): 21.

132. Benyamin Lichtenstein, G. T. Lumpkin, and Rodney Shrader, "Organizational Learning by New Ventures: Concepts, Strategies and Applications," in *Advances in Entrepreneurship Vol. 6: Cognitive Approaches to Entrepreneurship*, eds. Jerome A. Katz and Dean Shepherd (Oxford: Elsevier Science, 2003), 11.

133. Maria Minniti and William Bygrave, "A Dynamic Model of Entrepreneurial Learning," *Entrepreneurship Theory and Practice* 25, no. 3 (2001): 5.

134. Davide Ravasi and Carlo Turati, "Technology Development and Learning in Entrepreneurial Firms," SDA Bocconi, Research Division Working Paper No. 01–59 (2001).

135. Richard R. Nelson and Sidney G. Winter, *An Evolutionary Theory of Economic Change* (Cambridge, MA: Bellknap/Harvard, 1982).

136. Huber, "Organizational Learning."

137. Ibid.

138. Gaylen N. Chandler and Douglas W. Lyon, "Involvement in Knowledge Acquisition Activities by New Venture Team Members and Sales Growth," working paper (Utah State University, Logan, 2005).

5

Business Angels: Investment Processes, Outcomes, and Current Trends

Frances M. Amatucci and Jeffrey E. Sohl

The entrepreneurial economy and its contribution to economic growth have been well noted. High-growth entrepreneurial ventures have been the major source of job creation in the United States.[1] These firms also hold the greatest potential for innovation, commercialization of technology, and sustainable economic development. However, entrepreneurial ventures face significant financial hurdles in the early stage of their development. These high-growth ventures lack the assets necessary for collateral-based lending, and their high growth and accompanying high risk, results in reluctance by the banking sector to provide start-up capital. In addition, start-up firms often do not have the cash flow requirements that accompany debt financing, and any cash flow that does exist is needed to fund the growth of the start-up rather than servicing debt. This inability to attract debt capital in the early stage, and the mismatch between the need for growth capital and the short-term financial requirements of debt financing, contributes to the importance of equity financing. Equity capital supplies the venture with much needed capital for development and expansion while at the same time typically does not require a repayment until the exit event. As such, both the entrepreneur and the investor share the risk inherent in the start-up of these ventures. This critical role of early stage equity financing throughout the history of the entrepreneurial economy has been well documented.[2–5]

Angels (private investors) are the oldest and largest source of seed and start-up capital for entrepreneurs. Angels are equity investors that seek returns that are commensurate with the risk and illiquidity that are inherent in seed-stage investing. Angels are different from friends and family in that the investment is based on the financial risk/reward ratio as opposed to the affinity to the investment that is the predominant driver for friends and family. In the United States, angels invest more dollars in more companies than the formal, or institutional,

Table 5.1. Investment Activity

Year	Angel Investors		Venture Capital	
	Total Dollars (billions)	Number of Investments	Total Dollars (billions)	Number of Investments
2004	22.5	48,000	21.3	2910
2003	18.1	42,000	19.4	2840
2002	15.7	36,000	21.7	3046

venture capital market (Table 5.1). In 2004, in the United States, angels invested US$22.5 billion in 48,000 ventures, or approximately US$470,000 per deal.[6] In contrast, during this same time period venture capital funds invested US$21.3 billion in 2910 deals, for an average of US$7.3 million per deal. Since over 75 percent of venture capital deals are follow-on funding for existing portfolio companies, these 2910 deals represent close to 700 unique companies.[7]

As indicated in Table 5.1, this relationship between the angel and venture capital market, with respect to dollars invested and number of deals, has persisted for several years. In the seed and start-up stage, the difference between angels and venture capitalists is even starker. Close to 45 percent of angel deals in 2004 were in the seed and start-up stage (52 percent in 2003 and 50 percent in 2002), while venture capitalists allocated 6 percent of their 2004 deals to these stages (6.0 percent in 2003 and 4.9 percent in 2002). Even during the best of times, venture capitalists, over the last decade, have never invested more than 15 percent of the deals in the seed and start-up stage. Angels invest smaller amounts per investment and are the seed engine for entrepreneurs, while venture capitalists invest in larger deals in the later stages of growth. As such, angels invest in sixteen times more deals and over fifty times more firms than venture capitalists, and the majority of these angel deals are in the critical seed and start-up stage.

However, in spite of the size, scale and importance of the angel market, it is one of the least understood and underresearched equity markets. The major difficulty in conducting angel research is the inaccessibility of reliable angel data. At the present time, and in the foreseeable future, no directories of angels exist, nor are there any public records of their transactions. This lack of readily accessible public databases implies that to conduct angel research requires the arduous task of collecting primary data from individuals who wish to remain anonymous. Clearly, this need for anonymity is understandable, since successful angel investors rely on a reasonable flow of quality deals often obtained through an informal network of business associates and service providers. Once an angel assumes a public profile they are often inundated with a plethora of entrepreneurs seeking capital and the quality of these proposals can be quite varied. Thus, finding angels to participate in research studies is time consuming, labor intensive and the cost can be prohibitive. In essence, the angel researcher undertakes the unenviable task of searching for individuals who do not want to be found. Given that this initial hurdle can be overcome, significant obstacles remain. Since angels are high-net-worth individuals, they represent consumers with considerable buying power and influence. It is the goal of many organizations, from high-end retailers to financial planners, to reach these individuals both as a source product demand and to solicit opinions. As such, the angel researcher is one among many competing for the interest and attention of angel investors. One direct result is that the angel researcher is confronted with the likely prospect of low response rates to surveys that attempt to collect meaningful data on the angel market and the inherent potential of a significant presence of nonresponse bias. An additional difficulty is that even if angels can be found, and they respond in significant numbers, complete and usable responses are difficult to obtain given the sensitivity of the requested information. Specifically, information on private financial transactions, including investment amounts, terms and conditions of private equity deals, return rates, failure rates, and portfolio sizes, is not readily disclosed due to the highly sensitive and personal nature of such information. Thus, obtaining angel data places an additional burden on the academic researcher in terms of multiple contacts with the target population and a scrutiny with respect to the accuracy of the data that is received and the high standard of data confidentiality that the angel must be convinced exists.

In this chapter, we will summarize what is known about the business angel investment processes, outcomes, and current trends. First, a selective literature review focused on the equity investment process is provided. Then current trends in the business angel market, such as the evolving business angel–venture capitalist relationship, investment behavior of angels, and the institutionalization of the angel market, are described. We conclude with suggestions for future research based on both existing knowledge and future trends in the business angel sector.

LITERATURE REVIEW

The private equity investment process is frequently divided into preinvestment, contract negotiation, and postinvestment stages, and can be examined from the different perspectives of either the investor or the entrepreneur.[8–13] A flow diagram illustrating these stages is provided in Figure 5.1. Most research adopts the view of the investor, and is predominantly in the venture capital sector. In the following paragraphs, we examine existing research on the various stages with particular emphasis on the business angel sector.

Preinvestment Processes (Stage I): Search,
Initial Screening, and Due Diligence

The search process involving finding a business angel is complicated by the anonymity and informality of the business angel market. Sohl identified several

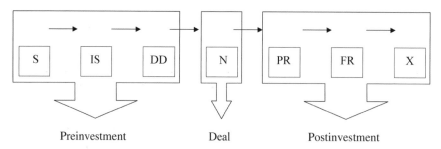

Figure 5.1. Business angel/venture capitalist investment process. S, Search; IS, Initial Screening; DD, Due Diligence; N, Negotiation; PR, Postinvestment Relationship; FR, Future Rounds; X, Exit.

mechanisms for matching entrepreneurs with investors; these included loosely organized referrals among professionals, venture capital clubs, business angel portals, and matching networks.[14]

As investors and entrepreneurs decrease the number of matching opportunities, initial screening is very important. Mason and Harrison point out that business angels consider two elements in the initial screening stage: the extent to which the proposal meets their personal investment criteria and the intuitive assessment of the proposal.[15] Although this stage takes only about ten minutes, 73 percent of all proposals are rejected. Focusing on technology-based ventures, Mason and Harrison examine the demand-side deficiencies that determine an entrepreneur not to be "investment ready" and conclude that management skills are critical in raising finance from outside investors in this stage. Investment criteria, quality of investment opportunities, and quality of the business plan are also important to investors during the screening stage.[16, 17]

Using qualitative data analysis on a sample of Canadian private investors, Feeney et al. evaluated attributes and shortcomings of the business and owners as important investment-screening criteria.[18] Mayfield maintained that the relationship between business angels and entrepreneurs forms during the due diligence process, and that relationship becomes the primary determinant of proposal acceptance or rejection.[19] Sapienza et al. confirmed these findings and even went further to point out that the relationship during the due diligence stage can also be adversarial.[20] Dibben et al. and Harrison et al. suggest "swift trust," which is the main type of trust developed between angel investors and entrepreneurs during due diligence, is built through the expression of different opinions between the two sides.[21, 22] See Table 5.2 for more research on Stage I of the investment process.

Negotiation/Contract Agreement Processes (Stage II)

Research on the processes associated with contract negotiation and agreement addresses topics, such as the role of context, trust and partnership formation,

Table 5.2. Selected Literature Review: Business Angel/Venture Capitalist Investment Process

Stage	Author(s)	Topic(s)
Stage I Preinvestment process: search, initial screening, and due diligence	Carter et al. (2003)	Human, social, and financial capital/gender
	Brush et al. (2002)	Role of social capital/gender
	Mason and Harrison (2002)	Barriers to investment
	Greene, Brush, Hart, and Saparito (2001)	Role of gender in venture capital funding
	Mayfield (2000)	Relationship development during due diligence
	Mason and Harrison (2000)	Investor readiness in initial screening
	Kolodinsky, Osteryoung, and Anthony (2000)	Rational and nonrational processes
	Feeney, Haines, and Riding (1999)	Private investor decision process
	Sohl (1999)	Uncover, clubs, alliances, and matching network
	Dibben, Harrison, and Mason (1998)	Trust/cooperation during initial screening
	Freear, Sohl, and Wetzel (1996)	Technology due diligence
Stage II Negotiation/contract agreement	Manigart et al. (2001)	Impact of trust
	Sohl and Areson-Perkins (2001)	Deal structure in high-tech ventures
	Kelly and Hay (2000)	Influence of context on contract comprehensiveness
	Shepherd and Zacharakis (1999)	Effect of anchoring and adjustment heuristic
	Landström, Manigart, Mason, and Sapienza (1998)	Agency and social exchange theory to examine contract terms and negotiation processes

(continued)

Table 5.2. (*continued*)

Stage	Author(s)	Topic(s)
Stage III Postinvestment process: relationship, future rounds, and exit	Parhankangas, A. and Landström, H. (2003)	Psychological contract violations
	Kelly and Hay (2001)	Agency theory regarding postinvestment relationship
	Farrell and Howorth (2001)	Behavior, cognitions, and motivations at exit
	Ardichvili, Cardozo, Tune, and Reinach (2002)	Assembly of nonfinancial resources
		Impact of conflict in postinvestment relationship
	Higashide and Birley (1998)	Timely information, trust, and monitoring
	Sapienza and Korsgaard (1995)	
Process: Multistage	Amatucci and Sohl (2004)	Women entrepreneurs and business angels
	Paul, Johnston, and Whittam (2003)	Business angel investment process
	Ramy and Gavious (2003)	Control, trust, and confidence
	Shepherd and Zacharakis (2001)	Business angels and venture capitalist comparisons
	Roberts, Stevenson, and Morse (2000)	Principle-agent versus incomplete contracts
	Van Osnabrugge (2000)	Partnership formation over time
	Sapienza, Korsgaard, Folger, Sagrera, Zhang (1999)	Process, postinvestment experience, performance
	Wright and Robbie (1998)	Social judgment theory perspective
	Mason and Harrison (1996)	Process versus outcomes in decision making
	Zacharakis and Meyer (1996)	
	Zacharakis and Meyer (1995)	
	Fried and Hisrich (1994)	
	Tyebjee and Bruno (1984)	

formality and comprehensiveness and decision processes.[23–33] From the business angel's perspective, this stage is very difficult because of information asymmetries between the investor and the entrepreneur. Kelly and Hay argued that the information gap is mainly created because angels may not have complete knowledge regarding how the venture will develop over time and the managerial competencies of the entrepreneur.[34] In addition, time and financial resource constraints inhibit extensive due diligence. They examine numerous contextual factors that may influence the contract comprehensiveness, including the relevant industry experience of the entrepreneur, the amount of involvement in the venture development process, and the amount of investment, equity stake, and referral source. The level of new venture experience of the entrepreneur, the general management experience of the entrepreneur, the number of investments made by the investor, the manner in which the investment is made (solo or syndicate), and the postinvestment employment of the investor were not found to be relevant. Moreover, contrary to research findings in Stage I, the level of interpersonal trust did not appear to influence contract comprehensiveness.

In general, it appears that some degree of formality does exist in the angel investor market with regard to contract comprehensiveness. Using frameworks of agency theory and social exchange theory, semistructured interviews with investors and entrepreneurs in Belgium, Sweden, the United Kingdom and the United States, found evidence to suggest that prior experience of contractors, number of investors involved, and the involvement preferences influence the level of contract formality.[35] Basically, an angel investment contract includes clauses about changes in ownership of the venture, postinvestment managerial agreements and monitoring, and exit agreements. To address new developments during the postdeal period, new clauses that increase contract complexity can be added. Based on the assertion that a contract is to protect investors, there is a strong case in their research for the notion that building trust between angels and entrepreneurs is not the main purpose of a written contract.

In a simulation involving 144 entrepreneurs and investors, Manigart et al. examine the relationship between trust and contractual agreements.[36] Results suggest that trust impacts contractual preferences of entrepreneurs but not investors. The investor preferences appeared to be independent of the level of trust of the entrepreneur.

As important participants in Stage II, lawyers may also influence the process, terms, and outcomes of contract negotiation. Bankman and Cole examine agency and nonagency explanations for the venture capital investment boom prior to the bust in 2001.[37] Fixed management fee structures and increased compensation supported the agency explanation that venture capitalists negotiated deals which put self-interest above investor interest. See Table 5.2 for more research on Stage II of the equity investment process.

Postdeal (Stage III) Processes: Postinvestment Relationship, Future Rounds, Exit

As indicated in the investment decision process flow diagram (Figure 5.1), the post investment stage involves the postcontract relationship between the entrepreneur and the investor, potential future rounds, and eventual exit. One of the major differences between business angels and venture capitalists lies in the expectation that the former brings industry experience and a network of potentially valuable contacts (i.e., the gold-plated rolodex) that can serve as intangible assets to the firm in the postinvestment stage.[38–40] The research indicates that the entrepreneur often values the business experience of the angel on par with the capital provided. This value-added investing is a key distinguishing feature of the angel market.[41]

In a survey of UK investors, Kelly and Hay question the use of agency theory in the context of informal venture capital since: (1) private investors and entrepreneurs often have already developed a high level of interpersonal trust; (2) often private investors bring badly needed managerial resources during the seed and start-up stages; and (3) investors can consider active postinvestment involvement as an effective risk-reduction strategy.[42] Ardichvili et al. employed formal qualitative data analysis of in-depth interviews with twenty-seven successful serial angel investors to examine the nonfinancial resources investors bring to new ventures.[43] The Ardichvili et al. research suggests that business model development and management of and sourcing of funding were most important. Given that the initial typology was limited to human, social, physical, and financial resources, the findings suggest the addition of an intellectual capital category that is separate from human capital.

Although focused on the venture capitalist, Parhankangas and Landström conducted a study to examine three forms of psychological contract violations, which occur between the venture capitalist and entrepreneur during the postcontract period.[44] These included: (1) a disagreement over goals or strategies; (2) entrepreneur incompetence; and (3) shirking or opportunistic behavior by the entrepreneur. Such psychological contract violations are likewise applicable to angel investors and entrepreneurs. Amatucci and Coleman described how disagreement over firm goals and strategies and *perceived* entrepreneur incompetence undermined the angel investor–entrepreneur relationship.[45] See Table 5.2 for more research on Stage III of the equity investment process, as well as studies that examine multiple stages.

Women and Minority Entrepreneurs

According to the U.S. Census Bureau, from 1997 to 2002, minority groups and women have increased business ownership faster than the national average.[46] From 1997 to 2004, majority-owned, privately held women-owned businesses increased by 23 percent compared with the national growth rate of 9 percent. In

2004, this group accounted for 30 percent of all businesses in the United States.[47] Women entrepreneurs are at a particular disadvantage in finding angel investors because they often do not have access to the networks where information about equity financing exists.[48] Although little research exists on minority entrepreneur access to seed and start-up capital in the business angel market, it is widely recognized that ethnic minority groups do experience more problems than other firms in obtaining financial resources from banks and other formal sources.[49, 50] In response to the low proportion of equity capital received by minorities and women, funds have been created to address the dearth of supply in equity capital for these groups. By providing a venue for women entrepreneurs to present to venture capitalists, Springboard Enterprises has served as a conduit for raising US$3 billion in venture capital. Likewise, the Minority Business Roundtable Venture Capital Fund and the New Africa Opportunity Fund assist in the minority and women entrepreneur's search for capital.[51]

On the supply side, as more women become entrepreneurs, an increasing number of women are becoming business angels. Although still relatively low, estimates are that 10 percent of all business angels in the United States are women and 5 percent of all business angels in Britain are women.[52] Sohl and Hill found that in 2003 only 13.3 percent of the investments made by women angels were in women-owned or operated businesses; however, since this was double the national average of 6.6 percent, it appears there is some partiality toward women-led businesses.[53]

In this section, we attempted to provide a selected review of the literature on the equity investment decision process, predominantly involving business angels. In the following section, current trends involving both investment processes and outcomes are described.

TRENDS IN THE BUSINESS ANGEL MARKET

The Business Angel–Venture Capitalist Relationship

As indicated, angels and venture capitalists occupy unique spaces in the spectrum of providers of risk capital. These singular positions of angels and venture capitalists are complimentary in the sense that the angel seed deal often migrates to the venture capital market for later stage expansion financing. With this mutual, though indirect, dependence between the two markets, it is expedient for both angels and venture capitalists to develop relationships on a broad level, rather than on a per deal basis. While angels often invest in small groups of five to six angels for a given deal, individual investor angels rely on their personal net worth as a source of funds. Given a desire to distribute these investment dollars over a portfolio of companies as a means to mitigate risk, there are inherent limits to the amount of capital that angels can invest. These limits, in turn, often prevent the angel from providing the larger dollars necessary for their start-up

investments to expand and grow into competitive ventures with a higher potential for an exit event. Thus, for angels, venture capitalists often represent a
source of follow-on funding for their investments. An amicable working relationship with the venture capital market is an important strategy for angels to
adopt in their quest to achieve an eventual merger, sale, or initial public offering
(IPO) for their investments. In addition, to ease this transition from an angel-
backed deal to venture capital funding, angels are often negotiating terms and
conditions in their seed deals that mitigate any friction that may arise and
provide for a smooth transition to later stage equity markets.[54]

Of note is that while this relationship is often viewed as the progression from
angel to venture capital deal, the contrary position also holds. For the venture
capitalist, with the predominance of later stage investments and the virtual
abandonment of the seed-stage market, the existence and knowledge of quality
seed and start-up ventures is pivotal for deal flow. Since the seed and start-up
market is the space occupied by angels, a connection to angels provides the venture capitalists with deals that have passed due diligence by angels and have
reached a stage of development that is within the investment objectives and expertise of the venture capital market. An ancillary benefit of the relationship is
that venture capitalists may refer deals deemed too early for their fund objectives
to angels, with the belief that these deals, after an initial investment and seasoning
by angels, will find their way back to the venture capitalists. Thus, a two-way
relationship between angels and venture capitalists is a beneficial strategy for both
markets—for angels to secure later stage funding for their investments and for
venture capitalists to maintain a source of quality deal flow.

However, while this bidirectional approach for business angels and venture
capitalists is an advantageous strategy, this relationship has experienced some
discontinuities over the last several years. Prior to 2000, over 80 percent of angel
investments were in the seed and start-up stage.[55] In the post-2000 business angel
market, a trend in the redistribution of angel investments, with respect to stage,
has emerged and has accelerated in recent years. As indicated in Table 5.3, the
business angel market is exhibiting a reallocation of investments by reducing the
percentage of seed-stage deals and increasing investments in postseed second
rounds. This movement by angels to second-stage financing is a redistribution of
capital, as opposed to the creation of investment dollars. Business angels are not
abandoning the seed market, since nearly half of their investments remain at this

Table 5.3.   Angel-Stage Investing

| | Percent of Investments | | |
	2002	2003	2004
Seed stage	50	52	43
Postseed stage	33	35	44

critical early stage, but they are redistributing their investment capital. A consequence of this redistribution is an exacerbation of the seed and start-up capital gap that currently exists for high-growth entrepreneurial ventures.[56]

It appears that there exist three motivations for this realignment of the business angel market and the business angel–venture capitalist relationship: an opportunistic, a necessitous, and a protectionist strategy. Inefficient markets yield opportunities for investors and a substantial secondary, postseed funding gap in the US$2–4 million range now exists for high-growth entrepreneurial ventures. This postseed stage gap has contributed to the inefficiency of the early stage equity market and angels are adopting an opportunistic motive in providing second round (postseed), follow-on funding for their seed deals. By exploiting market inefficiency and investing in the postseed stage, angels are able to preserve their seed stage position. In addition, through postseed funding from angels that have a vested interest in the firm as seed investors, entrepreneurs avoid the costly and time-consuming search for capital from new sources that are unfamiliar with their ventures. In addition, one of the goals of this additional funding round is to increase the potential for the angel to reach an exit event, most likely through an acquisition or sale, after the infusion of additional angel capital. In essence, the opportunistic motive is based on the strategy to both exploit market inefficiencies in the postseed gap and increase the likelihood of an exit event without any additional financing from investors external to the venture.

The necessitous strategy is based, in part, on the current nature of the venture capital market. The venture capital market has experienced an increase in deal size (US$7.3 million), a decrease in the number of first sequence investments (25 percent of deals), and a move to later stage investing.[57] These three factors combine to present substantial hurdles to the entrepreneur, and their angel investors, in securing venture capital in the postseed stage range of US$2–4 million. As a result, angels often find it necessary to provide a second round of funding to their seed investments, without which the venture will likely stagnate in growth or, in the worse case, be unable to continue operations. In this sense, angels may be viewed as providing a form of bridge financing for their investments. However, in this case, the postseed angel financing is often viewed as a necessary, rather than a sufficient, infusion of capital.

The third motivation for the realignment of the angel–venture capital relationship, the protectionist strategy, is based in part on the declining investment returns experienced by the venture capital industry in the post-2000 landscape and possible overvaluation by angels. These two factors have combined to result in the occurrence of significant devaluations of angel investments in later rounds, resulting in cram downs and substantial dilution of the angel investment position in the deal.[58] To avoid a second round that may be devalued, angels adopt a protectionist strategy and provide additional rounds of financing to reduce the total number of external rounds necessary to achieve exit. Since each subsequent round of capital results in an independent valuation of the firm's value, fewer rounds imply fewer valuations and thus reduce the chance of a decrease in the value of the firm, especially in light of the fact that valuation is a highly subjective process. In addition, through the infusion of angel capital in a postseed round, angels seek to protect their investment by affording the venture the opportunity to achieve additional growth. This continued growth and expansion of the venture adds value to the investment and places both the entrepreneur and angel investor with increased leverage in the negotiation for a later stage venture capital investment.

To summarize, the business angel and venture capital relationship, while still largely a complementary one in terms of market position in the spectrum of equity financing, has experienced significant changes in recent years. The recognition by both players for the need to develop a two-way relationship, in terms of deal flow, the need for compatible terms and conditions and later stage funding opportunities is a further confirmation of this complementary position. However, a retreat of venture capital to later stage deals, the existence of a postseed funding gap, the desire for angels to achieve exit without venture capital and potential acrimonious angel–venture capital valuation perspectives, has led to significant changes in the strategies adopted by angel investors. This realignment has led angels to follow an opportunistic, a necessitous, and a protectionist strategy to preserve their investment position while remaining the major source of seed and start-up equity capital for high-growth entrepreneurial ventures. It is surmised that these changes have resulted in a realignment of the angel market that is likely to continue in the future.

The Investment Behavior of Angels

The angel market is represented by the collection of individual investors who seek investment opportunities from a variety of sources. These investors are typically cashed-out entrepreneurs—individuals who have successfully started an entrepreneurial venture and have subsequently exited the investment either through a sale, a merger or acquisition, or through an initial public offering. Many have been the recipients of angel investments or venture capital. Thus, angel investors have substantial experience in the start-up and growth of successful ventures. It is important to note that angels invest their own money, usually allocating a prudent portfolio to angel investing. In this context, a prudent portfolio is defined as the amount of risk capital that the angel believes can be lost without a significant impact on their lifestyle. As an individual they decide when and how often to invest. These allocation decisions are often based upon the configuration of their portfolio, the stage of the angel investments they are involved in, their degree of involvement with the investment, and the attractiveness of the opportunity. In contrast, venture capitalists are a bit more constrained in their investment decisions. While a venture capitalist also decides on what ventures are attractive and how much to invest in each venture, as fund managers they have a fixed amount to the investment portfolio and they must invest the entire fund before the fund expires in ten years. As such, large funds result in large and late stage deals. Thus, while the angel decides on the size of their individual portfolio of angel investments and when to make these investments, the venture capitalist's portfolio is dictated by the size of the fund they manage and the life of the fund.

Business angels are often characterized as patient investors, and this is both out of necessity and a consequence of the investment spectrum within which they invest. Since business angels invest in the seed stage, the venture is often little more than a concept, possibly with limited sales but likely still in the business formation process. Much needs to be accomplished before the concept can grow into a viable business opportunity with the ability to attract additional funds and proceed to the exit event. Thus, since private investors provide early money, business angels have longer exit horizons than their venture capital counterparts and the capital they provide is often termed patient capital.

As a long-term investment, in the evaluation and investment decision phase the private investor market is a relationship-building market. Since the seed and start-up investor is investing predominately in the entrepreneur and this asset is a very mobile commodity, the vision of the entrepreneur must be in congruence with the investment objective of the business angel. Failure to grasp the need for vision alignment and the importance of the angel–entrepreneur relationship often increases the risk of failure, resulting in business closure or severe contraction for the entrepreneur and loss of investment for the investor.

Often angels actively interact with management in their investments and are value-added investors in the traditional sense. With their business start-up experience, angels operate under the assumption that this experience will increase the chance of success for their investments and thus increase the return on the investment. The need and desire for an active role in the investment, combined with limited financial resources, often determines the size of their angel investment portfolio. Since the investment is largely at the seed and start-up stage, the need to add value to the investment is especially acute, since these early stages are marked by the highest risk of survival. As part of this active investing profile, angels derive a type of intrinsic income from their angel investment activity. That is, in addition to the financial return, the investment portfolio provides the individual angel an opportunity to give back something to the entrepreneurial culture from which they derived substantial wealth.

One of the most significant behaviors of angels, and one that has persisted over the three decades during which angels have been researched, is their overwhelming propensity to invest in deals that are located close to their principal residence. By close, it is usually within a half-day's travel from their home. Over 80 percent of angel investments are within this geographic proximity and when angels invest at greater distances, they are often not the lead investor, but rather a passive member of a group that is involved in the deal. This regional nature of the market stems from several important behavioral characteristics of angel investors. As former entrepreneurs, these individuals enjoy the involvement with a start-up venture at the strategic level and since angels are value-added investors, these factors are more easily available to the venture if the investor lives nearby. Private investors often take bigger risks or accept lower rewards when they are attracted by the nonfinancial characteristics of an entrepreneur's proposal, such as the desire to create jobs in their own communities. In this regard they are investors that seek an attachment and a return, which again is commensurate with a geographic presence. However, it is important to note that return is the major consideration, and since these investments are start-ups, with substantial risk, proximity also affords the investor the opportunity to keep a close watch on the investment.

The yield (acceptance) rate is defined as the percentage of investment opportunities that are brought to the attention of investors that resulted in an investment. Historically, yield rates for angels have averaged close to 10 percent (Figure 5.2), indicating that of every ten proposals reviewed, one results in an investment. In 2000, the yield rates exhibited a significant increase (23 percent) with one in four proposals receiving an angel investment. In the post-2000 market yields retreated to a more sustainable level of 7 to 10 percent. The drop in yield rates in the post-2000 market was the result of pressure from the denominator and increased scrutiny from investors. Specifically, in the 2001–2004 time period, private investors received more proposals for consideration. During this same time period, angels exhibited a more measured approach to angel investing, as indicated by the time spent conducting due diligence, which increased by 25 percent in the post-2000 market. Thus, pressure from both the increase in the demand (denominator) and the more cautious approach to due diligence, contributed to a return of yield rates to their historical levels. As noted in Figure 5.2, yield rates in 2004 spiked to 18.5 percent. Data on yield rates in future years will be needed to determine if this change in yield rate is an anomaly or a systemic change in the angel market.

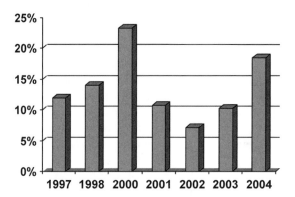

Figure 5.2.   Angel yield rates: number of deals funded/ number of proposals presented.

The Institutionalization of the Angel Market

The angel market is essentially a collection of individual investors who actively search for investment opportunities, conduct their own due diligence, and negotiate and decide whether or not to make an equity investment in an early stage entrepreneurial venture. This collection of individuals has organized into several varied portals (mechanisms or organizations that represent how angels conduct business in the market, from search to initial investment). Market inefficiencies and a persistent funding gap have provided the impetus for angels to adopt this portal structure. However, there does not exist, nor is there ever likely to exist, any directories of angels or any public records of their transactions. Business angels, in essence, often operate below the radar screen of the private equity market as a means to protect their anonymity and to assure quality deal flow.

One of the most noticeable trends in the organization of the business angel market has been the proliferation of a myriad of angel portals. In this context, an angel portal is defined as a mechanism for bringing together entrepreneurs seeking capital and angels searching for investment opportunities. Currently, the three largest of these portals, in terms of investment activity, are individual angels, informal angel groups, and formal angel alliances. All of these portals seek to reduce the inefficiency of the early stage equity market, increase quality deal flow to angels and preserve the anonymity of the individual investor. As a sense of scale, there were approximately 225,000 angels in the United States in 2004, who collectively invested US$22.5 billion.[59]

The collection of individual angels (classified as the individual angel portal) is the largest and oldest segment of the angel market. These individuals make over half of all the angel investments and represent the majority of the dollars invested. They rely on their own referral sources, often lawyers, accountants or other angels, for deal flow. These individuals have the lowest visibility of all the angel portals but appear to attract the highest quality of deal flow, mainly due to their development of a personal referral network. They also have the lowest percentage of latent angels (angels who have the net worth and have entered the market through a portal, but have not made any angel investments).

The informal angel group portal operates in a similar manner as the individual angel portal. The informal angel group typically has a membership of as little as ten investors and may be as large as fifty individuals. These informal angel groups are loosely organized, have a relatively low visibility (but higher than the individual angel), have a very low percentage of latent angels, and also represent a substantial portion of the dollars invested and the number of deals enacted in the angel market. Together, the individual angel and the informal angel group portals comprise close to 75 percent of the angel market activity.

The formal angel alliance is the most recent entrant to the angel market, with its beginnings traced to the formation of the Band of Angels (of Silicon Valley) in 1994. These formal angel alliances now number around 130 alliances scattered across the United States. They are the most highly structured of the angel portals and often have membership criteria, minimum investment requirements and screening committees. They have the highest visibility in the angel market and as such, often attract a wide range of quality in their deal flow. Formal angel alliances also have the largest percentage of latent angels, with over 50 percent of their members considered to be latent angels. Despite this high visibility, the formal angel alliance accounts for approximately 10 percent of the angel deals and dollars invested.

There has been a growing trend in the angel market to achieve a higher degree of sophistication and organization than was present in past years. More sophistication in the sense that angels are becoming more attentive to terms and conditions of their angel deals, more serious about due diligence, and are monitoring their investments more closely. These trends are both a reaction to the post-2000 market restructuring and the somewhat draconian terms and conditions imposed by later stage investors. Angels are requiring that entrepreneurs use their investment dollars over a longer period of time than in the past, and during this time they seek to add substantial value to the venture. Both of these are an effort to potentially reach an exit event with only angel capital, and at the same time to be in a position to have a reasonable amount of leverage, in terms of firm valuation, if the venture seeks later stage venture capital financing. Certainly all of these developments are signs of a growing and healthy market. As seed investors, this increased sophistication can only add value to the process, in terms of starting companies built on a solid foundation, mentoring these companies to achieve sustainable growth, and contributing substantially to the job generation capacity of the entrepreneurial sector.

Unfortunately, often confused with this sophistication, is the increase in the organizational structure of the angel market, as evidenced by the formation of formal angel alliances. Certain misguided conclusions point to the increased organization as the cause for increased sophistication. This movement to a more organized and structured angel market may result in the unfortunate consequence of the institutionalization of the angel market. As an example, some formal angel alliances have adopted a voting method by members to decide if the alliance will enact the angel investment. Minimum investment activity, also a requirement of some formal angel alliances, requires members to maintain a prescribed dollar level of angel investment for each member over a twelve-month period. Angels invest when they find a good deal with a technology that has the potential to capture a significant portion of a niche and is coupled with an excellent management team. They do not invest to maintain a minimum investment requirement. Business angels certainly do not invest based on the democratic process of voting; rather they make an individual investment decision, sometimes relying on the advice of other angels and trusted associates.

A portion of formal angel alliances are pooling investment capital into a so-called angel fund, with investment decisions made by an investment committee or a fund manager. These angel funds are a misnomer, since in essence they are venture capital funds with wealthy individuals as limited partners, albeit often without the carried interest requirement of the more traditional venture capital fund. Unfortunately, these angel funds represent a redistribution of business angel capital away from the individual angel investor to a fund structure. In addition, these funds could likely become a victim of their own success. Successful funds attract more investors and larger fund sizes, resulting in a retreat from the seed and start-up stage of financing. Such redistribution would only result in an exacerbation of the persistent, and troublesome, seed financing gap facing entrepreneurs seeking early stage capital. One needs to only look fifteen years in the past, when the venture capital industry consisted of funds in the US$20 million range and it was still economically feasible to make a seed deal work.

The potential institutionalization of the business angel market, as evidenced by the multifaceted forms of voting, fund creation, and minimum investment requirements that have been adopted by a reasonable number of the formal angel alliances, could present a significant impediment to the viability of the business angel investor as the major provider of seed capital to entrepreneurial ventures. In contrast, angel groups that provide a venue for reviewing business plans, work on generating quality deal flow, maintain individual decision making among members and provide a venue for informal syndication on a per deal basis, are providing a valuable service to the angel community. Groups that adopt these fundamental tenets of a healthy business angel market are assisting in creating a sustainable angel environment where worthy entrepreneurs have access to value-added angel investors. Fortunately, the business angel market tends to be self-correcting over time. Business angel investors are an educated lot and will likely discern the difference between the benefits of an increase in sophistication as opposed to the disadvantages of the movement to institutionalization. Quality deals, returns commensurate with the risk, and the fun and excitement of angel investing are the key drivers for angel investors, and all of these are available in a healthy and sophisticated market that is built on the basic tenets of individual investing.

CONCLUSIONS AND DIRECTIONS FOR FUTURE RESEARCH

Although angel research has made significant strides in the last decade, there remain many facets of the angel market that require further inquiry. The process of angel investing and the differentiation of these processes within the angel community is a potential avenue of investigation. These process components include the selection and screening of deals, the negotiation of the terms and conditions and the postinvestment relationship. In the selection and screening of deals, the proliferation of organized angel portals has resulted in a potential shift from individual angel selection and screening to investment committees making these decisions. One potential result of this shift is that individual angels, whose investment criteria may differ from that of the screening committee, may never get the opportunity to view deals that may be of interest to them. Research into the consequences of this relinquishing of the screening function by angels would indicate the extent and the opportunity cost consequences of this shift. In the negotiating of the terms and conditions, angels have traditionally utilized less burdensome terms and conditions than their venture capital counterparts. However, given the changes in the venture capitalists–angel relationship, an investigation of these changes in term sheets would shed light on both the evolving venture capitalists–angel relationship, as manifest in the term sheet, and the increased emphasis on angels with respect to preserving equity positions. With respect to the postinvestment relationship, research on changes in these relationships, in part due to the longer period of use for angel capital and the increase in angel postseed-stage investing needs investigation.

An important research topic is a more detailed analysis of the institutionalization of the angel market. Clearly, the consequences of a potential shift away from traditional angel investing and a potential morphing into the venture capital model poses the potential for significant changes into the angel market as the major source of seed and start-up capital. While this shift is in the early stages of development, examination as to whether the shift represents a basic systemic change in the angel market or is a reactionary to current, and temporary, market changes, needs to be studied.

While the attitudes, behavior, and characteristics of the basic angel market have been studied, there are segments within the angel market spectrum that have not received the attention they deserve. These segments include the minority and women angel market, from both a supply and demand perspective. While some research has been conducted on these segments from the perspective of venture capital, little research has focused on the angel components of these important, and growing, market segments. In addition, cross-cultural differences offer a potentially rich avenue of research, especially in light of the globalization of today's business market and as the angel market develops along this global dimension.

NOTES

1. David Birch, *Job Creation in America* (New York: Free Press, 1987).

2. William E. Wetzel, Jr., "Informal Risk Capital: Knowns and Unknown," in *The Art and Science of Entrepreneurship*, eds. D. L. Sexton and R. W. Smilor (Cambridge: Ballinger, 1986), 85–108.

3. C. Ou, "Holdings of Privately-Held Business Assets by American Families: Findings from the 1983 Consumer Finance Survey," unpublished report, Office of Economic Research, U.S. Small Business Administration, Washington, DC, 1987.

4. Robert J. Gaston and Sharon E. Bell, "The Informal Supply of Capital," Office of Economic Research, U.S. Small Business Administration, Washington, DC, 1988.

5. Colin M. Mason and Richard T. Harrison, "The Supply of Equity Finance in the UK: A Strategy for Closing the Equity Gap," *Entrepreneurship and Regional Development* 4 (1992): 357–380.

6. Center for Venture Research, "The Angel Investor Market in 2004: The Angel Market Sustains a Modest Recovery," http://wsbe.unh.edu/Centers_CVR/2004analysisreport.cfm.

7. PricewaterhouseCoopers, "Venture Capital Investing Rises to $21 Billion in 2004 after Three Years of Decline," *Money Tree Quarterly Report*, www.pwcmoneytree.com.

8. T. T. Tyebjee and A. V. Bruno. "A Model of Venture Capital Investment Activity," *Management Science* 30, no. 9 (1984): 1051–1066.

9. Vance Fried and Robert Hisrich, "Towards a Model of Venture Capital Investment Decision Making," *Financial Management* 23, no. 3 (1994): 28–37.

10. Mike Wright and Ken Robbie, "Venture Capital and Private Equity: A Review and Synthesis," *Journal of Business and Accounting* 25, no. 5 (1998): 521–570.

11. Mark Van Osnabrugge, "A Comparison of Business Angel and Venture Capitalist Investment Procedures: An Agency Theory-Based Analysis," *Venture Capital* 2, no. 2 (2000): 91–110.

12. Lisa Feeney, George Haines, and Allan Riding, "Private Investors' Investment Criteria: Insights from Qualitative Data," *Venture Capital* 1, no. 2 (1999): 121–146.

13. Frances M. Amatucci and Jeffrey E. Sohl, "Women Entrepreneurs Securing Business Angel Financing: Tales from the Field," *Venture Capital* 6, no. 2/3 (2004): 181–196.

14. Jeffrey E. Sohl, "The Early-Stage Equity Market in the USA," *Venture Capital* 1, no. 2 (1999): 101–120.

15. Colin M. Mason and Richard T. Harrison, "Investing in Technology Ventures: What Do Business Angels Look for at the Initial Screening Stage?," in *Frontiers of Entrepreneurship Research* (Wellesley, MA: Babson College, 2000).

16. Colin M. Mason and Matthew Stark, "What Do Investors Look for in a Business Plan? A Comparison of the Investment Criteria of Bankers, Venture Capitalists and Business Angels," *International Small Business Journal* 22, no. 3 (2004): 227–248.

17. Colin M. Mason and Richard T. Harrison, "Barriers to Investment in the Informal Venture Capital Sector," *Entrepreneurship and Regional Development* 14 (2002): 271–287.

18. Feeney, Haines, and Riding, "Private Investors' Investment Criteria."

19. William M. Mayfield, "The Formation of the Angel–Entrepreneur Relationship during Due Diligence," in *Frontiers of Entrepreneurship Research* (Wellesley, MA: Babson College, 2000).

20. Henry J. Sapienza, M. Audrey Korsgaard, Robert Folger, Chris Sagrera and Clement Zhang, "A Behavioral View of Partnership Formation in Investor–Entrepreneur Dyad," in *Frontiers of Entrepreneurship Research* (Wellesley, MA: Babson College, 1999).

21. *Swift trust* refers to situations where trust quickly develops among individuals involved in complex, nonroutine, and interrelated tasks, who have a limited history of working together and a low probability of working together again in the future. Mark R. Dibben, Richard T. Harrison, and Colin M. Mason, "Swift Trust, Cooperation and Coordinator Judgment in the Informal Investment Decision Making Process," in *Frontiers of Entrepreneurship Research* (Wellesley, MA: Babson College, 1998).

22. Richard T. Harrison, Mark R. Dibben, and Colin M. Mason, "The Role of Trust in the Informal Investor's Investment Decision: An Exploratory Analysis," *Entrepreneurship Theory and Practice* 21, no. 4 (1997): 63–82.

23. Peter Kelly and Michael Hay, "The Private Investor–Entrepreneur Contractual Relationship: Understanding the Influence of Context," in *Frontiers of Entrepreneurship Research* (Wellesley, MA: Babson College, 2000).

24. Jeffrey E. Sohl and Jill Areson-Perkins, "Current Trends in the Private Equity Financing of High Tech Ventures: An Analysis of Deal Structure," in *Frontiers of Entrepreneurship Research* (Wellesley, MA: Babson College, 2001).

25. Sapienza et al., "A Behavioral View of Partnership Formation in Investor–Entrepreneur Dyad."

26. Sophie Manigart, M. Audrey Korsgaard, Robert Folger, Henry J. Sapienza, and Katleen Baeyens, "The Impact of Trust on Private Equity Contracts," in *Frontiers in Entrepreneurship Research* (Wellesley, MA: Babson College, 2001).

27. Dean A. Shepherd and Andrew Zacharakis, "The Venture Capitalist-Entrepreneur Relationship: Control, Trust and Confidence in Cooperative Behaviour," *Venture Capital* 3, no. 2 (2001): 129–150.

28. Hans Landström, Sophie Manigart, Colin M. Mason, and Henry J. Sapienza, "Contracts between Entrepreneurs and Investors: Terms and Negotiation Processes," in *Frontiers of Entrepreneurship Research* (Wellesley, MA: Babson College, 1998).

29. John Freear, Jeffrey E. Sohl, and William E. Wetzel, "Technology Due Diligence: What Angels Consider Important," in *Frontiers of Entrepreneurship Research* (Wellesley, MA: Babson College, 1996).

30. Andrew L. Zacharakis and G. Dale Meyer, "The Venture Capitalist Decision: Understanding Process versus Outcome," in *Frontiers of Entrepreneurship Research* (Wellesley, MA: Babson College, 1995).

31. Andrew L. Zacharakis and G. Dale Meyer, "Do Venture Capitalists Really Understand Their Own Decision Process?: A Social Judgment Theory Perspective," in *Frontiers of Entrepreneurship Research* (Wellesley, MA: Babson College, 1996).

32. Van Osnabrugge, "A Comparison of Business Angel and Venture Capitalist Investment Procedures."

33. Dean A. Shepherd and Andrew Zacharakis, "The Affect of 'Anchoring and Adjustment' on Entrepreneur–Investor Negotiations," in *Frontiers in Entrepreneurship Research* (Wellesley, MA: Babson College, 1999).

34. Kelly and Hay, "The Private Investor–Entrepreneur Contractual Relationship."

35. Landström, "Contracts between Entrepreneurs and Investors."

36. Manigart et al., "The Impact of Trust on Private Equity Contracts."

37. Joseph Bankman and Marcus Cole, "The Venture Capital Investment Bust: Did Agency Costs Play a Role? Was It Something Lawyers Helped Structure?," *Chicago-Kent Law Review* 77 (2001): 211–234.

38. Colin M. Mason and Richard T. Harrison, "Informal Venture Capital: A Study of the Investment Process, the Post-Investment Experience and Investment Performance," *Entrepreneurship and Regional Development* 8 (1996): 105–126.

39. John Freear, Jeffrey E. Sohl, and William E. Wetzel, "The Informal Venture Capital Market: Milestones Passed and the Road Ahead," in *Entrepreneurship 2000*, eds. D. L. Sexton and R. Smilor (Chicago: Upstart, 1997).

40. Van Osnabrugge, "A Comparison of Business Angel and Venture Capitalist Investment Procedures."

41. Jeffrey E. Sohl, "The Private Equity Market in the USA: Lessons from Volatility," *Venture Capital* 5, no. 1 (2003): 29–46.

42. Peter Kelly and Michael Hay, "Helping Hands or Watchful Eye?: An Agency Theory Perspective on Private Investor Involvement in Entrepreneurial Ventures," in *Frontiers of Entrepreneurship Research* (Wellesley, MA: Babson College, 2001).

43. Alexander Ardichvili, Richard N. Cardozo, Kathleen Tune, and Judy Reinach, "The Role of Angel Investors in the Assembly of Non-Financial Resources of New Ventures: Conceptual Framework and Empirical Evidence," *Journal of Enterprising Culture* 10, no. 1 (2002): 39–56.

44. Annaleena Parhankangas and Hans Landström, "Responses to Psychological Contract Violations in the Venture Capitalist–Entrepreneur Relationship: An Exploratory Study," in *Frontiers of Entrepreneurship Research* (Wellesley, MA: Babson College, 2003).

45. Frances M. Amatucci and Susan Coleman, "Radha Jalan and ElectroChem, Inc.: Energy for a Clean Planet," *Entrepreneurship Theory and Practice* (in press).

46. "Preliminary Estimates of Business Ownership by Gender, Hispanic or Latino Origin, and Race: 2002," U.S. Census Bureau's 2002 Survey of Business Owners, released July 2005.

47. "Women Business Owners and Their Enterprises," Fact Sheet, National Women's Business Council, March 2005.

48. Candida G. Brush, Nancy M. Carter, Elizabeth Gatewood, Patricia G. Greene, and Myra M. Hart, *Clearing the Hurdles: Women Building High-Growth Businesses* (Upper Saddle River, NJ: Pearson/Prentice Hall, 2004).

49. Shannon Henry, "Backing the Immigrant Work Ethic," *Washington Post*, January 1, 2004.

50. David Smallbone, Monder Ram, David Deakins, and Robert Baldock, "Access to Finance by Ethnic Minority Businesses in the UK," *International Small Business Journal* 21, no. 3 (2003): 291–311.

51. For an overview of selected U.S. funds focused on minority markets, see Philip Alphonse and Jane Wei, "Allied Equity Partners: March, 1999," Stanford University Graduate School of Business, Case SM-61 (2001).

52. Natasha Muktarsingh, "Women of Substance," *Director* 55, no. 2 (2002): 60–63.

53. Jeffrey E. Sohl and Laura Hill, "Women Angel Investors: Do They Have What It Takes to Fly?," paper presented at the U.S. Association for Small Business and Entrepreneurship meeting, Palm Springs, California, 2005.

54. Sohl and Areson-Perkins, "Current Trends in the Private Equity Financing of High Tech Ventures."

55. Sohl, "The Private Equity Market in the USA."

56. Ibid.

57. PricewaterhouseCoopers, "Venture Capital Investing Rises to $21 Billion in 2004 after Three Years of Decline," *Money Tree Quarterly Report*, www.pwcmoneytree.com.

58. A cram down is a situation in which venture capitalists refuse to invest in a new project unless the preceding investors of the company lower the value of their original investment. If the earlier investors of the company do not invest new cash for the next round of financing, then their interest in the company is crammed down.

59. Center for Venture Research, "The Angel Investor Market in 2003: The Angel Market Rebounds, but a Troublesome Post Seed Funding Gap Deepens," http://wsbe.unh .edu/Centers_CVR/2003AR.cfm.

6
Venture Capital Financing

Andrew Zacharakis and Matthias Eckermann

Venture capital (VC) is the fuel for high potential growth firms, especially in the United States. New venture survival is tenuous at best, but those backed by venture capitalists (VCs) tend to achieve a higher survival rate than non-VC-backed businesses.[1–3] Studies find that survival for VC-backed ventures range from around 65 to 85 percent of the VC's portfolio.[4, 5] VC predominantly focuses on high-technology industries (91 percent of all investments in 2003 in the United States) and U.S. companies receive over 74 percent of all VC disbursed worldwide.[6] VCs focus on knowledge-based businesses that have the potential to change the way people live. Some examples of businesses that VCs have backed include Genetech, Apple, Google, Amazon, and Federal Express.[7] Although VC investments have fallen from a peak of US$100 billion in 2000 to around US$21 billion in 2004 in the United States, it is still higher than the level of investment in 1998.[8] Reflecting the overall importance to entrepreneurship, VC has received considerable academic attention. The stream of research can be categorized following the framework of Bygrave and Timmons, and Tyebjee and Bruno (see Figure 6.1).[9, 10] The basic model of VC starts with the formation of a fund (the predominant form in the United States is a limited partnership). In this mode, the VC acts as an entrepreneur and goes out and sells his fund concept to potential limited partners who provide the capital.[11] Once the VC firm has funds, it seeks deal flow and screens for those ventures that seem to have the greatest potential. The next phase is a deeper evaluation of those potential investments that survive the initial screening, often called due diligence. If the VC is still interested after due diligence, he or she will enter negotiations with the entrepreneur outlining the amount to be invested, the form of the investment, and a number of other terms that ideally protect the VC against opportunistic behavior. After the investment is

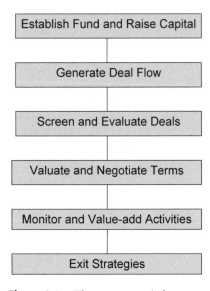

Figure 6.1.   The venture capital process.

made, the VC works with the entrepreneur to increase the value of the venture. This phase includes active monitoring and advising to the company on how to grow, working side-by-side to raise follow-on funding, and targeting some kind of liquidity event. The final stage in the VC process is exiting the investment and returning proceeds to limited partners.

This chapter showcases some of the research throughout the VC process outlined in the aforementioned model. We will focus on emerging trends, ideas, and practices in VC. We will make a special point of translating the findings from academic research into practical implications for both VCs and entrepreneurs.

LITERATURE REVIEW

The nature of the VC process involves transactions between two parties; limited partners and VCs, VCs and entrepreneurs, VCs and other VCs (syndicates), and insiders (entrepreneurs/VCs in earlier rounds) and exit vehicles such as initial public offerings (IPOs) and acquisitions. As such, agency theory is a commonly used theoretical lens to examine the process.[12–15] However, Arthurs and Busenitz assert that agency theory is limited in that it assumes the transacting parties to have different incentives.[16] As such, other theories are also common in examining the VC process, including resource-based theory and cognitive information processing theories.[17–19]

RAISING A FUND

Potential limited partners (LPs) face agency risks when investing into a VC fund, such as adverse selection and opportunistic behavior.[20, 21] The research around this topic has primarily focused on these agency risks and how LPs evaluate a potential VC investment a priori, protect themselves ex post of the investment and monitor ongoing performance. It is important to note that LPs do not have the same means at hand for disciplining VCs, as investors in matured corporations have to align management. In their analysis of governance structure in VC partnerships, Gompers and Lerner explicitly highlight the difficulty of dismissing the management of a VC fund owing to the central role of senior VCs in their company as well as the absence of a market for corporate control for most VC firms.[22] A priori, an LP's investment in a VC fund is more at risk. To explain investors' selection criteria, Gompers and Lerner use signal theory.[23] They stress that VCs must certify their ability to LPs in order to secure an LP investment. Gompers and Lerner argue that particularly high-quality VCs will have an incentive to release information about their ability to set themselves apart from average VCs and secure above-average financing conditions. Eventually, all VCs are somewhat forced to promote their track records on previous investments when establishing new funds as evidence of their ability to achieve high returns thereby addressing the sorting problem.[24]

Once LPs decide to invest in VCs, contracts are used to reduce the threat of opportunistic behavior ex post by VCs.[25] Gompers and Lerner studied contracts of 140 VC firms in the United States and identify three issues that are typically addressed: fund management, duties of the fund's management, and investment behavior.[26] However, they acknowledge that negotiating and monitoring these covenants is costly and investors appear to refrain from it except for situations characterized by severe agency threats, such as fraud.[27] Considering the costs of enforcement, agency theory predicts that the contracts will focus on aligning the interests of LPs and VC. Gompers and Lerner establish that both parties agree on a reward scheme that provides incentives for the VC firm to maximize the fund's profitability in the first place.[28] While the LP's investment is often returned first, the remaining gains are generally split so that the general partners receive 20 percent and the limited partners 80 percent.[29, 30]

The VCs also receive a yearly management fee of 2 to 3 percent of funds under management.[31] As the VC industry has grown, the best VC firms have been oversubscribed in new fund raising, leading them to create mega funds and/or being more selective in which LPs they allow to invest in their funds. Mega funds can create agency problems from the LP's perspective in that the management fee becomes so large that the VC may lose incentive to invest for future gains.[32] After the bubble collapsed, many funds voluntarily cut their size and reduced their management fees, yet the problem of alignment is an important one.[33]

Even though LPs have numerous ex-post contract provisions, it behooves LPs to monitor VC activities in order to protect and possibly enforce their rights.

However, Robbie, Wright, and Chiplin find that LPs are typically passive in their oversight of VCs, primarily due to the low percentage that VC accounts for in the LP's overall portfolio.[34] LPs rely on the VCs to accurately report activity on a quarterly and yearly basis. VCs have considerable latitude in reporting yearly performance of their portfolio companies to LPs, as there is no market validation of a portfolio company's valuation until it achieves some sort of exit.[35] Considering that internal rate of return (IRR) is the primary means that LPs use to judge VC performance, the potential volatility between reported and the ultimate actual IRR makes this measure problematic. Yet, Robbie, Wright, and Chiplin find that 66 percent of LPs do no monitoring and for those that take monitoring actions, it mostly consists of asking for more VC reports.[36] The IRR reporting problem becomes particularly severe as VC firms' promotion of new funds overlaps with their management of current funds.[37] Given illiquidity, no market price can be established for current investments. Objective track records thus suffer from a time lag allowing VCs to overstate their ability not only to current LPs, but to prospective LPs for follow-on funds. In result, VCs may overstate the success of recent activities or, in case of severe fluctuation in the firm, conceal the loss of management skills.

Although there is some research on the LP/VC dyad, it is still underdeveloped. The research by and large assumes that the LP and VC have already come together. Particularly for new firms, the questions arise of how new VCs can establish initial funds without having a track record to advertise? What are the conditions for a new VC firm to successfully raise funds and what factors account for failure at this stage? There is an opportunity to research how LPs identify which VCs they are interested in investing. This research might draw direction from the work on how VCs identify which entrepreneurial ventures they invest in. Whereas when looking at Akerlof's lemon problem, the process of VCs dropping out of the LPs' focus has not been given much attention either.[38] Our guess is that research focusing on the lifecycle of VC firms can add significant insights on both LPs' asset allocation strategies and VCs' decision making (as exemplified by Gompers's grandstanding theory).[39] On the flip side, there is room to understand how VCs develop their funding strategy and how they identify which LPs to approach. Specifically, what investment criteria do LPs use in evaluating potential VC investments? How do VCs approach LPs and sell them on their fund idea? In the context of selection, the question looms how VCs present their track records to potential LPs? How do VCs use track records to attract funding (i.e., is there a threat of VCs using distorted track records giving rise to a selection bias)? How critical is it to gain that first LP in order to signal quality of the fund? We also know that the VC/LP dyad is a repeated game with most successful VCs raising a succession of funds often giving previous LPs the first opportunity to invest in the current fund. How is this ongoing relationship impacted by a particular fund's performance? This question is appropriate, as many funds suffered greatly during the dot.com bust. Have LPs increased their due diligence and postinvestment monitoring as a result of poor performance since the bust? Have LPs required greater reporting? Have they been more proactive in defining the scope of the VC fund? As set out earlier, the recent development toward mega funds allowing VCs to select LPs may also put pressure on LPs to relinquish governance covenants. Is there an aggravated agency problem in mega funds? And what are the consequences? In sum, research into the VC/LP dyad has great potential to advance our understanding of the overall VC process.

DEAL FLOW AND SCREENING POTENTIAL INVESTMENTS

Deal flow and screening research also draws heavily on agency theory. Much of the research presupposes that entrepreneurs have an incentive to withhold information and then looks at methods VCs might use to avoid adverse selection. Network theory highlights the value of a strong network not only to increase deal flow but also to drive quality deals to the VC through trusted advisors. The research on decision criteria works to identify those factors that best predict which ventures have the greatest potential. Finally, more recent research looks at the decision biases involved in this process and examines how these biases might be minimized.

Amit, Glosten, and Muller assert that VCs face a lemon problem in that only those entrepreneurs who cannot raise cheaper capital from other sources will seek VCs out.[40] In fact, agency theory suggests that entrepreneurs possess an information advantage about their own capabilities as well as the true nature of the opportunity due to their involvement in the venture.[41, 42] Entrepreneurs may withhold negative information or overstate the venture's potential in order to attract investors and secure the cheapest financing available.[43–46] Given that traditional financers, such as banks or public investors insist on the availability of sufficient information to judge quality, lower quality entrepreneurs will have no other financing option but private equity.[47] As such, lower-quality entrepreneurs who have no other financing options are inclined to withhold information from VCs, which results in an adverse selection problem. Despite these problems, Amit, Brander, and Zott assert that VCs are better at identifying these agency problems (moral hazard and adverse selection).[48] Therefore, VCs need to find effective means to identify quality deal flow and to screen out lower-quality entrepreneurs.

Shane and Cable suggest that VC financing is a function of network ties, both direct and indirect.[49] The stronger the ties between entrepreneurs and investors, the more likely the VCs will fund entrepreneurs. Thus, network theory suggests that VCs generate deal flow by tapping their network. Specifically, better quality entrepreneurs will get warm referrals to VCs by knowing someone in the VC's network whom the VC respects and trusts.[50, 51] Tyebjee and Bruno observe that out of ninety deals, only 23 (26 percent) materialized pursuant to an unsolicited call of the entrepreneur. The majority of deals (65 percent) were recommended to the VC by other VCs (33 percent) or through sources, such as previous investees and personal contacts (roughly 40 percent). Ten percent received endorsement from investment banks or investment brokers. Social network theory extends economic perspectives, like agency theory, on which ventures receive financing, but VCs need to evaluate other factors in their decision process.[52]

Many researchers have investigated how VCs make their decisions, focusing heavily on the decision criteria that help distinguish those ventures that have a greater chance of providing strong returns.[53–62] The underlying justification for these studies is that a better understanding of the VC process may lead to better decisions and thereby more successful ventures. The information derived from these studies appears to fit four categories: (1) entrepreneur/team capabilities, (2) product/service attractiveness, (3) market/competitive conditions, and (4) potential returns if the venture is successful.[63]

Although insightful, many of these studies suffer from introspection biases since they use ex-post collection methods.[64–67] For instance, most VCs state that the entrepreneur is the most important factor in making their decision, but studies using real-time data collection methods, such as verbal protocols and policy-capturing experiments find that market-based factors are more important in the screening phase of the decision.[68, 69] Building upon these real-time methodologies has allowed researchers to investigate several other aspects of the VC decision process, including biases, the effect of experience, and demographics, among others.[70–73] The net result of these studies points out that VC decision making is at best imperfect and possibly suboptimal.

A main hypothesis derived from the finding that entrepreneurs have difficulty introspecting about their personal decision policies and also understanding that VCs suffer from decision biases, several studies have set out to build actuarial decision aids that can improve the screening process.[74–77] These studies consistently find that actuarial decision aids are better in screening ventures than are actual VCs themselves due to consistency in applying decision policies and removing decision biases.

This realm of VC research is perhaps the most developed, especially in regards to the screening decision. As such, much of the current work is adding greater depth to understanding how contextual factors influence the process. For example, Shepherd et al. find that VC experience has a curvilinear effect on decision performance.[78] While more experience is generally better, they find that after fourteen years of experience, VC decision effectiveness declines, possibly due to overreliance on gut feel rather than a concrete examination of all the decision factors. This study illustrates the value of building upon the platform findings of earlier coarser grained research to deepen our understanding of the VC phenomena.

Unlike the decision-screening process, deal flow has been relatively under investigated. While Amit et al. rightly point out the potential lemons problem VCs face, the question becomes what factors mitigate that problem?[79] Amit et al. assert that VCs have developed skills that help them weed out lemons, but we suspect that this is a matter of degree throughout the industry.[80] Specifically, we hypothesize that more established VCs would face less of a lemons problem than newer firms. What factors distinguish more effectively selecting funds and the also-rans? We suspect that the value and power of the VC's network is a fruitful area to start this investigation. For instance, does networking with the right angel investors, the right feeder VC funds, and the like, improve deal flow and thereby return?

DUE DILIGENCE

Due diligence takes a considerable amount of the VC's time; Smart estimates that VCs spend an average of 120 hours just evaluating the human capital potential of the entrepreneur.[81] This does not include the time VCs spend on due diligence of the market, product, or the financial standing of the portfolio company.[82] That means that due diligence on the entrepreneurial team requires anywhere from one to ten weeks of full time effort; however, VCs rarely spend all that time sequentially, so in calendar terms due diligence can last anywhere from six weeks to six months.[83] The level of due diligence is influenced by time constraints, cost of reducing information asymmetries and any number of situational aspects that can make thorough due diligence more difficult.[84] As such, due diligence is a cost/benefit trade-off; how much effort and time should VCs commit to reduce the adverse selection risk.[85] Investors will refrain from investing if they foresee an expensive due diligence process.

Due diligence involves evaluating both tangible (e.g., patents, accounts receivable, etc.) and intangible assets (quality of leadership, know how, culture, etc.).[86] Entrepreneurial firms seeking VC are likely to have more intangible assets, which are much harder to assess (more costly), especially for earlier stage deals.[87] Smart conducted an exploratory study of VC due diligence on the entrepreneurial team's human capital potential (an intangible asset); basically, VCs must assess the likelihood that the team's behaviors will lead to a desired outcome.[88] His study of fifty-one VCs finds three primary areas of due diligence effort: (1) work samples where the VC quizzes the entrepreneur on a number of what-if scenarios; (2) reference checks on people who can attest to the entrepreneur's capabilities; and (3) fact-based interviews to assess the entrepreneur's past performance. The emphasis on these avenues changes by stage of the investment. For earlier stage deals, Smart finds that work samples take more of the VC's time whereas for later stage deals, fact-based interviews become more important.[89] These findings have face validity in that in later stage deals, the VC can gauge the entrepreneur's efforts in the venture in question and assess how likely the entrepreneur is to continue on a successful course. On the other hand, for earlier stage deals, VCs are looking at the entrepreneur's decision-making process to assess whether the entrepreneur will develop a strategy that can lead to success.

Considering the difficulty of accurately measuring human capital capability, Fiet suggests that VCs are more concerned with market risk factors (demand, competition, and so on) than human capital issues because VCs can contract certain behaviors (term sheets) and take postinvestment action if there are human capital gaps (i.e., hire new team members, fire others).[90] As such, VCs focus on informants as a means of conducting due diligence. These experts can offer insight to market potential, and are often other VCs who might become coinvestors.[91] In essence, coinvesting (or forming a syndicate) can reduce the costs of due diligence as it brings more minds on the evaluation process.

Syndication is a common practice in financing transactions.[92–95] Two views of research examining the necessity and benefits of syndication stand out: the resource-based line and the financial economics line. Looking through the resource-base lens, syndication is highly relevant to VCs, for it allows VCs to pool information prior to investment decisions as well as throughout the investment process.[96, 97] Information on investments is considered a valuable resource as information reduces risk without negatively affecting returns.[98] Furthermore, two parties are likely to hold different information on the same subject resulting from different backgrounds, experiences, and perspective, so that pooling the knowledge of several parties increases the diversity of information considered.[99] Sah and Stigliz show that syndicated investments are superior to those that are based only on the knowledge base of one individual.[100] Scholars thus argue that a selection process for VC investments becomes more effective, the larger the number of VCs who actively participate.[101, 102] In essence, the pooling of experiences and knowledge eases information asymmetries between VCs and entrepreneurs and reduces the syndicate's exposure to adverse selection risk.

Since VCs can never make due diligence costless, VCs add a discount to their valuation.[103, 104] Therefore, better-quality entrepreneurs benefit if they can reduce information asymmetries. Busenitz, Fiet, and Moesel suggest that entrepreneurs can reduce the information gap and thereby cut the VC's cost of due diligence by signaling the entrepreneur's personal commitment to the venture.[105] In essence, such signaling reduces the VCs' concern over some agency risks, such as shirking, adverse selection, and hold-ups.[106] However, Busenitz et al. did not find that signaling was correlated to long-term venture success.[107] The lack of findings might suggest that signaling biases VCs in their due diligence process, possibly by encouraging them to take short-cuts (less time devoted to due diligence) or pay more attention to certain factors (such as the team) and less to others (such as the market).

While aspects of due diligence have received attention, more work can be done. Smart finds better due diligence performance by smaller VC firms and speculates that it is because they make fewer deals per partner, but he was unable to test that proposition.[108] A good future study might look at difference in due diligence by VC firm size, stage focus, technology focus, and so forth. Smart also questions whether there is a curvilinear effect on time/effort expended and value of due diligence. Following Kaplan and Stromberg, research might use investment memorandums written by VC to assess the level of due diligence and then see if there is a correlation to ultimate venture performance.[109] We also sense that due diligence research focuses on negative agency issues to the neglect of other positive outcomes. For instance, Busenitz and Barney assert that entre-preneurs are overoptimistic in their prospect for success.[110] Due diligence helps VCs work with entrepreneurs to identify pitfalls and reshape their opportunities so that they can achieve higher performance and thereby greater VC returns. Such preinvestment value-add not only improves the VC's potential return, but also better prepares the entrepreneur to succeed. Examining other positive spillover effects of due diligence would greatly expand our understanding of the value of this process.

NEGOTIATING AND CONTRACTING BETWEEN THE VC AND THE ENTREPRENEUR

If due diligence proves favorable, the VC and the entrepreneur enter negoti-ations on the investment's specific terms. Several issues are pertinent in this stage, including valuation, contract provisions that provide protection against agency risks, staging of future rounds, and board representation and oversight.[111]

As Wright and Robbie point out, valuation for a new venture is quite different from formal corporate valuation.[112] Wright and Robbie underscore the impor-tance of proper valuation models to incorporate the two facets that make VC investments distinctive: relatively high uncertainty compared with investments in matured companies and rapid growth. Techniques anticipating steady future developments and constant earnings on the basis of the company's history cannot entirely capture the potential inherent in such investment. Seppä and Laamanen therefore summarize that in a VC context, the absence of a performance history by which to judge the company and uncertainties about the young business par-ticularly hampers the use of conventional valuation methods, such as benchmark valuations on the basis of price/earnings (P/E) ratios of public companies or calculation of a company's discounted future cash flows (DCF).[113] A young company's earnings may for instance be subject to great jumps at the beginning, which is not predictable on the basis of its previous performance and eventually increasing the error of forecasts. Cornell and Shapiro, Kaplan and Ruback, and Keeley and Punjabi observe that VCs revert to benchmarks more specifically related to the business to assess the potential value an investment can attain given it prospects.[114–116] Manigart et al. surveyed VCs across five countries including the United States, and finds that the most common valuation techniques were earnings before interest taxes (EBIT) multiples and comparing the venture under consideration to recent transactions in the venture's sector, which is presumed to closely match the future potential of the firm.[117] The VCs then derive conclusions about the relative position of the firm and a valuation range instead of deriving a hard and fast value. Only in later stages and in the antecedent of an initial public offering or a trade sale do traditional corporate finance methods, such as DCF gain importance as the company becomes more predictable and uncertainties about the future development resolve.[118]

Most recently, real option theory has been introduced to the valuation quest in VC finance.[119, 120] Options may be particularly suitable for deriving a fair value because it depends on future decisions, which can be accounted for in option theory-based models. Such models are able to deal with the uniqueness and dynamic nature of each venture's future development.[121] As an option-based valuation is not derived from past business performances, it is not confounded if static forecasts are frustrated. Furthermore, since the option valuation is not grounded on benchmarks, it does not suffer from limited comparability of innovative businesses. An option approach not only provides the VC with an indicative valuation prior to the entry decision but can also allow for an incremental update every time new information surfaces.[122] A real option-theory approach however requires the VC to identify the most pertinent issues as well as the impact of an option-based valuation. Eventually, the accuracy of the input in terms of discretionary decisions or rights, the structure of decisions and consequences determines the quality of the valuation calling on research to identify the most important parameters (see McGrath, Ferrier, and Mendelow, for a review of option models in management; for a review on options in VC see Dixit and Pindyck; Lander and Pinches).[123-125]

Since valuation is highly susceptible to future performance of the venture, which is impacted by entrepreneur actions, unforeseen conditions, and so forth, VCs often contract to protect themselves from agreeing to an inflated valuation.[126-129] One way is to use hybrid financing which allows VCs to alter the financing structure throughout the investment period in reaction to newly emerging information. Norton and Tenenbaum research the preferred financing means of ninety U.S. VC firms and find that preferred convertible equity dominates in general as it allows VCs an effortless use of ratchets.[130-132] Cornelli and Yosha demonstrate that in the course of a staged investment, convertible securities afford VCs a strong position to work against window-dressing problems as they can increase their stake (diluting the entrepreneur's stake) in case predefined goals are not accomplished.[133] Depending on the business and the industry sector, the extent of these measures varies. For instance, high-technology investments with a higher risk for failure generally entail more contract provisions related to milestones than low-technology companies.[134] There is however some controversy on the sole validity of these findings. In a cross-border comparison, Cumming argues that the dominance of convertible preferred equity only applies to the United States whereas he observes that common equity dominates the Canadian VC industry.[135] In line with Gilson and Schizer, Cumming underlines factors that further impacts the choice of the capital structure most notably the in-force tax system.[136] Cumming and Gilson and Schizer argue that significant tax advantages for convertible preferred equity may also motivate U.S. VCs to favor such financing means.[137, 138]

Besides looking into capital structure related covenants, scholars research the application of other governance means, which are usually stipulated in advance to an investment. Barney et al. look into 270 VC contracts during 1983 and 1985 and observe that VCs occupy a disproportionably high number of board seats either with representatives or affiliates in relation to their actual ownership position.[139–141] It is argued that stronger board representation of VCs increases the entrepreneur's receptivity to financial, operational, and strategic advice.[142] Rosenstein finds that boards of VC-backed ventures have even greater power than the company's management (e.g., entrepreneur).[143] VCs use their board presence to supervise the management and initiate strategic changes if necessary.[144] In the long run however, Barney et al. find that VCs forego board seats the more the company's performance improves and the longer the management is in place. Barney et al. add that VCs grow keen to seek covenants protecting proprietary knowledge and impede entrepreneurs from engaging in rivaling activities the more competitive the venture's environment.[145] Kaplan and Strömberg provide an overview on the extent of specific governance methods that are commonly applied in VC finance on the basis of 213 investments in the United States.[146] They show that if companies lack significant turnover, VCs apply staging mechanisms, vesting, voting rights, and board influence in order to supervise the investment effectively. However, VCs tend to release these stringent conditions the more the venture matures and the more uncertainty is resolved.

Control and monitoring may have negative effects. Shepherd and Zacharakis warn that undue reliance on negative covenants, such as ratchets may so diminish entrepreneur motivation that it negatively impacts overall venture performance.[147] As such, Shepherd and Zacharakis propose a model of trust building that recognizes that any VC–entrepreneur relationship is based not only on control (from an agency perspective) but also on trust.[148] They assert that entrepreneurs (as well as VCs) can build trust in the other party by signaling commitment, taking fair and just actions, obtaining a good fit and open and frequent communication. While many scholars have focused on control mechanisms, less work has looked at the interaction of trust and control in the VC–entrepreneurship relationship.[149–151] One exception is that Sapienza and Korsgaard investigated VCs' responses to the timeliness with which entrepreneurs shared information, and the level of influence the VC had over the strategic direction of the venture.[152] By comparing the relations of two panels of master-level business students on the one hand and experienced VCs on the other hand with management teams of their portfolio companies, Sapienza and Korsgaard unveil that prompt feedback positively impacts the relationship. This turns into greater trust between investors and investees, which eventually softens principal agent concerns and relieves monitoring efforts. It is thus beneficial for VCs to seek timely cooperation with entrepreneurs.

While negotiation and contracting has drawn heavily on the shape of contracts and how the provisions tie to an agency perspective, most of the research seems to view the process from the VC's eyes. There is an opportunity to examine how entrepreneurs enter negotiations and how they improve the valuation through this process. We suspect that the ability of the entrepreneur to negotiate successfully will be contingent upon a number of contextual factors, such as the entrepreneur's previous experience, the perceived potential of the venture, current economic conditions (e.g., the dot.com boom and bust), and so forth. We also would encourage researchers to take the Shepherd and Zacharakis theoretical model regarding trust, and empirically test it.[153] Specifically, how does the negotiation process evolve? Does the way the process moves from initial meetings, to term sheets, to final valuation and terms influence the entrepreneur's incentives? In terms of valuation, we believe that research should not only improve methodologies but also relate a broader scope of factors to the venture value. We believe that an option theory approach offers much potential to integrate further factors. How and to what extent does the entrepreneur's initial endowment of skills or the VC's specific industry skills affect the eventual price they fetch for the venture? Research can account for the unique constellation of factors that drive every venture.

MONITORING AND VALUE-ADDED ACTIVITIES

After closing the investment contract and committing the first round of capital, the VC financing period commences. There is a great array of research, which looks into typical problems the venture encounters in the early phases of its life cycle.[154–156] Depending on the scope of innovation, a venture may be subject to substantial market and technology risks. In emerging markets, early stage ventures come across a multitude of rival products/services whereby the eventual dominant product design remains uncertain.[157, 158] The consequence is that many early stage firms entering the same industry do not succeed and drop out.[159, 160] In this demanding environment, Baum and Silverman add that the inexperience of the entrepreneur increases the risk of the early stage venture further.[161]

Throughout the VC process, the VC works with the entrepreneur to master the upcoming problems and assists on problems where the management may lack direction.[162, 163] Brander, Amit, and Antweiler refer to the VC's monitoring and assisting as value adding.[164] However, as of yet, much of the research on this topic is descriptive. For instance, scholars observe the scope of the VC's nonfinancial contribution to the venture and find that VCs typically assist on financial and managerial problems.[165–167] Gorman and Sahlman and Hellmann and Puri add that VCs help in recruiting top management.[168, 169] Furthermore, VCs offer ventures access to their networks of potential customers, suppliers, or financial service providers.[170]

Researchers further dwell on the intensity of the VC's involvement. Gorman and Sahlman find that VCs spend 60 percent of their time on such postinvestment activities.[171] On average, a VC commits 110 hours per year to assisting and monitoring one venture investment.[172] Elango et al. find that VCs devote an average of twenty hours per month in monitoring every portfolio company.[173] Although all VCs work with entrepreneurs postinvestment, the level of interaction varies. MacMillan et al. surveyed sixty-two VCs to assess their level of postin-vestment involvement.[174] They find that there are three categories of involvement that they label (1) laissez-faire, (2) moderate, and (3) close tracker. Surprisingly, MacMillan et al. find little difference in VC performance based on the level of involvement.[175] Sapienza and Gupta examine how context impacts the level of VC involvement.[176] VC involvement tends to be lower when the investment is in an earlier stage venture, the VC has less experience, the VC is geographically distant to the venture, and the VC perceives high goal congruence with the entrepreneur.[177] Furthermore, Sapienza, Manigart, and Vermeir find that VC monitoring and value-added activities increase based on the need of the portfolio company moderated by the VC's experience; more experienced VCs provide greater value-added services.[178]

The deep involvement of the VC in the venture raises the question of the quality of the relationship between the VC and the entrepreneur.[179–182] Sapienza and Gupta point out that in joining efforts, the VC and the entrepreneur better address the venture's initial struggles.[183] Cable and Shane construct a model based on game theory and highlight cooperation of both the VC and the en-trepreneur as a prerequisite for well-performing ventures.[184] Gompers indirectly supports this reasoning in his analysis of 794 investments, confirming the positive effect of a healthy VC relationship on the occurrence of IPOs.[185]

Yet as outlined earlier, the separation of ownership and management causes agency problems and induces VCs to take a variety of precautions. The ultimate threat to the entrepreneur, however, is his replacement in case of opportunistic and ineffective behavior (e.g., Fiet et al., Fredrickson, Hambrick, and Baumrin, and Sweeting and Wong report that dismissals occur surprisingly often).[186–188] Counter to management reshuffles in matured companies, dismissals in a VC context represent severe interference with the business's development, given that assets are still highly intangible and tied to the founders.[189–191] Competencies of managers of matured companies are more easily replaceable. The dismissal mir-rors an ultimate decision of the VC to secure and protect its investment and indicates a strongly malfunctioning VC relationship.[192–195] Bruton, Fried, and Hisrich find that CEO dismissal is by order of priority, most often a function of (1) ability (adverse selection), (2) disagreement in strategic direction, and (3) opportunistic behavior by the entrepreneur.[196] While opportunistic behavior is the least common reason for dismissal, Bruton et al. find that these CEOs tend to have the largest equity stake versus other dismissed CEOs.[197]

Even though most of the relevant issues are already covered by scholars, we perceive that much work can still be done. Most studies presume a sequence of events in that management assistance seems to be the VC's ex-ante choice, which then affects performance. This view neglects a feedback process in which a VC notes a growing demand for assistance based on a venture's performance and vice versa. This brings us to the question of the change in the interaction between VCs and entrepreneurs over time in terms of intensity, contents, and the like. Fur-thermore, research has so far taken a narrow perspective in that assisting and monitoring activities have mostly been related to performance issues. What else can be won by cooperating closer with entrepreneurs? We believe there may be potential in tapping other areas of interests of the VC. Monitoring and supervising may for instance represent a means to extend insights in certain businesses, which can be transferred to other investments. With regard to the exit, monitoring may as well help the VC establish an overview on potential acquirers.

EXITING THE INVESTMENT

The VC investing process lasts several years and ends with the VC's exit. The exit denotes the process in which the VC converts its illiquid stakes in a venture either into cash or liquid stakes which it can subsequently return to the LPs. Given the nonexistence of interim dividends in early stages, VC investments cannot distribute annual dividends designating the exit the VC's only source of gains.[198] VC research has already recognized the exit's importance and acknowledges that a VC's success is not only driven by its ability to identify and to manage venture investments but also by its capabilities in exiting portfolio companies efficiently.[199–202] From a company-specific perspective, three conditions end the VC's involvement. First, the company reaches a sufficient size and credibility to replace the VC funds with cheaper follow-on capital.[203, 204] Second, the duration of the VC investment approaches the end of the VC fund's lifetime forcing the VC to return the fund's resources to LPs. As Gompers and Lerner report, VC funds are limited to ten years effectively setting a deadline for the VC's exit.[205] Third, the venture has neither flourished to a point where it can attract follow-on funding nor is the fund running out of capital, but the VC perceives the investment as a so-called living dead. When moving toward exiting living-dead ventures, VCs use specific divestment vehicles to terminate the investment: (1) liquidation events enable the VC to secure some funds; (2) VCs may look for other VCs to take over; or (3) VCs may sell the venture privately to the entrepreneur or other companies.[206–208]

Scholars have examined the typical issues hampering the VC's exit mainly taking an information asymmetry perspective. The central problem of information asymmetry upon exit is that outside investors cannot risklessly establish a valuation of the venture but encounter an adverse selection problem.[209] Adverse selection takes place when VCs cannot distinguish between good and bad ventures due to information asymmetry. As a result, VCs have to bear the opportunity costs of uncertainty and, possibly, end up in investing in the wrong ventures.[210–212] Adverse selection hence becomes a central problem at exit again. Cumming and MacIntosh find that VCs use partial exits to grant follow-on investors insight into the value of the company in cases of severe information asymmetries as is the case in dynamic high-technology environments.[213] Habib and Ljungqvist ask how incumbent investors can reduce friction due to information asymmetry through hiring third-party certification.[214] Studies of IPOs show that in cases of severe information asymmetry, enlisting prestigious investment banks can lead to a lower underpricing.[215, 216]

Not only do scholars tie the VC's exit to the venture's conditions, they emphasize the impact of capital markets on exits as well.[217–220] Asset prices are not entirely based on objective assessments but also reflect the public markets' optimism about the quality of new issues. In fact, scholars argue that soaring investor optimism can cause price inflation across industries or markets.[221–225] Subsequent declines are driven by investors growing skepticism after they have become disappointed from too many lemon issues. Ibbotson and Jaffe refer to the peak of this cycle as a "hot issue market."[226] A hot issue market period is essentially characterized by a reduced impact of information asymmetry on IPOs. Since investors become less concerned about adverse selection, VCs find it easier to bring their companies public and reap above-average capital gains.[227] In support of this, scholars report a strong correlation between the average share price performance in national equity capital markets and the number of VC-backed companies that go public across all countries with established VC markets.[228–230] In the era between 1999 and 2000 when stock markets peaked, successful IPOs appeared virtually independent from the level of development of the issuing company.[231]

While research on prior steps in the VC process involves a variety of theories, such as network theory, resourced-based view, and the like, the existing research on exits is dominated by the financial economics lens centering on information asymmetry and capital markets explanations. Questions such as how the VC's network can facilitate exits have not yet been examined beyond the general theory on the VC's certification in IPOs. Do network ties and recurring transactions lead to strong ties and a trustful relationship that enables VCs to withdraw in a network environment? If networks with investment bankers, lawyers, and the like can create a deal inflow, can they also generate a deal outflow in terms of exits?

As far as investments are concerned, the gap in existing research on exits can be characterized by two dimensions: the venture's success and the exit's success. Scholars implicitly assume that unsuccessful ventures accomplish unsuccessful exits. Typical findings are that VCs harvest most of their returns from IPOs.[232–235] In addition, living dead investments are presumed to be failures with only inefficient exits accomplishable. Despite the relatively huge number of failing VC investments, research has not yet examined whether there is any upside potential in the disposals of stalling companies.[236, 237] If so, how can VCs withdraw best from struggling investments? A closely related question pertains to the dependence of VCs on hot issue markets to transaction's parameters. Future research should examine up to which level can VCs use hot issue markets to dispose of struggling ventures? In this context, we believe that a general literature gap exists on the comparison of the impact of hot issue markets versus the value-added hypothesis on VCs' capital gains. Do VCs sell some ventures only in hot issue markets? Do VCs essentially bet on the occurrence of hot issue markets to cash in on some investments?

GAPS AND FUTURE RESEARCH

VC has received a tremendous amount of research attention due to the power of VCs to help high-potential companies grow quickly and capture value. As we have gone through each of the major VC steps, we have suggested some areas that could use further research. Clearly, our review and suggestions are not exhaustive, but in general, we believe that the parameters of the VC phenomena are well laid out and future research should move toward adding depth. In particular, it appears that the majority of research views VC through the eyes of VCs. New research could shed further light on the topic by taking a look at the research questions from the eyes of the partner in the dyad (e.g., LPs, entrepreneurs, follow-on investors, and so forth). For instance, how do LPs make a decision to invest in a particular VC fund? How do LPs influence VC decisions as they build their portfolios? On the other end, how can entrepreneurs manage the negotiation process? What impact do the entrepreneur's actions have on the valuation and contract terms? How does the power of the parties involved in these transactions shape decision making at each step of the VC process? As we continue to answer these questions and others, our understanding of the VC process should inform the various stakeholders to this equity decision.

NOTES

1. Scott Kunkel and Charles Hofer, "Why Study the Determinants of New Venture Performance: A Literature Review and Rationale," presented at Academy of Management meetings (1990).

2. William Sandberg, *New Venture Performance* (Lexington, MA: Lexington Books, 1986).

3. Jeffry A. Timmons, *New Venture Creation: Entrepreneurship for the 21st Century* (Homewood, IL: Irwin, 1994).

4. William A. Sahlman, "The Structure and Governance of Venture Capital Organizations," *Journal of Financial Economics* 27 (1990): 473–521.

5. Terry Dorsey, *Operating Guidelines for Effective Venture Capital Funds Management* (Austin: University of Texas, 1979).

6. William D. Bygrave and Stephen A. Hunt, *Global Entrepreneurship Monitor: 2004 Financing Report* (Babson College and London Business School, 2005).

7. Ibid.

8. PricewaterhouseCoopers/Thomson Venture Economics/National Venture Capital Association MoneyTree Survey, updated March 28, 2005.

9. William Bygrave and Jeffry Timmons, *Venture Capital at the Crossroads* (Boston: Harvard Business School Press, 1992).

10. Tyzoon Tyebjee and Albert Bruno, "A Model of Venture Capitalist Investment Activity," *Management Science* 30, no. 9 (1984): 1051–1066.

11. Robert Robinson and Noam Wasserman, *The Venture Capitalist as Entrepreneur* (Boston: Harvard Business School Publishing, 2000).

12. Jonathan Arthurs and Lowell Busenitz, "The Boundaries and Limitations of Agency Theory and Stewardship Theory in the Venture Capitalist/Entrepreneur Relationship," *Entrepreneurship Theory and Practice* 28, no. 2 (2003): 145–162.

13. Douglas Cumming, "Agency Costs, Institutions, Learning, and Taxation in Venture Capital Contracting," *Journal of Business Venturing* 20, no. 5 (2005): 573–622.

14. Harry Sapienza and Anil Gupta, "Impact of Agency Risks and Task Uncertainty on Venture Capitalists-CEO Interaction," *Academy of Management Journal* 37, no. 6 (1994): 1618–1632.

15. Sahlman, "The Structure and Governance of Venture Capital Organizations."

16. Arthurs and Busenitz, "The Boundaries and Limitations of Agency Theory and Stewardship Theory."

17. Sharon A. Alvarez and Lowell W. Busenitz, "The Entrepreneurship of Resource-Based Theory," *Journal of Management* 27 (2001): 755–775.

18. Andrew Zacharakis and G. Dale Meyer, "A Lack of Insight: Do Venture Capitalists Really Understand Their Own Decision Process?" *Journal of Business Venturing* 13, no. 1 (1998): 57–76.

19. Dean Shepherd, "Venture Capitalists' Assessment of New Venture Survival," *Management Science* 45, no. 5 (1999): 621–632.

20. Ken Robbie, Mike Wright, and Brian Chiplin, "The Monitoring of Venture Capital Firms," *Entrepreneurship: Theory and Practice* 21, no. 4 (1997): 9–28.

21. Sahlman, "The Structure and Governance of Venture Capital Organizations."

22. Paul Gompers and Joshua Lerner, "The Use of Covenants: An Empirical Analysis of Venture Partnership Agreements," *Journal of Law and Economics* 39, no. 2 (1996): 463–498.

23. Ibid.

24. Sahlman, "The Structure and Governance of Venture Capital Organizations."

25. Ibid.

26. Gompers and Lerner, "The Use of Covenants."

27. Sahlman, "The Structure and Governance of Venture Capital Organizations."

28. Gompers and Lerner, "The Use of Covenants."

29. Christopher Barry, "New Directions in Research on Venture Capital Finance," *Financial Management* 23, no. 3 (1994): 3–15.

30. Gompers and Lerner, "The Use of Covenants."

31. Bob Zider, "How Venture Capital Works," *Harvard Business Review* 76, no. 6 (1998): 131–139.

32. Jason Green, "Venture Capital at a New Crossroads: Lessons from the Bubble," *The Journal of Management Development* 23, no. 10 (2004): 972–981.

33. Ibid.

34. Robbie, Wright, and Chiplin, "The Monitoring of Venture Capital Firms."

35. Mike Wright and Ken Robbie, "Venture Capital and Private Equity: A Review and Synthesis," *Journal of Business Finance and Accounting* 25, nos. 5 and 6 (1998): 521–570.

36. Robbie, Wright, and Chiplin, "The Monitoring of Venture Capital Firms."

37. Sahlman, "The Structure and Governance of Venture Capital Organizations."

38. George Akerlof, "The Market for Lemons: Quality Uncertainty and the Market Mechanisms," *Quarterly Journal of Economics* 84, no. 3 (1970): 488–500.

39. Paul Gompers, "Grandstanding in the Venture Capital Industry," *Journal of Financial Economics* 42, no. 1 (1996): 133–156.

40. Raphael Amit, Lawrence Glosten, and Eitan Muller, "Does Venture Capital Foster the Most Promising Entrepreneurial Firms?" *California Management Review* (Spring 1990): 103–111.

41. Ninon Kohers and Theodor Kohers, "Takeovers of Technology Firms: Expectations vs. Reality," *Financial Management* 30, no. 3 (2001): 35–54.

42. Matthias Eckermann and Andrew Zacharakis, "Venture Capitalist's Exit Strategy under Information Asymmetry: A Financial Economics Perspective" (Unpublished manuscript, 2005).

43. Barry, "New Directions in Research on Venture Capital Finance."

44. Paul Gompers, "Optimal Investment, Monitoring, and the Staging of Venture Capital," *Journal of Finance* 50, no. 5 (1995): 1461–1489.

45. Harry Sapienza and M. Korsgaard, "Procedural Justice in Entrepreneur–Investor Relations," *Academy of Management Journal* 39, no. 3 (1996): 544–574.

46. Roger Bowden, "Bargaining, Size, and Return in Venture Capital Funds," *Journal of Business Venturing* 9, no. 4 (1994): 307–330.

47. Cumming, "Agency Costs, Institutions, Learning, and Taxation in Venture Capital Contracting."

48. Raphael Amit, James Brander, and Christopher Zott, "Why Do Venture Capital Firms Exist? Theory and Canadian Evidence," *Journal of Business Venturing* 13, no. 6 (1998): 441–466.

49. Scott Shane and Daniel Cable, "Network Ties, Reputation, and the Financing of New Ventures," *Management Science* 48, no. 3 (2002): 364–381.

50. Vance Fried and Robert Hisrich, "Toward a Model of Venture Capital Investment Decision Making," *Financial Management* 23, no. 3 (1994): 28–37.

51. Tyebjee and Bruno, "A Model of Venture Capitalist Investment Activity."

52. Shane and Cable, "Network Ties, Reputation, and the Financing of New Ventures."

53. William Wells, "Venture Capital Decision-Making," unpublished doctoral dissertation (Pittsburgh: Carnegie Mellon University, 1974).

54. E. A. Poindexter, "The Efficiency of Financial Markets: The Venture Capital Case," unpublished doctoral dissertation (New York: New York University, 1976).

55. Tyebjee and Bruno, "A Model of Venture Capitalist Investment Activity."

56. Ian MacMillan, Robin Siegel, and P. SubbaNarasimha, "Criteria Used by Venture Capitalists to Evaluate New Venture Proposals," *Journal of Business Venturing* 1, no. 1 (1985): 119–128.

57. Ian MacMillan, L. Zeman, and P. SubbaNarasimha, "Criteria Distinguishing Unsuccessful Ventures in the Venture Screening Process," *Journal of Business Venturing* 2, no. 2 (1987): 123–137.

58. Robert Robinson, "Emerging Strategies in the Venture Capital Industry," *Journal of Business Venturing* 2 (1987): 53–77.

59. Jeffry Timmons, Daniel Muzyka, Howard Stevenson, and William Bygrave, "Opportunity Recognition: The Core of Entrepreneurship," *Frontiers of Entrepreneurship Research* (1987): 109–123.

60. William Sandberg, David Schweiger, and Charles Hofer, "The Use of Verbal Protocols in Determining Venture Capitalists' Decision Processes," *Entrepreneurship Theory and Practice* 13, no. 2 (1988): 8–20.

61. John Hall and Charles Hofer, "Venture Capitalists' Decision Criteria and New Venture Evaluation," *Journal of Business Venturing* 8, no. 1 (1993): 25–42.

62. Andrew Zacharakis and G. Dale Meyer, "The Venture Capitalist Decision: Understanding Process versus Outcome," *Frontiers of Entrepreneurship Research* 15 (1995): 465–478.

63. Zacharakis and Meyer, "A Lack of Insight."

64. Hall and Hofer, "Venture Capitalists' Decision Criteria and New Venture Evaluation."

65. Sandberg, Schweiger, and Hofer, "The Use of Verbal Protocols in Determining Venture Capitalists' Decision Processes."

66. Shepherd, "Venture Capitalists' Assessment of New Venture Survival."

67. Zacharakis and Meyer, "A Lack of Insight."

68. Hall and Hofer, "Venture Capitalists' Decision Criteria and New Venture Evaluation."

69. Zacharakis and Meyer, "A Lack of Insight."

70. Andrew Zacharakis and Dean Shepherd, "The Nature of Information and Venture Capitalists' Overconfidence," *Journal of Business Venturing* 16, no. 4 (2001): 311–332.

71. Dean Shepherd, Andrew Zacharakis, and Robert Baron, "Venture Capitalists' Decision Processes: Evidence Suggesting More Experience May Not Always Be Better," *Journal of Business Venturing* 18, no. 3 (2003): 381–401.

72. Candida Brush, Nancy Carter, Patricia Greene, Myra Hart, and Elizabeth Gatewood, "The Role of Social Capital and Gender in Linking Financial Suppliers and Entrepreneurial Firms: A Framework for Future Research," *Venture Capital: An International Journal of Entrepreneurial Finance* 4, no. 4 (2002): 305–323.

73. Patricia Greene, Candida Brush, Myra Hart, and Patrick Saparito, "Patterns of Venture Capital Funding: Is Gender a Factor?" *Venture Capital: An International Journal of Entrepreneurial Finance* 3, no. 1 (2001): 63–83.

74. Thomas Astebro, "Key Success Factors for Technological Entrepreneurs' R&D projects," *IEEE Transactions on Engineering Management* 51, no. 3 (2004): 314–321.

75. Hernan Riquelme and Tudor Rickards, "Hybrid Conjoint Analysis: An Estimation Probe in New Venture Decisions," *Journal of Business Venturing* 7, no. 6 (1992): 505–518.

76. Andrew Zacharakis and G. Dale Meyer, "The Potential of Actuarial Decision Models: Can They Improve the Venture Capital Investment Decision?" *Journal of Business Venturing* 15, no. 4 (2000): 323–346.

77. Andrew Zacharakis and Dean Shepherd, "A Non-Additive Decision-Aid for Venture Capitalists' Investment Decisions," *European Journal of Operational Research* 162, no. 3 (2005): 673–689.

78. Shepherd, Zacharakis, and Baron, "Venture Capitalists' Decision Processes."

79. Amit, Glosten, and Muller, "Does Venture Capital Foster the Most Promising Entrepreneurial Firms?"

80. Amit, Brander, and Zott, "Why Do Venture Capital Firms Exist?"

81. Geoffrey Smart, "Management Assessment Methods in Venture Capital: An Empirical Analysis of Human Capital Valuation," *Venture Capital: An International Journal of Entrepreneurial Finance* 1, no. 1 (1999): 59–82.

82. Ibid.

83. Popular press reports during the Internet boom investment period in 1999 and 2000 suggest that some VCs were cutting due diligence to the bare minimum (matter of days) in order to close deals before competing VCs (Kaplan, 1998). James Fiet, "Reliance

upon Informants in the Venture Capital Industry," *Journal of Business Venturing* 10, no. 3 (1995): 195–223.

84. Michael Harvey and Robert Lusch, "Expanding the Nature and Scope of Due Diligence," *Journal of Business Venturing* 10, no. 1 (1995): 5–22.

85. Raaj Sah and Joseph Stiglitz, "The Architecture of Economic Systems: Hierarchies and Polyarchies," *American Economic Review* 76, no. 4 (1986): 716–727.

86. Harvey and Lusch, "Expanding the Nature and Scope of Due Diligence."

87. Edgar Norton and Bernard Tenenbaum, "The Effects of Venture Capitalists' Characteristics on the Structure of the Venture Capital Deal," *Journal of Small Business Management* 31, no. 4 (1993): 23–41.

88. Smart, "Management Assessment Methods in Venture Capital."

89. Ibid.

90. Fiet, "Reliance upon Informants in the Venture Capital Industry."

91. Ibid.

92. James Brander, Raphael Amit, and Werner Antweiler, "Venture Capital Syndication: Improved Venture Selection versus the Value-Added Hypothesis," *Journal of Economics and Management Strategy* 11, no. 3 (2002): 423–452.

93. William Bygrave, "Syndicated Investments by Venture Capital Firms: A Networking Perspective," *Journal of Business Venturing* 2, no. 2 (1987): 139–154.

94. Joshua Lerner, "The Syndication of Venture Capital Investments," *Financial Management* 23, no. 3 (1994): 16–27.

95. Olav Sorensen and Toby Stuart, "Syndication Networks and Spatial Distribution of Venture Capital Investments," *American Journal of Sociology* 106, no. 6 (2001): 1546–1588.

96. Richard Florida and Donald Smith, "Venture Capital, Innovation and Economic Development," *Economic Development Quarterly* 4, no. 4 (1990): 345–360.

97. Brander, Amit, and Antweiler, "Venture Capital Syndication."

98. Bygrave, "Syndicated Investments by Venture Capital Firms."

99. Avanidhar Subrahmanyam and Sheridan Titman, "The Going-Public Decision and the Development of Financial Markets," *Journal of Finance* 54, no. 3 (1999): 1045–1082.

100. Sah and Stiglitz, "The Architecture of Economic Systems."

101. Lerner, "The Syndication of Venture Capital Investments."

102. Sorensen and Stuart, "Syndication Networks and Spatial Distribution of Venture Capital Investments."

103. Bradford Cornell and Alan Shapiro, "Financing Corporate Growth," *Journal of Applied Corporate Finance* 1 (Summer 1988): 6–22.

104. Douglas Cumming and Jeffrey MacIntosh, "Venture Capital Investment Duration in Canada and the United States," *Journal of Multinational Financial Management* 11, no. 4–5 (2001): 445–463.

105. Lowell Busentitz, James Fiet, and Douglas Moesel, "Signaling in Venture Capitalists—New Venture Team Funding Decisions: Does It Indicate Long-Term Venture Outcomes," *Entrepreneurship Theory and Practice* 29, no. 1 (2005): 1–12.

106. Steven Kaplan and Per Stromberg, "Characteristics, Contracts, and Actions: Evidence from Venture Capitalist Analyses," *Journal of Finance* 59, no. 5 (2004): 2173–2206.

107. Busentitz, Fiet, and Moesel, "Signaling in Venture Capitalists."

108. Smart, "Management Assessment Methods in Venture Capital."

109. Kaplan and Stromberg, "Characteristics, Contracts, and Actions."

110. Lowell Busenitz and Jay Barney, "Differences between Entrepreneurs and Managers in Large Organizations: Biases and Heuristics in Strategic Decision-Making," *Journal of Business Venturing* 12, no. 1 (1997): 9–30.

111. Sahlman, "The Structure and Governance of Venture Capital Organizations."

112. Wright and Robbie, "Venture Capital and Private Equity."

113. A DCF valuation computes the risk and time-adjusted value of a company's future cash flows. Tuukka Seppä and Tomi Laamanen, "Valuation of Venture Capital Investments: Empirical Evidence," *R&D Management* 31, no. 2 (2001): 215–230.

114. Cornell and Shapiro, "Financing Corporate Growth."

115. Steven Kaplan and Richard Ruback, "The Market Pricing of Cash Flow Forecasts: Discounted Cash Flow vs. the Method of 'Comparables,'" *Journal of Applied Corporate Finance* 8, no. 4 (1996): 45–60.

116. Robert Keeley and Sanjeev Punjabi, "Valuation of Early-Stage Ventures: Option Valuation Models vs. Traditional Approaches," *Journal of Entrepreneurial and Small Business Finance* 5, no. 2 (1996): 114–138.

117. Sophie Manigart, Koen De Waele, Mike Wright, Ken Robbie, Philippe Desbrières, Harry Sapienza, and Amy Beekman, "Venture Capitalists, Investment Appraisal and Accounting Information: A Comparative Study of the US, UK, France, Belgium and Holland," *European Financial Management* 6, no. 3 (2000): 389–403.

118. Wright and Robbie, "Venture Capital and Private Equity."

119. Avinash Dixit and Robert Pindyck, "The Options Approach to Capital Investment," *Harvard Business Review* 73 no. 3 (1995): 105–119.

120. Wright and Robbie, "Venture Capital and Private Equity."

121. Ibid.

122. Ibid.

123. Rita McGrath, Walter Ferrier, and Aubrey Mendelow, "Real Options as Engines of Choice and Heterogeneity," *Academy of Management Review* 29, no. 1 (2004): 86–101.

124. Dixit and Pindyck, "The Options Approach to Capital Investment."

125. Diane Lander and George Pinches, "Challenges to the Practical Implementation of Modelling and Valuing Real Options," *Quarterly Review of Economics and Finance* 38, Special Issue (1998): 537–567.

126. Wright and Robbie, "Venture Capital and Private Equity."

127. Steven Kaplan and Per Stromberg, "Venture Capitalists as Principals: Contracting, Screening and Monitoring," *American Economic Review* 91, no. 2 (2001): 426–430.

128. Andrei Kirilenko, "Valuation and Control in Venture Finance," *Journal of Finance* 56, no. 2 (2001): 565–587.

129. Francesca Cornelli and Oved Yosha, "Stage Financing and the Role of Convertible Securities," *Review of Economic Studies* 70, no. 1 (2003): 1–32.

130. Edgar Norton and Bernard Tenenbaum, "Factors Affecting the Structure of U.S. Venture Capital Deals," *Journal of Small Business Management* 30, no. 3 (1992): 20–29.

131. Norton and Tenenbaum, "The Effects of Venture Capitalists' Characteristics on the Structure of the Venture Capital Deal."

132. Jeffrey Trester, "Venture Capital Contracting under Asymmetric Information," *Journal of Banking and Finance* 22, no. 6–8 (1998): 675–699.

133. Cornelli and Yosha, "Stage Financing and the Role of Convertible Securities."

134. Paul Gompers and Joshua Lerner, *The Venture Capital Cycle* (Cambridge, MA: MIT Press, 2000).

135. Cumming, "Agency Costs, Institutions, Learning, and Taxation in Venture Capital Contracting."

136. Ronald Gilson and David Schizer, "Understanding Venture Capital Structure: A Tax Explanation for Convertible Preferred Stock," *Harvard Law Review* 116, no. 3 (2003): 874–916.

137. Cumming, "Agency Costs, Institutions, Learning, and Taxation in Venture Capital Contracting."

138. Gilson and Schizer, "Understanding Venture Capital Structure."

139. Jay Barney, Lowell Busenitz, James Fiet, and Douglas Moesel, "The Structure of Venture Capital Governance: An Organizational Economic Analysis of the Relations between Venture Capital Firms and New Ventures," *Academy of Management Proceedings: Best Papers* (1989): 64–68.

140. Sorensen and Stuart, "Syndication Networks and Spatial Distribution of Venture Capital Investments."

141. Malcolm Baker and Paul Gompers, "The Determinants of Board Structure at the Initial Public Offering," *Journal of Law and Economics* 46, no. 2 (2003): 569–598.

142. Vance Fried, Garry Bruton, and Robert Hisrich, "Strategy and the Board of Directors in Venture Capital-Backed Firms," *Journal of Business Venturing* 13, no. 6 (1998): 493–503.

143. J. Rosenstein, "The Board of Strategy: Venture Capital and High Technology," *Journal of Business Venturing* 3, no. 2 (1988): 159–170.

144. Christopher Barry, Chris Muscarella, John Peavy III, and Michael Vetsuypens, "The Role of Venture Capital in the Creation of Public Companies: Evidence from the Going-Public Process," *Journal of Financial Economics* 27, no. 2 (1990): 447–471.

145. Jay Barney, Lowell Busenitz, and Douglas Moesel, "The Relationship between Venture Capitalists and Managers in New Firms: Determinants of Contractual Covenants," *Managerial Finance* 20, no. 1 (1994): 19–30.

146. Steven Kaplan and Per Stromberg, "Financial Contracting Theory Meets the Real World," *Review of Economic Studies* 70, no. 2 (2003): 281–315.

147. Dean Shepherd and Andrew Zacharakis, "The Venture Capitalist–Entrepreneur Relationship: Control, Trust and Confidence in Co-operative Behavior," *Venture Capital: An International Journal of Entrepreneurial Finance* 3, no. 2 (2001): 129–149.

148. Ibid.

149. Fiet, "Reliance upon Informants in the Venture Capital Industry."

150. Sahlman, "The Structure and Governance of Venture Capital Organizations."

151. Jay Barney, Lowell Busenitz, James Fiet, and Douglas Moesel, "New Venture Teams' Assessment of Learning Assistance from Venture Capital Firms," *Journal of Business Venturing* 11, no. 4 (1996): 257–272.

152. Sapienza and Korsgaard, "Procedural Justice in Entrepreneur–Investor Relations."

153. Shepherd and Zacharakis, "The Venture Capitalist–Entrepreneur Relationship."

154. Joel Baum and Brian Silverman, "Picking Winners or Building Them: Alliance, Intellectual, and Human Capital as Selection Criteria in Venture Financing and Performance of Biotechnology Start-ups," *Journal of Business Venturing* 19, no. 3 (2004): 411–436.

155. Norton and Tenenbaum, "The Effects of Venture Capitalists' Characteristics on the Structure of the Venture Capital Deal."

156. Robert Ruhnka and John Young, "Some Hypotheses about Risk in Venture Capital Investing," *Journal of Business Venturing* 6, no. 2 (1991): 115–133.

157. Baum and Silverman, "Picking Winners or Building Them."

158. Nancy Huyghebaert and Linda Van de Gucht, "Incumbent Strategic Behavior in Financial Markets and the Exit of Entrepreneurial Start-ups," *Strategic Management Journal* 25, no. 7 (2004): 669–688.

159. Lowell Busentiz and James Fiet, "The Effects of Early Stage Venture Capital Actions on Venture Disposition," *Journal of Entrepreneurial and Small Business Finance* 5, no. 2 (1996): 97–115.

160. Kathleen Eisenhardt and Claudia Bird Schoonhoven, "Organizational Growth: Linking Founding Team, Strategy, Environment, and Growth among U.S. Semiconductor Ventures," *Administrative Science Quarterly* 35, no. 3 (1990): 504–529.

161. Baum and Silverman, "Picking Winners or Building Them."

162. John Ruhnka, Howard Feldman, and Thomas Dean, "The Living Dead Phenomenon in Venture Capital Investments," *Journal of Business Venturing* 7, no. 2 (1992): 137–155.

163. Michael Gorman and William Sahlman, "What Do Venture Capitalists Do?" *Journal of Business Venturing* 4, no. 4 (1989): 231–248.

164. Brander, Amit, and Antweiler, "Venture Capital Syndication."

165. Barry, "New Directions in Research on Venture Capital Finance."

166. Ian MacMillan, David Kulow, and Roubina Khoylian, "Venture Capitalists' Involvement in Their Investments: Extent and Performance," *Journal of Business Venturing* 4, no. 1 (1989): 27–47.

167. Sahlman, "The Structure and Governance of Venture Capital Organizations."

168. Gorman and Sahlman, "What Do Venture Capitalists Do?"

169. Thomas Hellmann and Manju Puri, "Venture Capital and the Professionalisation of Start-Up Firms: Empirical Evidence," *Journal of Finance* 57, no. 1 (2002): 169–197.

170. Antonio Davila, George Foster, and Mahendra Gupta, "Venture Capital Financing and the Growth of Startup Firms," *Journal of Business Venturing* 18, no. 6 (2003): 689–708.

171. Gorman and Sahlman, "What Do Venture Capitalists Do?"

172. Ibid.

173. B. Elango, Vance Fried, Robert Hisrich, and Amy Polonchek, "How Venture Capital Firms Differ," *Journal of Business Venturing* 10, no. 2 (1995): 157–179.

174. MacMillan, Kulow, and Khoylian, "Venture Capitalists' Involvement in Their Investments."

175. Ibid.

176. Sapienza and Gupta, "Impact of Agency Risks and Task Uncertainty on Venture Capitalists-CEO Interaction."

177. Ibid.

178. Harry Sapienza, Sophie Manigart, and W. Vermeir, "A Comparison of Venture Capital Governance and Value-Added in the U.S. and Western Europe," *Academy of Management Journal* 38, no. 1 (1995): 105–109.

179. Daniel Cable and Scott Shane, "A Prisoner's Dilemma Approach to Entrepreneur–Venture Capitalist Relationships," *Academy of Management Review* 22, no. 1 (1997): 142–176.

180. Gorman and Sahlman, "What Do Venture Capitalists Do?"

181. Sahlman, "The Structure and Governance of Venture Capital Organizations."

182. Sapienza and Gupta, "Impact of Agency Risks and Task Uncertainty on Venture Capitalists-CEO Interaction."

183. Ibid.

184. Cable and Shane, "A Prisoner's Dilemma Approach to Entrepreneur–Venture Capitalist Relationships."

185. Gompers, "Optimal Investment, Monitoring, and the Staging of Venture Capital."

186. James Fiet, Lowell Busenitz, Douglas Moesel, and Jay Barney, "Theoretical Perspectives on the Dismissal of New Venture Team Members," *Journal of Business Venturing* 12, no. 5 (1997): 347–366.

187. James Fredrickson, Donald Hambrick, and Sara Baumrin, "A Model of CEO Dismissal," *Academy of Management Review* 13, no. 2 (1988): 255–270.

188. R. Sweeting and Chi-Fong Wong, "A UK 'Hands-Off' Venture Capital Firm and the Handling of Post-Investment Investor–Investee Relationships," *Journal of Management Studies* 34, no. 1 (1997): 125–152.

189. Gaylen Chandler and Erik Jansen, "The Founder's Self-Assessed Competence and Venture Performance," *Journal of Business Venturing* 7, no. 3 (1992): 223–236.

190. Arnold Cooper, F. Javier Gimeno-Gascon, and Carolyn Woo, "Initial Human and Financial Capital as Predictors of New Venture Performance," *Journal of Business Venturing* 9, no. 5 (1994): 371–395.

191. Jeffrey McGee, Michael Dowling, and William Megginson, "Cooperative Strategy and New Venture Performance: The Role of Business Strategy and Management Experience," *Strategic Management Journal* 16, no. 7 (1995): 565–580.

192. Cable and Shane, "A Prisoner's Dilemma Approach to Entrepreneur–Venture Capitalist Relationships."

193. Gorman and Sahlman, "What Do Venture Capitalists Do?"

194. Sahlman, "The Structure and Governance of Venture Capital Organizations."

195. Sapienza and Gupta, "Impact of Agency Risks and Task Uncertainty on Venture Capitalists-CEO Interaction."

196. Garry Bruton, Vance Fried, and Robert Hisrich, "CEO Dismissal in Venture Capital-Backed Firms: Evidence from an Agency Perspective," *Entrepreneurship Theory and Practice* 24, no. 4 (2000): 69–77.

197. Ibid.

198. Bernard Black and Ronald Gilson, "Venture Capital and the Structure of Capital Markets: Banks versus Stock Markets," *Journal of Financial Economics* 47, no. 3 (1998): 243–277.

199. Douglas Cumming and Jeffrey MacIntosh, "A Cross-Country Comparison of Full and Partial Exits," *Journal of Banking and Finance* 27, no. 3 (2003): 511–548.

200. Timothy Lin, "The Certification Role of Large Block Shareholders in Initial Public Offerings: The Case of Venture Capitalists," *Quarterly Journal of Business and Economics* 35, no. 2 (1996): 55–65.

201. Timothy Lin and Richard Smith, "Insider Reputation and Selling Decisions: The Unwinding of Venture Capital Investments During Equity IPOs," *Journal of Corporate Finance* 4, no. 3 (1998): 241–263.

202. J. William Petty, William Bygrave, and Joel Shulman, "Harvesting the Entrepreneurial Venture: A Time for Creating Value," *Journal of Applied Corporate Finance* 7, no. 1 (1992): 48–58.

203. Philippe Aghion, Peter Bolton, and Jean Tirole, "Exit Options in Corporate Finance: Liquidity versus Incentives" *Review of Finance* 8, no. 3 (2004): 327–353.

204. Anil Gupta and Harry Sapienza, "Determinants of Venture Capital Firms' Preferences Regarding the Industry Diversity and Geographic Scope of Their Investments," *Journal of Business Venturing* 7, no. 5 (1992): 347–362.

205. Paul Gompers and Joshua Lerner, "An Analysis of Compensation in the U.S. Venture Capital Partnership," *Journal of Financial Economics* 51, no. 1 (1999): 3–44.

206. Ruhnka, Feldman, and Dean, "The Living Dead Phenomenon in Venture Capital Investments."

207. Clement Wang and Valerie Sim, "Exit Strategies of Venture-Backed Companies in Singapore," *Venture Capital* 3, no. 4 (2001): 337–358.

208. Cumming and MacIntosh, "A Cross-Country Comparison of Full and Partial Exits."

209. Akerlof, "The Market for Lemons."

210. Barry, "New Directions in Research on Venture Capital Finance."

211. Gompers, "Optimal Investment, Monitoring, and the Staging of Venture Capital."

212. Sapienza and Korsgaard, "Procedural Justice in Entrepreneur–Investor Relations."

213. Cumming and MacIntosh, "A Cross-Country Comparison of Full and Partial Exits."

214. Michael Habib and Alexander Ljungqvist, "Underpricing and Entrepreneurial Wealth Losses in IPOs: Theory and Evidence," *Review of Financial Studies* 14, no. 2 (2001): 433–458.

215. Richard Carter, Frederick Dark, and Ajai Singh, "Underwriter Reputation, Initial Returns, and the Long-Run Performance of IPO Stocks," *Journal of Finance* 53, no. 1 (1998): 285–311.

216. Habib and Ljungqvist, "Underpricing and Entrepreneurial Wealth Losses in IPOs."

217. Black and Gilson, "Venture Capital and the Structure of Capital Markets."

218. Joshua Lerner, "Venture Capitalists and the Decision to Go Public," *Journal of Financial Economics* 35, no. 3 (1994): 293–316.

219. Dean Shepherd and Andrew Zacharakis, "Speed to Initial Public Offering of VC-Backed Companies" *Entrepreneurship Theory and Practice* 25, no. 3 (2001): 59–69.

220. Wang and Sim, "Exit Strategies of Venture-Backed Companies in Singapore."

221. Gompers and Lerner, *The Venture Capital Cycle.*

222. Robert Ibbotson and Jeffrey Jaffee, " 'Hot Issue' Markets," *Journal of Finance* 30, no. 4 (1975): 1027–1042.

223. Alexander Ljungqvist and William Wilhelm, "IPO Pricing in the Dot-com Bubble," *Journal of Finance* 58, no. 2 (2003): 723–752.

224. Eli Ofek and Matthew Richardson, "DotCom Mania: The Rise and Fall of Internet Stock Prices," *Journal of Finance* 58, no. 3 (2003): 1113–1137.

225. Jay Ritter, "The 'Hot Issue' Markets of 1980," *Journal of Business* 57, no. 2 (1984): 215–240.

226. Ibbotson and Jaffee, "'Hot Issue' Markets."

227. Ofek and Richardson, "DotCom Mania."

228. Lerner, "The Syndication of Venture Capital Investments."

229. Shepherd and Zacharakis, "Speed to Initial Public Offering of VC-Backed Companies."

230. Wang and Sim, "Exit Strategies of Venture-Backed Companies in Singapore."

231. O. Sacirbey, "Market Forces New Exit Strategies," *IPO Reporter* 24, no. 19 (2000): 3.

232. Bygrave and Timmons, *Venture Capital at the Crossroads.*

233. Sacirbey, "Market Forces New Exit Strategies."

234. Swee Sum Lam, "Venture Capital Financing: A Conceptual Framework," *Journal of Business Finance and Accounting* 18, no. 2 (1991): 137–149.

235. Busentitz and Fiet, "The Effects of Early Stage Venture Capital Actions on Venture Disposition."

236. John Cochrane, "The Risk and Return of Venture Capital," Working Paper (2001).

237. Blaine Huntsman and James Hoben, "Investment in New Enterprise: Some Empirical Observations on Risk, Return, and Market Structure," *Financial Management* 9, no. 2 (1980): 44–51.

7

Small-Firm Growth Strategies

Johan Wiklund

This chapter focuses on how the strategic choices of small firms influence their growth. The relationship between strategy and growth is of particular importance because strategic choices have direct consequences on whether and by how much a firm expands. By focusing on small firms' strategic choices, this chapter differentiates itself from the bulk of previous studies on small-firm growth.

A number of studies have related the different characteristics of small firms to their growth.[1, 2] Examples include studying psychological characteristics or human capital aspects of the small business founder, such as personality traits, experience in the industry, or education level, and assessing how these relate to firm growth.[3–5] However, such variables only have an indirect effect on growth; they must in some way be converted into action in order to influence the firm's development.[6] Generally, the mechanisms involved in these characteristics getting converted into growth are not explicated. Instead, the researcher assumes, for example, that experienced business owners have developed specific knowledge which they can use in the firm, or that a business owner with high need for achievement works harder and is more goal orientated, and thus this is why their firm grows. However, individuals with similar characteristics in terms of psychological profile and/or human capital choose to operate businesses that vary considerably in terms of the strategies chosen. Therefore, it is not reasonable to assume that empirical studies shall find especially strong relationships between these types of indirect variables and growth. A review of the literature also shows that this is the case—the relationship between these indirect variables and growth is generally weak.[7]

An alternative to studying such general and indirect variables is to instead open up the "black box" and examine what the firm actually does and how this directly influences growth. A suitable way to do this is by relating a firm's strategy to its growth. Porter holds that a firm is made up of a collection of activities.[8] A firm's strategy then decides how these activities form and how they fit together. In other words, a firm's strategy directs what it does. This is the reason the relationship between strategy and growth is the main focus of this chapter.

There is another advantage to studying how a firm's strategy influences its growth. A firm's strategy can change through conscious choice. This is, therefore, of significant interest to business owners and consultants, who take an active interest in the growth and performance of these businesses. Although it may be interesting to know how the personality of a business owner or the industry that the firm competes in influences the firm's growth, such aspects can only be influenced by small business owners to a much smaller extent.

Therefore, the logic of this chapter builds on the basic premises of human action theory.[9] It suggests that while the characteristics of the small business or its manager may affect growth, such characteristics only have an indirect effect. They must be transformed into some type of action and activity in order to affect growth. Strategy is a variable that captures actions and activities. Merely having the goal of expanding the business does not create growth unless appropriate actions are taken. A model is developed and tested, suggesting that, in line with previous research findings, general aspects of the firm indeed affect growth, but that these effects are mediated by the strategy pursued by the small business. This model is tested empirically on a Swedish dataset and the implications of the findings are discussed.

The chapter proceeds as follows. In the next section small firms' strategic options are discussed. With support from previous research it is argued that an entrepreneurial strategic orientation is particularly important to small firm growth. The Research Methods section is then presented. The subsequent section is devoted to the empirical results. The two final sections then discuss the implications of the present study for small business owners and those interested in supporting small business in their growth strategies (i.e., policymakers and consultants). First, I talk about what small businesses can do to influence their growth. Ideas are presented in relation to how small firms can change their strategy to achieve higher levels of growth. Finally, measures to stimulate growth in different types of firms are discussed.

THE IMPORTANCE OF AN ENTREPRENEURIAL STRATEGIC ORIENTATION

Given that strategy is the central concept of this chapter, it is important to identify the strategic dimensions that are reflected in organizational customs, processes, and methods, and decide which of them can be implemented in a small firm and hence can influence a small firm's growth.

Mintzberg developed a typology consisting of five distinctively different types of firms: the *bureaucracy*, the *simple* type, the *adhocracy*, the *professional bureaucracy*, and the *diversified* type.[10] Others have suggested different typologies much along the same lines, the major difference being the labeling of the different types of firms identified. Small firms are most likely to be found among the adhocracy or simple categories.

Adhocracies are characterized as being flexible, having flexible organizational structures, and a strategy responsive to competitors, customers, and market opportunities. A key strategic element for these types of firms is innovation.[11]

Simple firms, on the other hand, are dominated by the chief executive, having a simple, informal structure and decision-making style, their competitiveness largely stemming from their flexibility in relation to customer preferences. In particular, the risk taking dimension of strategy is very important for simple firms. Some simple firms show extreme entrepreneurial risk taking, whereas others are extremely conservative and risk-averse.[11]

Mintzberg's classification, which identifies two types of small firms, appears relevant, and these two types of firms are similar to descriptions in the small business research literature. It also highlights several important characteristics of small firms. Strategic themes that can be extracted from the earlier description of these firms are responsiveness to customers, taking advantage of opportunity, innovativeness, and risk taking. Indeed, this leads the thoughts to entrepreneurship and the importance of an entrepreneurial strategy. Therefore, it seems appropriate to focus on the entrepreneurial dimensions of strategy when conducting research on small firms. Furthermore, it may be more difficult to differentiate small firms according to other strategic dimensions since resource constraints may well prevent small firms from pursuing cost leadership or differentiation strategies.[12]

Firms with an entrepreneurial strategic orientation innovate boldly and regularly while taking considerable risks in their product-market strategies.[13] Miller proposes that a firm's actions relating to innovation, risk taking, and proactiveness represent the primary dimensions of an entrepreneurial strategic orientation: "An entrepreneurial firm is one that engages in product-market innovation, undertakes somewhat risky ventures, and is first to come up with 'proactive' innovations, beating competitors to the punch."[14] These firms monitor market changes and respond quickly, thus capitalizing on emerging opportunities. Several researchers have agreed that an entrepreneurial strategic orientation is a combination of three dimensions: innovativeness, proactiveness, and risk taking.[14–21] The innovativeness dimension of an entrepreneurial strategic orientation reflects a tendency to support new ideas, novelty, experimentation, and creative processes, thereby departing from established practices and technologies.[22] Proactiveness refers to a posture of anticipating and acting on future wants and needs in the marketplace, thereby creating a first-mover advantage vis-à-vis competitors. With such a forward-looking perspective, proactive firms have the desire to be pioneers, thereby capitalizing on emerging opportunities. Risk taking is associated with a willingness to commit large amounts of resources to projects where the cost of failure may be high.[23] It also implies committing resources to projects where the outcomes are unknown. It largely reflects the organization's willingness to break away from the tried-and-true, and venture into the unknown. This suggests that organizations that have an entrepreneurial strategic orientation are more prone to focus attention and effort toward opportunities.

There is reason to believe that an entrepreneurial strategic orientation has positive implications for the growth of small firms. A general tendency in today's business environment is the shortening of product and business model life-cycles.[24] Consequently, the future profit streams from existing operations are uncertain and businesses need to constantly seek out new opportunities. An entrepreneurial strategic orientation can assist companies in such a process. Innovative companies, creating and introducing new products and technologies, can generate extraordinary economic performance and have even been described as the engines of economic growth.[25, 26] A firm with an entrepreneurial strategic orientation identifies market changes and responds quickly to these changes to take advantage of these emerging opportunities. Proactive companies can create first-mover advantages, target premium market segments, charge high prices, and skim the market ahead of competitors.[21] They can control the market by dominating distribution channels and establish brand recognition. The link between risk taking and performance is less obvious. However, there is research to suggest that while the tried-and-true strategies may lead to high mean performance, risky strategies leading to performance variation may be more profitable in the long run.[27, 28] Previous empirical results provide support for a positive relationship between an entrepreneurial strategic orientation and performance.[19, 21, 23, 29, 30]

> Those in strategic management are concerned with the performance implications of management processes, decisions, and actions at the level of the firm. Prior theory and research have suggested that an E[ntrepreneurial] O[rientation] is a key ingredient for organizational success. (p. 151)[22]

It appears that the relationship between an entrepreneurial strategic orientation and growth is especially strong among smaller firms. Smallness in itself encourages flexibility and innovation, while the limited pool of resources that a small firm has access to, limits its ability to compete using other strategic orientations, such as cost leadership.

This section has established that an entrepreneurial strategic orientation is likely to have a positive impact on the growth of small firms. The introduction of this chapter mentioned the advantages of studying the relationship between strategy and growth, but that there are other variables that are likely to affect growth, mediated through the strategic orientation of the firm, such as the human capital or psychological profile of the small business manager. In order to incorporate such factors, a model is developed that takes into account these factors as well as the strategic orientation of the small firm in explaining growth. Based on a thorough review of the literature on small business growth and performance a model of the relationship between the indirect variables, an entrepreneurial strategic orientation and growth is developed. This model is presented in Figure 7.1. The model illustrates the most significant variables that have been studied in previous research and shows how these variables influence each other. For a more thorough presentation of the logic underlying the model and how it was developed, see Wiklund.[7] According to the logic presented, it can be assumed that many variables influence a firm's entrepreneurial strategic orientation. However, only entrepreneurial strategic orientation influences the firm's performance. This model is the base for the empirical study that is presented in this chapter.

RESEARCH METHODS

Design and Sample

The data for the study were collected in multiple waves. In the first year, a telephone interview was followed up by a mail questionnaire concerning the independent variables. One year after the initial study, a shorter telephone interview follow-up was conducted, which makes the study longitudinal and reduces the risk of reverse causality encountered in cross-sectional studies. The data collected during the second year were concerned with outcomes (i.e., growth since the initial data collection).

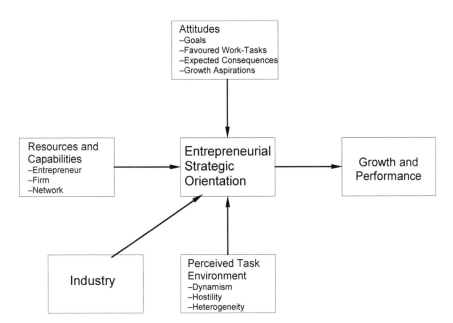

Figure 7.1. Research model predicting an entrepreneurial strategic orientation and growth.

The sample was stratified over the Swedish equivalents of International Standard Industrial Classification (ISIC) codes. Small firms from specific manufacturing, service, and retail industries were selected. The sample was also stratified over the size brackets 10–19 and 20–49 employees. Furthermore, the sample was stratified over the firms' growth rate, so that the share of high-growth firms was overrepresented in the sample for both size brackets and all industries. All data were collected from the managing director. The managing director was explicitly asked for at the beginning of the telephone interviews, and the mail questionnaire was sent directly to the managing director accompanied by a personalized letter.

Out of the 808 firms in the initial sample, 630 were telephone interviewed, which gives a response rate of 78 percent; 465 firms also returned the mail questionnaire (total response rate 58 percent). These 465 firms were approached again for a telephone interview one year later. No less than 447 responded, which equals 96 percent of the remaining firms from the previous year and 55 percent of the original sample. Thirty-four firms, where the managing director had been replaced during the studied year, were excluded from the analyses since it seems perilous to attribute outcomes of a firm to an individual no longer working there.

Variables and Measures

The theoretical constructs in the model presented in Figure 7.1 were measured as follows.

Small Business Growth

Four measures were used to capture small business growth. Growth in terms of sales and employment was calculated as the relative growth between the survey rounds. When assessing performance, comparisons with competing businesses in the market reveal important additional information.[31] Therefore, respondents were asked to rate their sales and employment growth compared to competitors on five-point scales. Each of the variables were standardized and summed to an index. The Cronbach's alpha value of the scale was 0.91.

Entrepreneurial Strategic Orientation

Miller's original scale consisting of eight items was used.[14] These items are of the forced choice type, with pairs of opposite statements. A seven-point scale divides the two statements.

Environment

A total of six dimensions of the task environment are included. The scales for measuring environmental dynamism, heterogeneity, and hostility were taken from Miller and Friesen.[13] Changes over the past three years along these three environmental dimensions have their origin in Miller.[32] All items were measured on seven-point opposite statement scales. Association with one of four broad-industry categories was taken from the data register. Specific questions were also asked about other industry characteristics (i.e., customer concentration, supplier concentration, and exports). The theoretical construct of industry is formed by these indicators.

Resources and Capabilities

Resources of the firm consist of size in terms of employees, sales, management team size, number of employees having university degrees, board size, and investment by external owner. To capture a relative measure of size and financial slack, I asked respondents to compare the firm's size and capital availability to that of its competitors. Miller's items were used to operationalize the perceived use of employees and the board in the decision-making process.[32] The human capital of the manager was operationalized by various measures of experience and knowledge. Indicators included the type and length of education and training, experience with managing different types of firms (i.e., management, same industry, rapid-growth firm, and maximum number of subordinates), and tenure in present position. We also collected information on age, ethnicity, and gender as well as whether the respondent started, inherited, bought, or is employed by the firm. These measures used to operationalize human capital are taken from Davidsson.[33] To operationalize social capital I asked respondents how important was a particular contact in providing advice on important decisions from a list of nine types of contacts (Delmar and one original item).[33] These nine items were factor analyzed, resulting in three factors and the corresponding indices were constructed. Respondents also indicated the firm's number of external board members.

Motivation

According to Miner's task motivation theory, the work task of managing a small business is likely to involve taking moderate risks, assuming personal responsibility for performance, paying close attention to feedback in terms of costs and profits, and finding new or innovative ways to make a new product or provide a new service.[34–36] Because motivation consists of several related constructs that affect behavior (see Locke for a review),[37] I relied on a number of concepts associated with the small business manager work tasks. The different motives are viewed as attitude objects and the strengths of the motives are tapped by the respondent's attitude toward the object. We build on the tripartite view, according to which attitudes can be broken down into three different classes of evaluative responses: (1) cognitive responses, also known as beliefs, are thoughts that people have about the attitude object; (2) affective responses consist of feelings, moods, or emotions that people have in relation to the attitude object;

and (3) behavioral responses are the overt actions or intentions exhibited by people in relation to the attitude object.[38] The goals of the respondent are viewed as affective responses since they have to do with their feelings regarding a number of possible goals (eight items original, ten from Davidsson).[33] These eighteen items were factor analyzed, resulting in six factors, and corresponding indices were constructed. Favored work tasks are also seen as affective responses for the same reason (fifteen items from Delmar).[39] These items were factor analyzed, resulting in four factors, and corresponding indices were constructed. Expectations of changes that would occur in the firm as a result of growth refer to the beliefs held by respondents. Thus expected consequences of growth are classified as cognitive responses (two items original, eight from Davidsson).[33] These items were factor analyzed resulting in two factors, and corresponding indices were constructed. The final set of variables concerns growth intentions over the next five years. These variables are viewed as behavioral responses and were calculated based on present size and ideal size five years into the future in terms of employment and sales (two items from Davidsson).[33] This leads to a total of fourteen variables. The theoretical construct of motivation is formed by these fourteen variables, that is, each variable brings some unique information to the construct.[40]

ANALYSIS AND RESULTS

To be able to investigate a model, such as the one present in Figure 7.1, with many latent constructs (i.e., constructs consisting of several manifest indicators) and where a number of variables have an indirect influence on growth, an advanced method of analysis is required. In this study partial least squares (PLS), which was developed by Herman Wold, has been used.[41, 42] The interpretation of the PLS analysis is principally the same as multiple regression analysis. Explained variance is the best estimation of model fit in PLS analysis, and goodness-of-fit indices are largely irrelevant.[43]

There are two steps to the analysis. The first step tests the explanatory ability of the model as specified in Figure 7.1. Step two utilizes the information provided by the first step to revise the model in an attempt to increase its explanatory ability. One feature of PLS analysis is that it computes the correlation between all constructs, which can be used as a cue for adding structural relationships in the model.

An assessment of the correlations among the variables suggests some additional direct linkages, not anticipated in Figure 7.1. More precisely, it appears that aspects of the task environment and motivation have direct effects on growth.

Adding these direct effects, model fits is substantially improved. The total explained variance in growth is consistent with, or greater than, many models of small business growth (see Delmar for a review of explained variance in growth

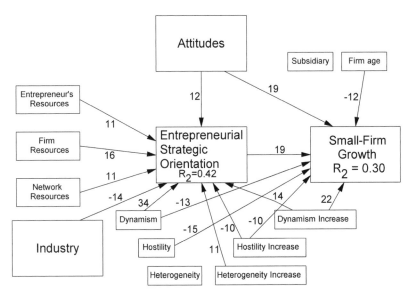

Figure 7.2. Revised research model predicting an entrepreneurial strategic orientation and growth, with path coefficients and explained variance indicated. Path coefficients below 0.10 are suppressed.

models).[44] The graphical representation of the model is displayed in Figure 7.2 and the results in Table 7.1. Due to space limitations, the regression weights and factor loadings for manifest indicators are not reported. The model explains 42 percent of entrepreneurial strategic orientation and 30 percent of growth. On average, 36 percent of the variance in the two endogenous variables is explained.

In sum, the model depicted in Figure 7.2 demonstrates that motivation and components of the task environment (dynamism, hostility, and heterogeneity increase) have a direct effect on small business growth. Components of resources (resources of the individual, network resources, resources of the firm), motivation, industry, and components of the task environment (dynamism increase, hostility increase, heterogeneity increase) have an indirect effect on small business growth through an entrepreneurial strategic orientation. Most path coefficients are larger in relation to an entrepreneurial strategic orientation than to small business growth (exceptions are motivation, increase in environmental dynamism, and environmental hostility). This highlights the importance of understanding the antecedents of an entrepreneurial strategic orientation, offers a solid basis for an exploration of the indirect effect of constructs on small business growth via an entrepreneurial strategic orientation, and, although an entrepreneurial strategic orientation explains an important amount of the variance in small business growth, there is still a need to explore the direct effect of

Table 7.1. Partial Least Square Results for the Revised Model of Small Business Growth

Predictor Construct	Predicted Construct	Path Coefficient
Attitudes	EO	0.12
Industry	EO	−0.14
Dynamism	EO	0.34
Heterogeneity	EO	0.07
Hostility	EO	−0.07
Dynamism increase	EO	0.14
Heterogeneity increase	EO	0.11
Hostility increase	EO	−0.10
Entrepreneur's resources	EO	0.11
Firm resources	EO	0.16
Network resources	EO	0.11
Firm age	Growth	−0.12
Subsidiary	Growth	−0.01
Attitudes	Growth	0.19
Dynamism	Growth	−0.13
Hostility	Growth	−0.15
Dynamism increase	Growth	0.22
Heterogeneity increase	Growth	0.07
Hostility increase	Growth	−0.10
Entrepreneurial orientation	Growth	0.19
Explained variance and model fit		
R^2 EO	.42	
R^2 Growth	.30	
RMS Cov (E, U)	.06	

Note: EO, extent of entrepreneurial strategic orientation. Path coefficients are equal to standardized regression coefficients in multiple linear regression analysis. RMS Cov (E, U) measures model fit. The closer to zero, the better the model fits the data.

other constructs on growth. The results can be summarized according to the following:

- Growing small firms have an entrepreneurial strategic orientation. It is foremost a strategy with a focus on innovation and being proactive.
- These firms are usually found in relatively stable industries that become substantially more dynamic in later years.
- Industry dynamics have the largest positive effect on entrepreneurial strategic orientation and it has a nonnegligible negative effect on growth. An explanation could be that an industry, which changes quickly and is difficult

to predict, places a lot of strategic pressure on the firm. If the firm does not have the capacity to adopt an entrepreneurial strategic orientation, then it cannot grow in a rapidly changing environment. The negative influence that dynamic has on growth in combination with the large positive influence it has on entrepreneurial strategic orientation shows that an increase in industry dynamics has an overall positive effect; however, the industry should not be too dynamic if the firm does not have at the same time an entrepreneurial strategic orientation. In other words, if a firm wants to benefit from the opportunities in a dynamic industry it requires an entrepreneurial strategic orientation.

- Small business owners' attitudes are important for growth. Attitudes that are especially important for growth are: to have a goal for increased sales; a desire to be creative at work; to enjoy working with strategic tasks; and a preference for not being directly involved in production.
- Younger firms grow more than older firms.
- Firms grow foremost through an increase in demand in their market niche and not through taking market share from their competitors. That is, growing small firms prefer to find new market niches than fight for market share in existing markets.

ADVICE FOR INCREASING GROWTH

A consistent finding is that small business managers themselves and the choices they make are crucial to the development of their firms. The possibility to form the destiny of their firms should be encouraging for small business managers. The growth of their firms is not caused by deterministic forces outside the control of the small firm. On the contrary, growth is largely influenced by conscious decisions made by the small business manager. Hence, it is possible for the small business manager to take actions in order for the company to expand. Moreover, in broad terms, motivation seems more important than personal abilities. It seems that "what I want" has a larger influence on actual outcomes than "what I know."

For a small business manager, survival of potential crises is of course of utmost importance. Therefore, it is important to stress that a common misunderstanding is that a firm that grows and becomes larger could have larger difficulties surviving a crisis. Research indicates the opposite.[45] Larger firms have buffers and can survive longer during a sales decrease. Also, it is easier for a larger firm to get rid of resources, such as machinery or employees and survive at a smaller scale. Hence, a small business manager who feels that survival is an important goal may consider growth as a suitable survival strategy. Furthermore, factors contributing to growth also contribute to survival, reinforcing that growth and survival go hand in hand. Renewal of customers and products is, for instance, stressed as central for survival as well as growth.[45] Findings also suggest that financial performance and growth are closely related and further that larger and expanding firms perform better than smaller firms. As a consequence, a small business manager who wishes to enhance financial performance may consider expanding his or her firm.

These are forceful arguments in favor of why small business managers should strive for growth. Then, if growth is the aim, what actions should be taken to achieve this? Based on the findings, it is possible to provide some concrete advice on suitable strategies in order for a small firm to enhance growth and performance. First of all, it is important to be flexible and have a strategic orientation toward opportunities. Products and customers need to be exchanged and renewed, preferably ahead of competitors. To do this, small business managers need to free themselves from the institutional thinking that tends to develop within an industry.[46] Ideas, values, and beliefs of an industry tend to streamline organization and management. Companies conform to the expectations of appropriate organization structure and management to gain legitimacy. In order to enhance growth and performance, small business managers need to be strong enough to resist such pressures for conformity and instead search for innovative alternatives.

The firm's environment, possibly as defined by industry or sector, is not a given, and firms within all sectors can achieve high growth. The crux of the matter lies in positioning the firm favorably in relation to competitors and customers. Of particular importance is to move into environments where demand increases and the rate of technological renewal is high. For firms that utilize strengths, weaknesses, opportunities, threats (SWOT) analysis, it may be profitable to mainly focus on the opportunity dimension, matching them with internal capabilities, and more actively search for new opportunities.

The significance of the general development of the firm's market niche and the importance of detecting new business opportunities indicate the importance of external information. Being updated regarding business opportunities does not involve knowledge of all possible sources of information. Instead, the interpretation of available information may be more important. It is a matter of being in a state of mind where information is interpreted from the viewpoint of whether it offers an opportunity or not. The daily newspaper may be a sufficient source of business opportunities for many small firms, provided that it is being read the right way. The important factor is to match these opportunities with the firm's core competencies in order to determine whether it is a suitable opportunity or not. If this is the case, the opportunity should be pursued.

A small, rapidly growing, and profitable small firm that I recently visited may serve as an example of how this could be carried out. This small firm operates in the chemical industry. The entrepreneur realized that the food industry faced an increased demand for a relatively new type of synthetic nonalcoholic beverages. He also realized that their core competencies of mixing chemicals, filling and labeling bottles, and distributing these products to supermarkets were equally well suited for this new opportunity as for their existing products. By starting to produce these new synthetic nonalcoholic beverages, the firm was able to pursue a new business opportunity based on its existing competencies. This can serve as a

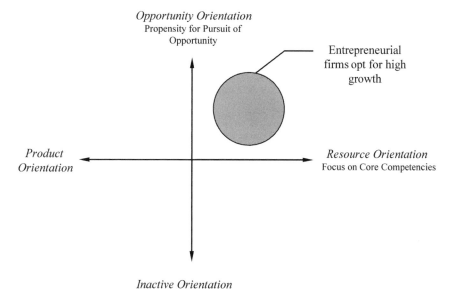

Figure 7.3. Characteristics of a small entrepreneurial growth firm in terms of the firm's opportunity and resource orientation.

general illustration of some of the key strategic issues determining the success of a small firm. Figure 7.3 is an illustration of how small firms can exploit opportunities based on their core competencies. The figure shows the ideal position for a small entrepreneurial firm that is striving for growth.

Many small business managers have a concern for the qualities associated with small scale, and this concern is justifiable. There is research to suggest that on issues like comradeship, involvement, and job satisfaction, employees and people in general think highly of small firms.[47] Even more impressive evidence for the advantages of small scale is presented in the classic study by Barker and Gump.[48] Therefore, the small-firm owner-manager may have a very real reason to be concerned about the atmosphere of the small firm when faced with expansion opportunities. This concern may be a source of an eternal goal conflict for many small business owner-managers. Thus, it is essential that small business managers are able to organize the expanding firm in such a way that these small-scale qualities are not lost on the way.

A CLASSIFICATION OF SMALL FIRMS AND IMPLICATIONS FOR SMALL BUSINESS MANAGERS

Of course, not all firms are alike. It is, however, possible to identify different types of firms and discuss suitable measures for each group. First and foremost, it

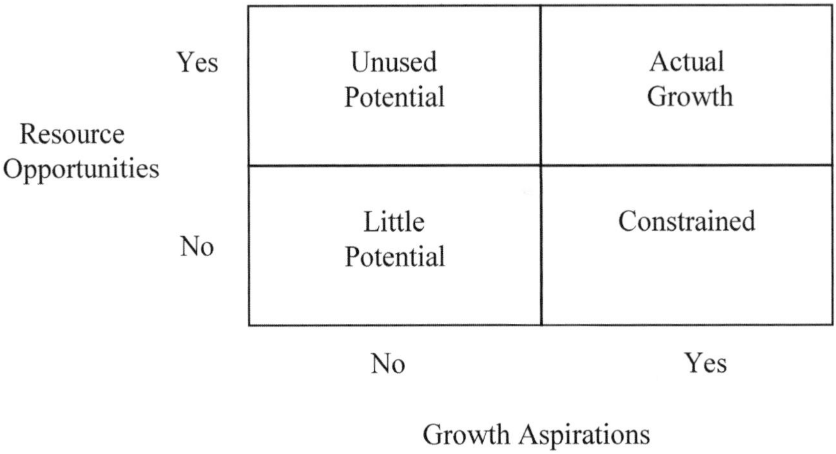

		No	Yes
Resource Opportunities	Yes	Unused Potential	Actual Growth
	No	Little Potential	Constrained

Growth Aspirations

Figure 7.4.   Four types of firms in terms of resources and opportunities for growth and growth aspirations.

is important to emphasize that development and growth is, for a large part, dependent on conscious decisions made by the firm leader. An important conclusion is that soft factors, such as the firm's strategic direction and attitude can be more important than hard facts, such as industry or access to capital. Growing firms can be found in all places and in all industries.

In a relative sense, a small business owner's education and experience are of limited importance for growth. The business owner's motivation appears to be more important. The typical growing firm leader could be seen as a combination of a strategist and an inventor. It should also be noted that access to capital does not significantly affect the firm's development. The growing and developing entrepreneurial firm seems to have the ability to find the necessary capital for its development. The important conclusion to take from this is that increased access to capital as a single measure is unlikely to have a significant influence on a firm's development. Nor can it be assumed that a massive emphasis on education can create a large number of new entrepreneurs or growing firms.

Based on the information in this chapter, a categorization is made of small business growth outcomes based on the small business managers' motivation to grow their businesses and the ability to do so. Specifically, Figure 7.4 categorizes small business growth along two dimensions—resources and opportunities for growth provide one dimension and growth aspirations the other. Depending on their position along these two dimensions, four types of small businesses are identified:

1. Starting with the small businesses in the upper right quadrant, which possesses both the necessary opportunities and resources, and the aspiration to grow, I propose that these small businesses are the ones most likely

to exhibit actual growth. To these small businesses, I say good luck. They are pursuing a desired outcome that is within their reach. This is not to say that they will always achieve growth, there are other intervening factors that could lead to less growth than expected or even bankruptcy, but these firms are in the best position to succeed.

2. In the upper left quadrant are the small businesses that have an unused potential since they, if they were motivated, have the ability, resources, and opportunity to expand. A relatively large proportion of all small businesses are probably in this situation. For example, one small business manager commented, "I enjoy doing what I'm doing. The minute I stop enjoying it I'll do something else. I'm not as well off as I'd like to be but I don't have that goal of having so much money in the bank . . . I think I've reached the stage of life where money's not that important. It's about lifestyle, it's being able to do a whole lot of things. You just need enough money to do what you want to do. . . . So success for me is that the business runs at a profit—it doesn't have to be a huge profit, just a profit—that I make enough out of it to keep myself the way I want to be kept and that I get the satisfaction of client feedback saying 'hey you're doing a good job.' "[49] To these small business managers I say: "If you are happy with the size of the business, then well done and I hope that you continue to enjoy." The only proviso to this congratulatory statement is if there is dispute among the stakeholders of the business in terms of its growth outcomes, then the situation becomes a source of conflict. For example, the small business manager may have a nonactive partner in the business that is looking to grow his investment by increasing the size of the business. In such a situation, the motivations of others may also need to be considered. Although partners often have different objectives for a business, this is less often the case with small businesses where ownership is dominated by one individual or by a family where motivations are often relatively consistent.

3. Small businesses, which strive for growth but lack certain skills, capital, other abilities, resources, and opportunities, I call constrained. These small businesses are situated in the lower right quadrant. Although I have suggested earlier in the chapter that deficiencies in the ability to achieve growth can, to a certain extent, be compensated for by increased motivation (i.e., increase enthusiasm and effort toward achieving the desired goal), the inconsistency between one's aspirations and one's ability is more than likely going to lead to disappointment, and possibly the failure of the business. To these small business managers, I suggest that they move out of this quadrant by changing their classification on either of the dimensions. That is, increase one's ability so that the desired growth outcome becomes more likely. This might occur simply through the passage of time as the manager accumulates more experience, and this experience leads to knowledge and skills that are important in formulating and implementing growth strategies. Although I have focused on the human capital of the small business

manager I suspect that his or her human capital can be complemented by human capital of the small business's other managers. For example, the small business manager's ability might be limited in managing cash flows in a way to effectively fuel growth, but could hire a CFO to undertake these activities. We believe that other members of the management team might be able to increase the ability of the small business to achieve growth, but this should not understate the importance of the human capital of its leader because in the end the leader is the one most responsible for the direction of the firm. The other change that could be made to move a small business out of this quadrant is to adjust the small business manager's motivation in a way that is more consistent with his or her abilities (the next category). For example, rather than being motivated to grow and take the company public, the small business manager with limited abilities might be better off focusing on using the business to generate a good income without the loss of independence that would occur through employment.

4. Small businesses in the fourth category, finally, neither have motivation nor abilities or resources for growth, and thus have little potential for growth. All businesses are not suited for expansion. Due to limited management abilities, these businesses may actually perform better if they remain at a smaller scale. One small business manager commented on his biggest problem with running a small business "Probably for me I struggle with coming up with new ideas. That can be a bit of a problem, and then developing the whole thing to make it pay."[49] This group still has an important role in society for creating employment. To these small business managers, I use an American saying: "Way to go." We believe they are making an important contribution to society by utilizing their resources to the fullest to generate economic wealth for the nation and themselves, gain utility from other aspects of the business not related to money, but not overextending themselves that is likely to lead to financial ruin and emotional heartache.

IMPLICATIONS FOR POLICYMAKERS

The practical implications of this chapter for policymakers are numerous. First, I find that small business managers with greater growth aspirations are more likely to realize growth. The importance of motivation has largely been overlooked in policy programs. So far, there has been an overemphasis on implementing support programs that provide small businesses with resources or aim at increasing the ability for small businesses to grow, including training programs for small business managers and tax cuts. Implicit in most supportive programs is the assumption that if only small businesses had these resources and abilities, they would grow. To date there has been a trend to implement programs for the development of small firms that emphasize increasing the firm's access to resources, such as risk capital, or they strive to increase the firm's ability to expand, through, for example, the education of the firm owner. Built into these types of programs lies the assumption that if only the firm had access to the right resources or knowledge could it develop and grow. Such programs, however, tend to brush aside the important soft qualities, such as motivation. Referring back to Figure 7.4, I am able to develop policy implications for each of the four groups identified in the figure.

1. The small businesses in the upper right quadrant (actual growth) are not in great need of policy programs. They are achieving their desired outcomes and simultaneously create wealth and employment for society. Appropriate policy measures include policies aimed at easing and simplifying government communications and operations, such as reducing bureaucratic red tape, as well as ensuring a flexible labor market such that these businesses are able to recruit the talent needed to maintain their growth trajectory.

2. Small businesses with unused potential, in the upper left quadrant, require different policy measures. The major factor limiting the growth of these small businesses is a lack of growth aspiration. The goals of society (e.g., creation of new jobs) do not necessarily conform to the goals of individual small business managers. In order to align these goals, it might be possible for policymakers to make growth more attractive to small business managers by reducing some of the barriers.

3. Most small business policies are at present designed under the assumption that the majority of small firms belong to the constrained category. Prevalent advice and financial support services are probably most effective in relation to this group, provided they are appropriately designed. In particular, I found that education plays an important role in enabling growth aspirations to be realized. Governments and others wishing to grow an economy need to emphasize the importance of education, which could increase the ability of small business managers to realize their growth aspirations.

4. Small businesses in the fourth category, little potential for growth, still have an important role in society for creating employment and the like. These small businesses are unlikely to benefit greatly from policy changes other than those policies that more broadly improve the macroeconomic environment.

Realizing that the needs of different types of small businesses differ, there are still some policy measures that are generally positive. Considering the influence of dynamic environments on growth, general policies should be aimed at creating more munificent environments. Policy measures can help create more vibrant markets. Keeping in mind that most small firms operate in the private service and retail sector in the domestic market, measures aimed at increasing domestic, consumer demand are likely to be most effective. This could involve measures to increase the purchasing power of consumers, such as the reduction of income or sales tax.

NOTES

1. S. Birley and P. Westhead, "Growth and Performance Contrasts between 'Types' of Small Firms," *Strategic Management Journal* 2 (1990): 535–557.

2. R. Siegel, E. Siegel, and I. C. MacMillan, "Characteristics Distinguishing High-Growth Ventures," *Journal of Business Venturing* 9, no. 2 (1993): 169–180.

3. A. C. Cooper, F. J. Gimeno-Gascon, and C. Y. Woo, "Initial Human and Financial Capital as Predictors of New Venture Performance," *Journal of Business Venturing* 9, no. 5 (1994): 371–395.

4. M. R. Foley, *What Makes a Small Business Successful?* (Sheffield: Sheffield Centre for Environmental Research, 1984).

5. D. J. R. Macrae, "Characteristics of High and Low Growth Small and Medium Sized Businesses," *Management Research News* 15, no. 2 (1992): 11–17.

6. A. C. Cooper, *Challenges in Predicting New Venture Performance*, in *Entrepreneurship: Perspectives on Theory Building*, eds. I. Bull, H. Thomas, and G. Willard (London: Elsevier, 1995), 109–127.

7. J. Wiklund, "Small Firm Growth and Performance: Entrepreneurship and Beyond" (doctoral dissertation, Jönköping International Business School, 1998).

8. M. E. Porter, "Towards a Dynamic Theory of Strategy," *Strategic Management Journal* 12 (1991): 95–117.

9. W. Greve, "Traps and Gaps in Action Explanation: Theoretical Problems of a Psychology of Human Action," *Psychological Review* 108, no. 2 (2001): 435–451.

10. H. Mintzberg, *The Structure of Organizations* (Englewood Cliffs, NJ: Prentice Hall, 1979).

11. D. Miller, "Organizational Configurations: Cohesion, Change, and Prediction," *Human Relations* 43, no. 8 (1990): 771–789.

12. M. E. Porter, *Competitive Advantage* (New York: Free Press, 1985).

13. D. Miller and P. H. Friesen, "Innovation in Conservative and Entrepreneurial Firms: Two Models of Strategic Momentum," *Strategic Management Journal* 3 (1982): 1–25.

14. D. Miller, "The Correlates of Entrepreneurship in Three Types of Firms," *Management Science* 29 (1983): 770–791, 771.

15. J. G. Covin and D. P. Slevin, "Strategic Management of Small Firms in Hostile and Benign Environments," *Strategic Management Journal* 10 (January 1989): 75–87.

16. J. G. Covin and D. P. Slevin, "New Venture Strategic Posture, Structure, and Performance: An Industry Life Cycle Analysis," *Journal of Business Venturing* 5 (1990): 123–135.

17. J. G. Covin and D. P. Slevin, "A Conceptual Model of Entrepreneurship as Firm Behaviour," *Entrepreneurship Theory and Practice* (Fall 1991): 7–25.

18. J. L. Namen and D. P. Slevin, "Entrepreneurship and the Concept of Fit: A Model and Empirical Tests," *Strategic Management Journal* 14 (1993): 137–153.

19. J. Wiklund, "The Sustainability of the Entrepreneurial Orientation—Performance Relationship," *Entrepreneurship Theory and Practice* 24, no. 1 (1999): 37–48.

20. S. Zahra, "A Conceptual Model of Entrepreneurship as Firm Behaviour: A Critique and Extension," *Entrepreneurship Theory and Practice* 16 (Summer 1993): 5–21.

21. S. Zahra and J. Covin, "Contextual Influence on the Corporate Entrepreneurship-Performance Relationship: A Longitudinal Analysis," *Journal of Business Venturing* 10 (1995): 43–58.

22. G. T. Lumpkin and G. G. Dess, "Clarifying the Entrepreneurial Orientation Construct and Linking It to Performance," *Academy of Management Review* 21, no. 1 (1996): 135–172.

23. D. Miller and P. H. Friesen, "Archetypes of Strategy Formulation," *Management Science* 24, no. 9 (1978): 921–933.

24. G. Hamel, *Leading the Revolution* (Cambridge, MA: Harvard University Press), 2000.

25. S. L. Brown and K. M. Eisenhardt, *Competing on the Edge* (Boston, MA: Harvard Business School Press, 1998).

26. J. Schumpeter, *The Theory of Economic Development* (Cambridge, MA: Harvard University Press, 1934).

27. J. G. March, "Exploration and Exploitation in Organizational Learning," *Organization Science* 2 (1991): 71–87.

28. R. G. McGrath, "Exploratory Learning, Innovative Capacity, and Managerial Oversight," *Academy of Management Journal* 44 (2001): 118–131.

29. T. Burns and G. M. Stalker, *The Management of Innovation* (London: Tavistock, 1961).

30. H. Mintzberg, "Strategy-Making in Three Modes," *California Management Review* (Winter, 1973): 44–53.

31. S. Birley and P. Westhead, "A Comparison of New Businesses Established by 'Novice' and 'Habitual' Founders in Great Britain," *International Small Business Journal* 12, no. 1 (1994): 38–60.

32. D. Miller, "The Structural and Environmental Correlates of Business Strategy," *Strategic Management Journal* 8 (1987): 55–76.

33. P. Davidsson, *Continued Entrepreneurship and Small Firm Growth* (Stockholm: Economics Research Department, Stockholm School of Economics, 1989).

34. R. R. Bellu, "Task Role Motivation and Attributional Style as Predictors of Entrepreneurial Performance: Female Sample Findings," *Entrepreneurship and Regional Development* 5 (1993): 331–344.

35. J. B. Miner, "Entrepreneurs, High Growth Entrepreneurs, and Managers: Contrasting and Overlapping Motivational Patterns," *Journal of Business Venturing* 5, no. 4 (1990): 221–234.

36. J. B. Miner, N. R. Smith, and J. S. Bracker, "Role of Entrepreneurial Task Motivation in the Growth of Technologically Innovative Firms: Interpretations from Follow-Up Data," *Journal of Applied Psychology* 79, no. 4 (1994): 627–630.

37. E. A. Locke, "The Motivation Sequence, the Motivation Hub, and the Motivation Core," *Organizational Behavior and Human Decision Processes* 50 (1991): 288–299.

38. A. H. Eagly and S. Chaiken, *The Psychology of Attitudes* (Orlando, FL: Harcourt Brace Jovanovich, 1993).

39. F. Delmar, *Entrepreneurial Behavior and Business Performance* (Stockholm: Economics Research Department, Stockholm School of Economics, 1996).

40. C. Fornell, P. Lorange, and J. Roos, "The Cooperative Venture Formation Process: A Latent Variable Structural Modeling Approach," *Management Science* 36 (1990): 1246–1255.

41. H. Wold, "Model Construction and Evaluation When Theoretical Knowledge Is Scarce," in *Evaluation of Econometric Models*, eds. J. B. Ramsey and J. Kmenta (New York: Academic Press, 1980), 47–74.

42. H. Wold, "Partial Least Squares," in *Encyclopaedia of Statistical Sciences*, eds. S. Kotz and N. L. Johnson (New York: Wiley, 1985), 581–591.

43. J. Hulland, "Use of Partial Least Squares (PLS) in Strategic Management Research: A Review of Four Recent Studies," *Strategic Management Journal* 20 (1999): 195–204.

44. F. Delmar, "Measuring Growth: Methodological Considerations and Empirical Results," in *Entrepreneurship and SME Research: On Its Way to the Next Millenium*, eds. R. Donckels and A. Miettinen (Aldershot, VA: Avebury, 1997), 190–216.

45. D. J. Storey, *Understanding the Small Business Sector* (London: Routledge, 1994).

46. R. Greenwood and C. R. Hinings, "Understanding Radical Organizational Change: Bringing Together the Old and New Institutionalism," *Academy of Management Review* 21, no. 4 (1996): 1022–1054.

47. J. Curran et al., *Employment and Employment Relations in the Small Service Sector Enterprise—a Report* (Kingston: Kingston Business School, ESRC Centre for Research on Small Service Sector Enterprises, 1993).

48. R. G. Barker and P. V. Gump, *Big School, Small School*, 1st ed. (Stanford, CA: Stanford University Press, 1964).

49. R. Cameron, *Small Business Research Report* (Cameron Research Group: www.cameraonresearch.com.au, 2003).

8
Going Global

Pat H. Dickson

The phenomenon of entrepreneurial firms internationalizing their operations is not new; however, the academic study of these activities of entrepreneurial firms is relatively young and vigorous. The academic interest in the internationalization of entrepreneurial firms is driven by reports of the growth and extent of activities of such firms as well as an emerging debate as to whether the existing theories of internationalization apply, given the unique nature of these firms.

Competing internationally, long considered to be the province of large multinational firms, is now widely considered to be open to firms of all sizes. Etemad, Wright, and Dana suggest that advances in technology, manufacturing and logistics have created a world in which even the smallest and youngest of firms can compete.[1] This view of an emerging world market accessible to even the most resource constrained and remote nations and organizations has recently been underscored by Thomas Friedman in *The World Is Flat*, in which he traces the convergence of technology and world events and its role in bringing about significant changes in traditional value chains.[2] The evidence of the involvement of entrepreneurial firms in international trade has been building during the past two decades. Kohn notes that as early as the middle part of the 1980s, smaller firms accounted for more than 50 percent of all U.S. foreign investing firms.[3] Reynolds suggests that this involvement in international trade continued to be strong through the early 1990s with more than 10 percent of all small to medium-sized enterprises (SMEs) involved in direct foreign investment and over 20,000 of the estimated 35,000 transnational firms having less than 500 employees.[4] He further notes that by 2005 an estimated 80 percent of all SMEs would either be affected by or involved in international trade. Shrader, Oviatt, and McDougall support this with their report of estimates that by 2005, one-third of all small manufacturing firms would derive at least 10 percent of their revenues from foreign sources.[5]

The growing internationalization of entrepreneurial firms has been mirrored by growing academic interest. Wright and Ricks, when contemplating the previous twenty-five years of international business research, identified research relating to international entrepreneurship and the internationalization of small business as a key area for future research.[6] In response to this and other calls for an increased focus on internationalization of entrepreneurial firms, there have been special journal issues devoted to the topic by *Entrepreneurship Theory and Practice*, the *Journal of Business Venturing*, *Small Business Economics*, and the *Academy of Management Journal*. A new journal devoted exclusively to this field of study, the *Journal of International Entrepreneurship*, was founded in 2003. Compilations of international entrepreneurship research have also recently been published including *Globalization and Entrepreneurship*, edited by Hamid Etemad and Richard Wright and *Handbook of Research on International Entrepreneurship*, edited by Léo-Paul Dana.[7, 8]

Research devoted specifically to understanding the internationalization of entrepreneurial firms has led to a vigorous debate focused on the unique characteristics of entrepreneurial firms, in particular, their resource constraints and the timing of the entry of such firms into the international marketplace, and whether traditional theories of internationalization, developed almost exclusively in respect to larger firms, are applicable to entrepreneurial firms.[9] In response to this debate, a number of integrated models of the internationalization of entrepreneurial firms have been offered including those developed by Zahra and George, Bell et al., and Oviatt, Shrader, and McDougall.[10–12] Each of these integrative models provides a unique perspective for understanding the internationalization process. The model developed by Oviatt and McDougall has as its primary focus the rapid internationalization of new ventures, while the model proposed by Zahra and George encompasses a broader definition of international entrepreneurship to include established firms that are entrepreneurial in their internationalization process.[13, 14] Bell et al. suggests a model that includes a consideration of existing firms that may operate domestically for long periods of time before, sometimes very rapidly, internationalizing their operations.[15]

These emerging integrated models of internationalization, while providing an overarching framework for understanding the internationalization activities of entrepreneurial firms, tend to place their greatest emphasis on the motives and outcomes for internationalization. Although each acknowledges the critical role of certain firm processes to internationalization, none provides a detailed review of the full range of processes research has identified. Accordingly, the focus of this chapter is neither the motives nor outcomes of going global, but rather the processes through which entrepreneurial firms go global. The focus on processes is not intended as a review or support of the models of internationalization labeled as "process" models, but rather intended to be theoretically agnostic in focusing specifically on research associated with the enabling and enacting processes that entrepreneurial firms utilize in internationalizing their operations. The ultimate goal of the discussion is to provide a review of existing research, a possible bridge between competing models of the internationalization of entrepreneurial firms by focusing on common processes of internationalization, and to illuminate insight that current research might have for the owners and managers of entrepreneurial firms.

The first section of this chapter will provide a brief review of the debate regarding the applicability of the traditional models of internationalization to entrepreneurial firms and three recently proposed integrative models of international entrepreneurship. The second section of the chapter will provide a review of representative research focused on the enabling processes utilized by entrepreneurial firms in internationalizing as well as the apparent gaps in current knowledge. The third section reviews research specifically focusing on the enacting processes of internationalization by entrepreneurial firms. In addition, in the second and third sections, research questions will be posed with the goal of encouraging the integration of existing models of venture internationalization. Finally, in the conclusion of the chapter, future research areas will be suggested.

A BRIEF HISTORY: GRADUAL GLOBALS, BORN GLOBALS, AND BORN-AGAIN GLOBALS

Oviatt and McDougall in their seminal article put into play a debate that had been simmering for some time.[16] They observed that there was clear evidence that many early stage ventures did not appear to be following the traditional stage or process models of internationalization developed with multinational enterprises (MNEs) in mind but rather internationalized from the very start of operations. This observation has engendered a long-running debate in the entrepreneurship literature as to the applicability of traditional models of internationalization. This debate has centered around three process-based conceptualizations of how entrepreneurial firms globalize. These three processes have been popularly termed as *gradual global*, *born global*, and *born-again global*.

Gradual Globals

International business research is replete with a variety of theories framing the internationalization process of firms, many of which have been utilized in an attempt to understand the internationalization process of entrepreneurial firms.[17] The most widely utilized of theses theories, both in the international business literature as well as the entrepreneurial literature are those that have been labeled as the stage theories of internationalization or the Uppsala Internationalization Models.[18] The most influential of the stage models is the one articulated by Johanson and Vahlne.[19, 20] Johanson and Vahlne suggest that firms internationalize through various processes slowly and incrementally over time. The foundation for the model is the processes of acquisition, integration, and knowledge development and an ever-increasing commitment of resources to international markets. The underlying assumption is that as the firm learns more about distant markets the risk-reward valuations improve allowing the firm to incrementally increase commitments of resources. For example, the firm may first enter an international market through an export relationship that over time may evolve into a joint-venture marketing or manufacturing relationship and ultimately into an investment in offshore manufacturing. A second component of the process is the successive movement of the firm into what Johanson and Vahlne suggest are "psychically distant" markets.[21] They suggest that firms will first move into international markets that are most similar to their home markets but with time and knowledge acquisition will take increasingly greater risks by entering markets that are more dissimilar to their home markets.[22]

Although the stage models of internationalization seem to appropriately characterize the behavior of larger firms, entrepreneurship scholars have suggested that the unique nature of entrepreneurial firms is not adequately addressed by existing theories. Oviatt and McDougall report that a wide range of case studies of entrepreneurial firms demonstrate that many begin international activities at founding.[23] This combined with a consideration of the typically limited resource base of early-stage ventures, which requires the ventures to rely more on hybrid structures for their international transactions, leads them to conclude that a unique theory of internationalization may be appropriate.[24]

Born Globals

Oviatt and McDougall, in their review of research pertaining to firms that were international in scope from inception, found that such firms typically had strong networks allowing for the marketing of their products or services—innovative products and services and a tightly managed organization.[25] Most important, the founding team had from inception a vision of international operations. Such ventures were termed international new ventures but have come to be more commonly known as born globals in the entrepreneurship literature. Consistent with their observations of these international from inception ventures, Oviatt and McDougall define such a venture as "a business organization that, from inception, seeks to derive significant competitive advantage from the use of resources and the sale of outputs in multiple countries."[26] In a concurrent study of twenty-four born-global firms, McDougall, Shane, and Oviatt conclude that the traditional stage models of internationalization fail to provide an explanation as to why and how born-global firms can internationalize without first going through the incremental processes predicted by the stage models.[27] Their observations, along with those of others, regarding the applicability of the traditional models has led to a significant body of research in recent years.[28]

In their 1994 article and in a later study, Oviatt and McDougall provide the basic elements for a process theory of born globals.[29] This was followed by the publication of a proposed risk-management model of new venture internationalization.[30, 31] The model, focusing on the rapid internationalization of new ventures, describes a set of complex interactions between the venture founders and the general environment of the venture, which are mediated by the industry environment as well as the characteristics of the entrepreneur. The framework, based on the analysis and understanding of the risks involved in internationalization, is consistent with their definitions of international new ventures as those ventures that are from inception international in scope.

Born-Again Globals

Recently a third process of internationalization has been described—that of the born-again venture. Bell and Young describe such entrepreneurial firms as those that are well established in their domestic markets but which suddenly, based on some triggering event, demonstrate rapid and dedicated internationalization.[32] This process of internationalization is also described by Madsen and Servais as a "leapfrog" process.[33] Because of their sudden conversion to dedicated internationalization, Bell et al. consider these firms to be born-again international ventures.[34] Interestingly, the characteristics of this process, as described by these researchers, closely parallels the attributes of punctuated equilibrium, first described in the biological sciences and later applied in group development and entrepreneurship research.[35, 36] In order to accommodate the temporal aspects of such internationalization, Bell, McNaughton, Young, and Crick have proposed a model of internationalization that in their estimation recognizes the existence of differing pathways for establishing international operations.[37] The proposed model is an effort to accommodate all three processes of internationalization—gradual global, born global, and born-again global. They suggest that the trajectory that an entrepreneurial firm takes is dependent upon the knowledge-based aspects of the firm, the strategic posture of the firm, and the unique attributes of the firm's internal and external environments.

Another model of international entrepreneurship has been proposed by Zahra and George.[38] Expressing concern that the definition of international entrepreneurship proposed by Oviatt and McDougall does not adequately encompass the international entrepreneurial behavior of established firms, Zahra and George propose a model intended to accommodate such behavior.[39, 40] They define international entrepreneurship as "the process of creatively discovering and exploiting opportunities that lie outside a firm's domestic markets in the pursuit of competitive advantage."[41] The focus of their model is the international activity of established firms and the forces that influence the degree, speed, and geographic scope of international activities. The model describes a complex interaction between firm, environmental, and strategic factors that lead to internationalization and ultimately to establishing a competitive advantage for the firm.

Explicit in each of these models are the processes through which entrepreneurial firms internationalize. Because these models are intended as general models there is little in-depth analysis of the specific processes through which entrepreneurial

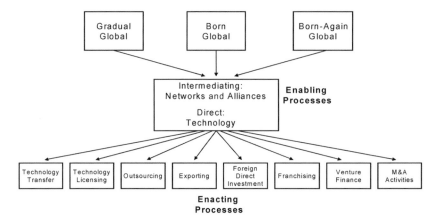

Figure 8.1. Going global: The processes through which entrepreneurial firms internationalize.

firms enter international markets. Following the lead of Wright and Ricks who define international entrepreneurship as a firm-level activity, the following sections of this chapter will provide a brief review of the firm-level processes associated with the internationalization of entrepreneurial firms that have been described in existing research.[42, 43] Processes are those routes or courses of action undertaken by entrepreneurial firms in crossing national boundaries. Figure 8.1 provides an overview of these firm-level processes, identified in current research, through which entrepreneurial firms internationalize and are characterized as either *enabling* or *enacting* processes. Enabling processes are those processes that permit or facilitate the entrepreneurial firm to extend operations beyond the firm's domestic borders. In some respects, these enabling processes are analogous to the pathways described by Bell et al.[44] These enabling processes are both intermediating, as in networking and alliance building, and direct, as enabled by emerging technologies. Enacting processes are those processes that allow entrepreneurial firms to enact international behavior. These processes or actions include exporting, outsourcing, and foreign direct investment (FDI); technology licensing and transfer; franchising; and venture financing, and merger and acquisition (M&A) activities.

It would appear that the real contrast between the proposed models of internationalization is not over the processes through with entrepreneurial firms internationalize but rather over the temporal aspects of the processes as well as the combination of enabling and enacting processes. For example, the gradual global perspective would predict that firms would add these processes incrementally over time beginning with those that carry the least risk to the firm. The born-global perspective would suggest that firms internationalize through a combination of processes simultaneously in order to manage risk. Although the born-again global perspective would also predict a combination of processes attached to international market entry, it would predict that the timing of the entry would be based on some unique triggering event not necessarily occurring at founding. These enabling and enacting processes would also seem to describe the middle ground common to all three models. The current research associated with these models has as its primary focus the "why" of going global. Focusing on the "how" or the processes through which entrepreneurial firms internationalize paints in clear relief the commonalities between the various perspectives of venture internationalization as well as intriguing research questions that may help facilitate the integration of these perspectives. Although the following discussion has as its primary focus research that is associated with entrepreneurial firms, each of the processes has a much broader foundation of research.

ENABLING PROCESSES

The limited resources of entrepreneurial firms require that in order to expand across national boundaries, these firms must utilize a range of resources and processes external to, yet available to the firm. In general these enabling processes have been termed as intermediate and direct. Intermediating processes are those processes that flow through other organizations and that extend the reach of the entrepreneurial firm while minimizing the risk of internationalization. The two most discussed intermediating processes are networking and alliance building.

Intermediating Processes

Networking has long been placed at the core of the entrepreneurial process.[45] Networks have been so omnipresent in case studies of international ventures that many have called for the application of network theory in explaining the internationalization process.[46-48] Building upon a rich foundation of theory and research on business networks, entrepreneurship scholars have explored the role of the networking process in the efforts of entrepreneurial firms in expanding beyond their domestic markets. In this research, the internationalization process is seen as being embedded within the social, institutional, and industry webs, which support the firm in the acquisition of market knowledge, operational capabilities, human capital, finances, and other necessary resources. The role of the networking process in terms of enabling the firm is underscored by the findings of Coviello and Munro in a case study analysis of small software firms.[49] Their findings led them to conclude that the firms in their study made simultaneous use of multiple entry processes, all of which were accessed through the firm's existing international network. Johanson and Mattsson suggest that a firm's ability to enter international markets is more dependent upon its network and position in the network than on market attributes.[50]

The range of research focused on the role of networks in the internationalization of entrepreneurial firms is growing. For example, Johanson and Mattsson suggest that success in international market entry is more dependent upon relationships in current markets than within the chosen market.[51] Moen, Gavlen, and Endresen, in a case study of Norwegian software development companies, conclude that the choice of international markets to enter as well as the process of entry is dependent to a great extent upon the firm's existing networks.[52] Yeoh directly links the firm's external networks with the firm's overall international performance.[53] Focusing on network relationships between large and small firms, Etemad, Wright, and Dana argue that small firms, when highly specialized and efficient, can utilize their relationships with large firms to achieve international competitiveness.[54] Finally, Autio, Yli-Renko, and Salonen provide evidence of a strong linkage between managerial capabilities, the quality of international relationships, and international growth.[55]

A natural outgrowth of the networking process is a second mediating process—alliance formation. Oviatt and McDougall argue that the limited resource base of entrepreneurial firms necessitates the use of hybrid structures in the international process.[56] García-Canal, Duarte, Criado, and Llaneza define international alliances as "those formed by firms which aim at coordinating their actions in several markets and/or at gaining access to competencies that can be exploited in different international markets."[57] These same researchers, while noting the wide range of alliance research, lament the fact that there is limited research into how firms make use of alliances in order to accelerate international expansion.[58]

Examples of the research focused on the use of alliances for internationalization by entrepreneurial firms include the work of García-Canal et al., which draws on a case analysis of eleven Spanish firms and concludes that firms that utilize alliances for globalization typically develop several independent multicountry alliances for market entry as well as for improving core competences in the markets into which they sell their products.[59] Kohn in his empirical analysis of U.S. SMEs concludes that many utilize alliances for acquiring capabilities they lack in international markets or to fend off backward-vertical integration by larger customers.[60] Contrary to other findings, Prater and Ghosh in their study of over 100 small U.S. firms with European operations found a greater use of informal relationships rather than more formal alliance relationships.[61] Finally, in a study of over 1,400 SMEs from five countries, Steensma, Marino, Weaver, and Dickson focused on the relationship between three of Hofstede's dimensions of national culture and technology alliance formation and the use of equity ties.[62, 63] Specifically their research suggested three relationships. First, in countries with higher levels of uncertainty avoidance, technological uncertainty was found to have a more positive relationship with the propensity to form technology alliances and to utilize equity ties in those alliances. Second, in countries with lower masculinity ratings, technological uncertainty was found to have a more positive relationship with the propensity to form technological alliances. Finally, it was found that the relationship between technological uncertainty and the use of equity was impacted by the individualistic traits of a country.

The existing networks and alliances of firms are often referred to as the "social capital" of the firm.[64] Knowledge gleaned from research linking the existence, origins, and levels of social capital, whether connected to the individual entrepreneur or the entrepreneurial firm, would suggest the critical importance of such capital to the owners and managers of entrepreneurial firms interested in internationalization. Unfortunately, existing research is often mute on a number of important issues, including how such social capital is acquired and which types of social capital are most effective and efficient in the internationalization process.

One relatively new and interesting approach to understanding how entrepreneurial firms acquire and utilize social capital in the internationalization process is the use of learning theory.[65] At first blush, the use of learning theory to explain the acquisition of social capital would seem to support the stage models of internationalization. The clear evidence that some firms are international from inception suggests a number of intriguing avenues for additional inquiry. For example, how do entrepreneurs of born globals acquire the experiential learning necessary for successful international relationships prior to founding? One avenue for such learning has been explored by Bloodgood, Sapienza, and Almeida, who found that prior international work experience was positively linked to internationalization.[66] Additional questions of seeming importance include: what types of social capital are most important to internationalization at various stages of venture development; for ongoing domestic-only ventures, how might the triggering events driving the need for internationalization interact with existing networks and alliances to determine the timing and success of internationalization; what types of social capital are most critical to internationalization for the born global, the gradual global and the born-again global firm?

Direct Processes

Technology has emerged as both an enabling process as well as an enacting process as will be discussed later. As an enabling process, technology, and in particular the use of the Internet, has allowed direct and instant contact between firms at opposite locations of the world and enabled a wide range of commercial exchanges. Hamill suggests that the emergence of the global information superhighway has had a profound impact on the conduct of international business.[67, 68] Tetteh and Burn note that the extent to which small firms can benefit from the use of technology in internationalizing their reach is based on the firm's product offerings, the nature of the market and industry, the nature of the firm's partnerships and internal arrangements—all of which ultimately impact the information intensity of the firm's value chain.[69] They go on to suggest three business models which characterize how the entrepreneurial firm utilizes online technology. The first is an independent business unit with an online presence primarily utilized in advertising its products. The second model involves participation in a cluster or group of autonomous businesses online and the organization of operations and products around shared resources. The final model is the use of a virtual community that includes an online collection of various stakeholders.

Although this is a relatively new area of research for international entrepreneurship, some representative studies include that of Kotha, Rindova, and Rothaermel, whose survey of 101 top Internet firms resulted in the conclusion that the pursuit of internationalization is not automatic but based on the firm's reputation and Website traffic.[70] Loane, McNaughton, and Bell conclude that all of the firms in their study, which included forty Internet start-ups from five countries, had undertaken rapid and dedicated internationalization, greatly enabled by the Internet.[71] Some research has shown that the Internet enables entrepreneurial firms to more quickly and easily reach international markets.[72, 73] Similar studies include those of Khon and Bennett.[74, 75]

The use of online technology is readily apparent for the managers of ventures providing content and content-related services, where country boundaries have little relevance. For other types of firms, the role of online technologies may be less readily apparent but nonetheless compelling in the internationalization process. For example, such technologies greatly expand the firm managers' ability to manage such activities as marketing and sales, product development, and outsourcing across international boundaries. Research questions, the answers to which have impact for all three perspectives of venture internationalization, include the following: how might technology serve as a substitute for social capital facilitating early entry into international markets; in what ways does technology facilitate the ability of the firm to be born global; in what ways does technology change the temporal aspects of the internationalization process?

ENACTING PROCESSES

At the heart of entrepreneurship is the enactment of opportunities. The following section will provide a brief review of research relating to those processes through which entrepreneurial firms enact internationalization. In reality, these processes are often so intertwined that the boundaries are unintelligible and in fact the premise of both the born-global perspective and the born-again perspective of internationalization is that firms often use unique combinations of these processes for rapid internationalization. The importance of these enacting processes is underscored by the findings of Zahra, Ireland, and Hitt who suggest that the mode of international market entry has significant impact, for example, on the breadth, depth, and speed of technological learning.[76]

Exporting, Outsourcing, and FDI

Lu and Beamish argue that the two most utilized processes for internationalization are exporting and FDI.[77] Additionally, in recent years, outsourcing has emerged as a widely utilized process for internationalization.[78] A significant body of research has been focused on the exporting behavior of entrepreneurial firms and although research has now shifted to a consideration of a broader range of internationalization behaviors, export research continues to be prevalent.[79] Examples of recent export-focused research includes that of Poutziouris, Soufani, and Michaelas who in a study of UK SMEs determined that exporting companies relied on lower ratios of fixed assets, achieved higher growth rates, and increased sales and turnover.[80] Interestingly, in a study of Japanese SMEs, Lu and Beamish found that exporting had a negative impact on firm performance, but cautioned that the time period of the study included a period in which the Japanese yen experienced strong appreciation causing exports to lose competitiveness.[81] Dalli in a study of Italian SMEs determined that the commitment of the firm, in terms of the internal organization in support of exporting, was correlated with the variation in export sales as well as export intensity.[82] Finally, Yeoh focuses on the use of learning-based theory to explain the relationship between exporting and firm performance.[83]

The stage models of internationalization often note outsourcing as a logical next step in the gradual internationalization of firms. Dunning suggests that with current technological advances, such as computer-aided design and manufacturing processes, firms can relinquish control over the development and manufacturing of products while still exercising control over the key attributes of those products.[84] This growing capacity to outsource while maintaining acceptable levels of controls suggests the continued growth of outsourcing in the internationalization process. Given the importance of outsourcing as an internationalization process, there is surprisingly little research specific to the use of outsourcing by entrepreneurial firms. In a study of ten New Zealand firms, Chetty and Campbell-Hunt conclude that entrepreneurial firms tend to internalize the sale and marketing functions in international markets if the product is highly technical and requires long periods of customization prior to sale.[85] If the product requires extensive after-sale service and customization, the sales and marketing function is typically outsourced. Dahab and Esperança argue that if firm leadership has the goals to expand rapidly or to be able to respond effectively to sudden environmental changes, the firm will tend to rely more on outsourcing as an internationalization strategy.[86]

Stage models of internationalization also prescribe that over time firms may evolve from exporting into international markets and the outsourcing of key process internationally to making investments in infrastructure in those markets. Dunning, in the reappraisal of his eclectic paradigm, suggests that the decision to utilize FDI as a process of internationalization is dependent upon the level of need the firm has to manage risks by internalizing transactions.[87] It is also dependent upon other firm-specific characteristics, including production and inventory processes and ownership strategies. Ultimately he suggests that all of these internal firm characteristics influencing FDI decisions are impacted by any location-specific advantages that might be accrued from such investments.[88] The use of FDI allows entrepreneurial firms to manage risks and leverage location-based advantages, such as competitively priced labor, unique resources, and knowledge. On the other hand, FDI requires greater resource commitment and makes market exit far more difficult.

In a study of 164 Japanese SMEs, Lu and Beamish conclude that FDI is a more competitive way of operating in international markets than exporting.[89] Their results also suggest that when firms first initiate FDI activities, firm profitability, as measured by return on assets (ROA) and return on sales (ROS), declines, but overtime and with increasing FDI commitments there is a positive relationship between FDI and profitability. They utilized two measures of FDI, looking across all types of investments, which included a total count of FDIs in which the company had a 10 percent or greater equity share and the total number of countries in which the company had FDIs. Coviello and Martin in their study of SME service firms conclude that firms tend to internationalize in a manner that reduces risk and internalizes firm-specific assets, but that certain location-specific advantages do accrue from FDI activity.[90] Finally, Manalova suggests that FDI tends to be clustered in several industries, particularly those that are technology based.[91]

The motives behind the use of each of these enacting processes for internationalization would appear to be driven by the desire to obtain location-specific benefits, while at the same time managing the risks associated with international operations. Although the use of these processes begs a number of interesting research questions, central to this discussion are those that might help to integrate the various models of venture internationalization. The gradual evolution of the firm into exporting, outsourcing, and FDI, as suggested by the stage models would seem logical. How might this gradual evolution be circumvented by the born-global firm? How might the mix of these strategic processes differ between born globals and gradual globals? Finally, since each of the models acknowledge the critical role of the external environment an important question would seem to be how might the external environment influence the temporal aspects of when and how each of these strategic processes are employed by entrepreneurial firms.

Technology Licensing and Transfer

A central decision in the technology commercialization process of firms is whether to profit from the sale of product technology or to seek to self-exploit through internalizing the manufacturing processes.[92] As Webster and Sugden note, the decision is whether to use or sell.[93] When put into an internationalization context, the decision takes on added degrees of risk. Developing production capabilities in distant markets requires FDI and the associated financial risks, while licensing minimizes the firm's international exposure from an operational standpoint, but increases the potential loss of control over the technology being licensed. Arora et al. suggest that licensing is more likely to be the chosen process if the market is distant, when the market share of the licensor is small, and when the downstream market is highly competitive.[94] Castellani and Zanfei, in a study involving thirteen European companies and nineteen North American companies, conclude that firms need no specific knowledge of a market in order to commercialize technology through licenses, but in high-velocity industries fewer licensing transactions can be accomplished given the rapid changes in technology.[95] Given the relative importance of licensing as an internationalization strategy for entrepreneurial firms, either inbound or outbound licensing, it is interesting to note a very limited level of research activity.

Technology transfer, often facilitated through both formal methods such as licensing and alliances as well as through more informal methods, can serve as an enacting process for internationalization by entrepreneurial firms. The technology transfer process, according to Eden, Levita, and Martinez "involves the acquisition, assimilation, diffusion, and development of technology."[96] Eden et al. suggest that for SMEs the cost of technology production and transfer are high, resulting in a greater use of alliances and joint ventures and a focus on niche markets.[97] Ultimately they conclude that while SMEs face unique challenges as a result of their limited resource base their flexibility can allow them to be successful in internationalizing their technology transfer processes. Buckley in his comparison of SME transnationals with all size firms concludes that while SMEs will not be the major suppliers of technology in international market, they can successfully fill important niche roles.[98] Other research that provides insight into technology transfer as an internationalization process includes that of Crick and Jones, Etemad, and Burgel and Murray.[99–101]

Research suggests that for entrepreneurial managers who choose to utilize technology-related processes to internationalize the key issues in managing risk are driven by both firm and environmental factors as well as the nature of the technology. Yeoh suggests that one possible factor in the success of internationalization is the imitability of the technology possessed by the entrepreneurial venture. His assumption provides an interesting research question.[102] Does the imitability of the technology possessed by a venture impact the temporal aspects of internationalization?

Franchising

The licensing and transfer of specific technologies often lead entrepreneurial firms into international markets. Franchising is similar in that the desire to license complete operational systems is often both a motive for internationalization and a process through which entrepreneurial firms internationalize. Grünhagen and Mittelstaedt suggest that drives toward globalization accounted for much of the expansion seen in franchising during the thirty-year period beginning in 1960.[103] Franchising, according to Michael is seen by many as a way of entering international market with relatively low risk.[104] Michael identifies economic, strategic, and cultural factors impacting the rate of franchising as a process for entering international markets.[105] Clarkin, in a study of 1200 North American franchises found that opportunity recognition was the most important motivator for international expansion.[106, 107]

It would appear that franchising as an internationalization process would be one open to entrepreneurial ventures from inception. In a broader sense, an interesting question for empirical research relates to the attributes of the enacting processes through which entrepreneurial firms internationalize. Do the attributes of certain processes make those processes more or less likely, or even possible, to be utilized at specific stages of venture development?

Venture Finance and M&A

Venture capital (VC), while a resource, also embodies a process that impacts the firm both financially and strategically. For example, Carpenter, Pollock, and Leary suggest that VC backing is associated with greater risk-taking by the venture and thus a greater willingness to enter international markets, particularly given the expectations for financial returns implicit in VC financing.[108] Surprisingly, the results of their study indicated that the impact of VC financing on internationalization was negative. They speculated that venture capitalists (VCs) are "reasoned" risk-takers and that the positive impact of VC on internationalization would only be evident in the presence of significant international experience held by the management team. Burgel and Murray in their study of 311 British start-ups found an inconclusive relationship between VC involvement and internationalization.[109] At this point, the evidence as to the relationship between the VC process and internationalization is inconclusive, given the limited nature of the research conducted.

Often closely linked with the process through which ventures are financed is the process through which ventures either merge with or are acquired by other firms. The M&A process has long been recognized as important in internationalization. Acs, Morck, Shaver, and Yeung suggest, given that entrepreneurial firms hold a significant place in the development of innovations, the most efficient means through which these innovations might be disseminated into the international marketplace is through their absorption by larger multinationals.[110] The ability of firms to expand internationally and the viability of those expansion moves appear to be enhanced, according to Vermeulen and Barkema, by earlier acquisitions—whether those acquisitions are domestic or international.[111] They speculate that the acquisitions may broaden the firm's knowledge base and foster the development of new knowledge critical to later expansion. Barkema and Vermeulen note that when firms choose to expand into a foreign market by establishing a local subsidiary, they must choose between starting a new business or acquiring an existing local company.[112] Their research with twenty-five Dutch firms suggests to them that the key determinants of the choice of entry processes are the firm's strategic posture, its multinational diversity, and the diversity of its products. In a similar study with over 2,100 entries into the U.S. market by Anand and Delios, the results suggest that it was the upstream and downstream capabilities of the entering firm that determined the choice of a new start-up or an acquisition of an existing firm.[113] Finally, Bell et al. noted that an interesting strategy utilized by some small firms, whose resource constraints prevent them from internationalizing, is to make the firm attractive as a takeover target by a larger domestic or foreign multinational firm.[114]

For venture managers contemplating the acquisition of VC, current research provides little guidance as to the role of VC in either promoting or hindering internationalization. At most, the findings suggest that the relationship may be specific to the VC source. Moving forward, an interesting research question for international scholars is if the timing of VC input has an influence on the temporal aspects of internationalization by the venture. Regarding M&A activity, the research of Vermeulen and Barkema suggests that firms that utilize start-ups for market entry rather than acquisitions tend to have lower survival rates.[115] Left unanswered is the question, does this hold true for ventures at all stages of development?

CONCLUSION

The debate engendered by the evidence that some entrepreneurial firms do not follow the traditional stage models of internationalization but rather are born global, has led to much important research in recent years. The primary goal of this discussion has been to review the literature associated with the enabling and enacting processes available to entrepreneurial firms for internationalization that are common to most models of internationalization and to pose research questions that might aid in integrating the born global, gradual global, and born-again global perspectives. Taken in total, existing research suggests that entrepreneurial firms utilize a unique mix of enabling and enacting processes for internationalization. Questions of key interest that span all three internationalization perspectives include: how does the unique mix of processes available to a specific firm influence the timing, extent, and scope of internationalization; how does the firm's unique compliment of processes impact the choice of markets; how does the complement of processes impact the absorptive capacity of the firm to cultivate new markets and capabilities; does the developmental stage of the venture influence the choice and mix of processes utilized for internationalization? Existing research suggests to entrepreneurs that the mode of internationalization needs to be carefully aligned with the stage of development of the firm, the unique internal resources of the firm, and the location-specific external resources and opportunities available. Finally, the focus of this discussion has been primarily at the firm level of analysis. Extending internationalization research to focus on the enabling and enacting processes at the industry and environmental levels may provide important additional information for policymakers interested in understanding and supporting the internationalization of entrepreneurial firms.

NOTES

1. Hamid Etemad, Richard W. Wright, and Léo-Paul Dana, "Symbiotic International Business Networks: Collaboration between Small and Large Firms," *Thunderbird International Business Review* 43, no. 4 (2001): 481–499.

2. Thomas L. Friedman, *The World Is Flat* (New York: Farrar, Straus & Giroux, 2005).

3. Tomas O. Kohn, "Small Firms as International Players," *Small Business Economics* 9, no. 1 (1997): 45–51.

4. Paul D. Reynolds, "New and Small Firms in Expanding Markets," *Small Business Economics* 9, no. 1 (1997): 79–84.

5. Rodney C. Shrader, Benjamin M. Oviatt, and Patricia P. McDougall, "How New Ventures Exploit Trade-offs among International Risk Factors: Lessons for the Accelerated Internationalization of the 21st Century," *Academy of Management Journal* 43, no. 6 (2000): 1227–1247.

6. Richard W. Wright and David A. Ricks, "Trends in International Business Research: Twenty-Five Years Later," *Journal of International Business Studies* 25, no. 4 (1994): 687–701.

7. Hamid Etemad and Richard Wright, eds., *Globalization and Entrepreneurship* (Cheltenham, UK: Edward Elgar, 2003).

8. Léo-Paul Dana, ed., *Handbook of Research on International Entrepreneurship* (Cheltenham, UK: Edward Elgar, 2004).

9. The foundations for this debate can be reviewed for example in Jim Bell, Rod McNaughton, and Stephen Young, "'Born-Again Global' Firms: An Extension to the 'Born Global' Phenomenon," *Journal of International Management* 7 (2001): 173–189; A. Bakr Ibrahim, "Internationalization: Motive and Process," in *Handbook of Research on International Entrepreneurship*, ed. Léo-Paul Dana (Cheltenham, UK: Elgar, 2004), 129–136; Tage Koed Madsen and Per Servais, "The Internationalization of Born Globals: An Evolutionary Process," *International Business Review* 6, no. 6 (1997): 561–583; Benjamin M. Oviatt and Patricia P. McDougall, "Toward a Theory of International New Ventures," *Journal of International Business Studies* 25, no. 1 (1994): 45–64.

10. Shaker Zahra and Gerard George, "International Entrepreneurship: The Current Status of the Field and Future Research Agenda," in *Strategic Entrepreneurship*, eds. Michael A. Hitt, R. Duane Ireland, S. Michael Camp, and Donald L. Sexton (Malden, MA: Blackwell, 2002), 255–288.

11. Jim Bell, Rod McNaughton, Stephen Young, and Dave Crick, "Towards an Integrative Model of Small Firm Internationalization," *Journal of International Entrepreneurship* 1, no. 1 (2003): 339–362.

12. Benjamin M. Oviatt, Rodney C. Shrader, and Patricia P. McDougall, "The Internationalization of New Ventures: A Risk Management Model," in *Theories of the Multinational Enterprise: Diversity, Complexity and Relevance*, eds. Michael A. Hitt and Joseph L. C. Cheng (Amsterdam: Elsevier, 2004), 165–185.

13. Benjamin M. Oviatt and Patricia P. McDougall, "Toward a Theory of International New Ventures," *Journal of International Business Studies* 25, no. 1 (1994): 45–64.

14. Zahra and George, "International Entrepreneurship."

15. Bell, McNaughton, Young, and Crick, "Towards an Integrative Model of Small Firm Internationalization."

16. Oviatt and McDougall, "Toward a Theory of International New Ventures."

17. Some of the more popular theories that have been utilized in attempting to understand the globalization of entrepreneurial firms include innovation-related internationalization models, which can be reviewed in Warren J. Bilkey and George Tesar, "Attempted Integration of the Literature; the Export Behavior of Firms," *Journal of International Business Studies* 9, no. 1 (1977): 33–46; foreign direct investment theory, which can be reviewed in Peter J. Buckley and Mark Casson, "Theory of International Operations," in *The Internationalization of the Firm: A Reader*, eds. P. J. Buckley and P. Ghauri (London: Academic Press, 1993), 45–50; network theory, which can be reviewed in Jan Johanson and Jan-Erik Vahlne, "Business Relationship Learning and Commitment in the Internationalization Process," *Journal of International Entrepreneurship* 1, no. 1 (2003): 83–101. Additionally, such traditional economic theories as transaction cost theory as noted by Andrew L. Zacharakis, "Entrepreneurial Entry into Foreign Markets: A Transaction Cost Perspective," *Entrepreneurship Theory and Practice* 21, no. 3 (1997): 23–39; and resource theory, as reviewed by Patrick C. Woodcock, Paul W. Beamish, and Shige Makino, "Ownership-Based Entry Mode Strategies and International Performance," *Journal of International Business Studies* 25, no. 2 (1994): 253–273, have been applied in explaining the entry of entrepreneurial firms into international markets.

18. For complete reviews of the literature associated with the stage or Uppsala models of internationalization, see Nils-Erik Aaby and Stanley F. Slater, "Management Influences on Export Performance: A Review of the Empirical Literature 1978–1988," *International Marketing Review* 6, no. 4 (1989): 7–26; Bent Petersen and Torben Pedersen, "Twenty Years After—Support and Critique of the Uppsala Internationalization Model," in *The Nature of the International Firm*, eds. Ingmar Björkman and Mats Forsgren (Copenhagen: Copenhagen Business School Press, 1997): 117–134.

19. Jan Johanson and Jan-Erik Vahlne, "The Internationalization Process of the Firm," *Journal of International Business Studies* 8, no. 1 (1977): 23–32.

20. See also Jan Johanson and Jan-Erik Vahlne, "The Mechanism of Internationalization," *International Marketing Review* 7, no. 4 (1990): 11–24; Jan Johanson and F. Wiedersheim-Paul, "The Internationalization of the Firm—Four Swedish Cases," *Journal of Management Studies* 6 (1975): 305–322.

21. Johanson and Vahlne, "The Mechanism of Internationalization."

22. To see how these theories are framed within the context of entrepreneurial firms, see for example, Nicole E. Coviello and Andrew McAuley, "Internationalization and the Smaller Firm: A Review of Contemporary Empirical Research," *Management International Review* 39, no. 3 (1999): 223–256; Tage Koed Madsen and Per Servais, "The Internationalization of Born Globals: An Evolutionary Process," *International Business Review* 6, no. 6 (1997): 561–583; Øystein Moen and Per Servais, "Born Global or Gradual Global? Examining the Export Behavior of Small and Medium-Sized Enterprises," *Journal of International Marketing* 10, no. 3 (2002): 49–72.

23. Oviatt and McDougall, "Toward a Theory of International New Ventures."

24. Not all scholars agree that the Uppsala or stage models are not applicable to entrepreneurial firms. See for example, Tage Koed Madsen and Per Servais, "The Internationalization of Born Globals: An Evolutionary Process," *International Business Review* 6, no. 6 (1997): 561–583, for a defense of the applicability of such models in the entrepreneurial context.

25. Ibid.

26. Ibid, p. 49.

27. Patricia P. McDougall, Scott Shane, and Benjamin M. Oviatt, "Explaining the Formation of International New Ventures: The Limits of the Theories from International Business Research," *Journal of Business Venturing* 9, no. 6 (1994): 469–487.

28. A review of born-global research can be found in Alex Rialp-Criado, Josep Rialp-Criado, and Gary A. Knight, "The Phenomenon of International New Ventures, Global Start-ups, and Born-Globals: What We Know after a Decade (1993–2002) of Exhaustive Scientific Inquiry," Working paper #2002/11 (Dep. D"Economia de l'Empresa, Universitat Autònoma de Barcelona, Barcelona, Spain, 2002). Examples of this research in more recent publications as well as discussions of the born-global concept can be found in Sylvie Chetty and Colin Campbell-Hunt, "A Strategic Approach to Internationalization: A Tradition versus a 'Born-Global' Approach," *Journal of International Marketing* 12, no. 1 (2004): 57–81; Gary Knight, Tage Koed Madsen, and Per Servais, "An Inquiry into Born-Global Firms in Europe and the USA," *International Marketing Review* 21, no. 6 (2004): 645–665; Øystein Moen and Per Servais, "Born Global or Gradual Global? Examining the Export Behavior of Small and Medium-Sized Enterprises," *Journal of International Marketing* 10, no. 3 (2002): 49–72. A review of the impact of Oviatt and McDougall, "Toward a Theory of International New Ventures" can be found in a special edition of the *Journal of International Business Studies* in 2005.

29. Benjamin M. Oviatt and Patricia P. McDougall, "A Framework for Understanding Accelerated International Entrepreneurship," in *Research in Global Strategic Management*, vol. 7, eds. A. M. Rugman and R. W. Wright (Stamford, CT: JAI Press, 1999), 23–40.

30. Oviatt, Shrader, and McDougall, "The Internationalization of New Ventures."

31. Rodney C. Shrader, Benjamin M. Oviatt, and Patricia P. McDougall, "How New Ventures Exploit Trade-offs among International Risk Factors: Lessons for the Accelerated Internationalization of the 21st Century," *Academy of Management Journal* 43, no. 6 (2000): 1227–1247.

32. Jim Bell, Rod McNaughton, and Stephen Young, " 'Born-Again Global' Firms: An Extension to the 'Born Global' Phenomenon," *Journal of International Management* 7 (2001): 173–189.

33. Tage Koed Madsen and Per Servais, "The Internationalization of Born Globals: An Evolutionary Process," *International Business Review* 6, no. 6 (1997): 561–583.

34. Bell, McNaughton, and Young, " 'Born-Again Global' Firms."

35. Connie J. G. Gersick, "Revolutionary Change Theories: A Multi-Level Exploration of the Punctuated Equilibrium Paradigm," *Academy of Management Review* 16, no. 1 (1991): 10–36.

36. Connie J. G. Gersick, "Pacing Strategic Change: The Case of a New Venture," *Academy of Management Journal* 37, no. 1 (1994): 9–45.

37. Bell, McNaughton, Young, and Crick, "Towards an Integrative Model of Small Firm Internationalization."

38. Zahra and George, "International Entrepreneurship."

39. Oviatt and McDougall, "Toward a Theory of International New Ventures."

40. Zahra and George, "International Entrepreneurship."

41. Ibid., p. 261.

42. Wright and Ricks, "Trends in International Business Research."

43. The range of definitions applied to international ventures is matched by a wide range of foci for the studies that might be included in a review of this literature. Some research has as its focus the international activities of small firms, while others are labeled as small to medium-sized enterprises. Additionally, since a significant area of interest is the born globals, research that addresses new venture and early stage ventures must also be included. In general, I have based the analysis on the broader definition provided by Wright and Ricks, "Trends in International Business Research," which suggests that international entrepreneurship is a firm-level activity that crosses national borders. Finally, Oviatt and McDougall's 1994 article provides a strong starting point for research on the internationalization of entrepreneurial firms. For reviews that include earlier works as well as foundation works in international business, please see Robert D. Hisrich, S. Honig-Haftel, Patricia P. McDougall, and Benjamin M. Oviatt, "International Entrepreneurship: Past, Present, and Future," *Entrepreneurship Theory and Practice* 20, no. 4 (1996): 5–11; Patricia P. McDougall and Benjamin M. Oviatt, "International Entrepreneurship Literature in the 1990s and Directions for Future Research," in *Entrepreneurship 2000*, eds. Donald L. Sexton and Raymond W. Smilor (Chicago: Upstart Publishing, 1997), 291–320.

44. Bell, McNaughton, Young, and Crick, "Towards an Integrative Model of Small Firm Internationalization."

45. Howard E. Aldrich and Catherine Zimmer, "Entrepreneurship through Social Networks," in *The Art and Science of Entrepreneurship*, eds. Donald L. Sexton and R. W. Smilor (Cambridge, MA: Ballinger, 1986), 3–24.

46. Jim Bell, "The Internationalization of Small Computer Software Firms: A Further Challenge to 'Stage' Theories," *European Journal of Marketing* 29, no. 8 (1995): 60–75.

47. Nicole E. Coviello and Hugh J. Munro, "Network Relationships and the Internationalization Process of Small Software Firms," *International Business Review* 6, no. 4 (1997): 361–386.

48. Jan Johanson and Jan-Erik Vahlne, "Business Relationship Learning and Commitment in the Internationalization Process," *Journal of International Entrepreneurship* 1, no. 1 (2003): 83–101.

49. Nicole E. Coviello and Hugh J. Munro, "Network Relationships and the Internationalization Process of Small Software Firms," *International Business Review* 6, no. 4 (1997): 361–386.

50. Jan Johanson and L.-G. Mattsson, "Internationalization in Industrial Systems— a Network Approach," in *Strategies in Global Competition*, eds. N. Hood and Jan-Erik Vahlne (London: Croom Helm, 1988), 287–314.

51. Ibid.

52. Øystein Moen, Morten Gavlen, and Iver Endresen, "Internationalization of Small, Computer Software Firms: Entry Forms and Market Selection," *European Journal of Marketing* 38, no. 9/10 (2004): 1236–1251.

53. Poh-Lin Yeoh, "International Learning: Antecedents and Performance Implications among Newly Internationalizing Companies in an Exporting Context," *International Marketing Review* 21, no. 4/5 (2004): 511–535.

54. Hamid Etemad, Richard W. Wright, and Léo-Paul Dana, "Symbiotic International Business Networks: Collaboration between Small and Large Firms," *Thunderbird International Business Review* 43, no. 4 (2001): 481–499.

55. Erkko Autio, Helena Yli-Renko, and Ari Salonen, "International Growth of Young Technology-Based Firms: A Resource-Based Network Model," *Journal of Enterprising Culture* 5, no. 1 (1997): 57–73.

56. Oviatt and McDougall, "Toward a Theory of International New Ventures."

57. Esteban García-Canal, Cristina López Duarte, Josep Rialp Criado, and Ana Valdés Llaneza, "Accelerating International Expansion through Global Alliances: A Typology of Cooperative Strategies," *Journal of World Business* 37, no. 2 (2002): 91–107, p. 92.

58. For reviews of the use of alliances for internationalization by firms of all sizes, see Anna Grandori and Giuseppe Soda, "Inter-Firm Networks: Antecedents, Mechanisms and Forms," *Organization Studies* 16, no. 2 (1995): 183–214; Richard N. Osborn, John Hagedoorn, Johannes G. Denekamp, Geert Duysters, and C. Christopher Baughn, "Embedded Patterns of International Alliance Formation," *Organization Studies* 19, no. 4 (1998): 617–638.

59. Ibid.

60. Kohn, "Small Firms as International Players."

61. Edmund Prater and Soumen Ghosh, "Current Operational Practices of U.S. Small and Medium-Sized Enterprises in Europe," *Journal of Small Business Management* 43, no. 2 (2005): 155–169.

62. H. Kevin Steensma, Louis Marino, K. Mark Weaver, and Pat H. Dickson, "The Influence of National Culture on the Formation of Technology Alliances by Entrepreneurial Firms," *Academy of Management Journal* 43, no. 5 (2000): 951–973.

63. Gert Hofstede, *Culture's Consequences: International Differences in Work-Related Values* (Beverly Hills, CA: Sage, 1980).

64. Poh-Lin Yeoh, "International Learning."

65. Johanson and Vahlne, "Business Relationship Learning and Commitment in the Internationalization Process."

66. James M. Bloodgood, Harry J. Sapienza, and James G. Almeida, "The Internationalization of New High-Potential U.S. Ventures: Antecedents and Outcomes," *Entrepreneurship Theory and Practice* 20, no. 4 (1996): 61–76.

67. Jim Hamill, "The Internet and International Marketing," *International Marketing Review* 14, no. 5 (1997): 300–323.

68. General reviews of the reach and impact of the use of the Internet in international business can be found in John Hagel and Arthur G. Armstrong, *Net Gain: Expanding Markets through Virtual Communities* (Boston: Harvard Business School Press, 1997); Don Tapscott, *Digital Economy: Promise and Peril in the Age of Networked Intelligence* (New York: McGraw-Hill, 1996).

69. Emmanuel Tetteh and Janice Burn, "Global Strategies for SME-Business: Applying the Small Framework," *Logistics Information Management* 14, no. 1/2 (2001): 171–180.

70. Suresh Kotha, Violina P. Rindova, and Frank T. Rothaermel, "Assets and Actions: Firm-Specific Factors in the Internationalization of U.S. Internet Firms," *Journal of International Business Studies* 32, no. 4 (2001): 769–791.

71. Sharon Loane, Rod B. McNaughton, and Jim Bell, "The Internationalization of Internet-Enabled Entrepreneurial Firms: Evidence from Europe and North America," *Canadian Journal of Administrative Sciences* 21, no. 1 (2004): 79–96.

72. Joseph Alba, John Lynch, Barton Weitz, Chris Janiszewski, Richard Lutz, Alan Sawyer, and Stacy Wood, "Interactive Home Shopping: Consumer, Retailer, and Manufacturer

Incentives to Participate in Electronic Marketplaces," *Journal of Marketing* 61, no. 3 (1997): 38–53.

73. Brad Kleindl, "Competitive Dynamics and New Business Models for SMEs in the Virtual Marketplace," *Journal of Developmental Entrepreneurship* 5, no. 1 (2000): 73–85.

74. Kohn, "Small Firms as International Players."

75. Roger Bennett, "Export Marketing and the Internet: Experiences of Web Site Use and Perceptions of Export Barriers among UK Businesses," *International Marketing Review* 14, no. 5 (1997): 324–344.

76. Shaker Zahra, R. Duane Ireland, and Michael A. Hitt, "International Expansion by New Venture Firms: International Diversity, Mode of Market Entry, Technological Learning, and Performance," *Academy of Management Journal* 43, no. 5 (2000): 925–950.

77. Jane W. Lu and Paul W. Beamish, "The Internationalization and Performance of SMEs," *Strategic Management Journal* 22, no. 6/7 (2001): 565–586.

78. Sônia Dahab and José Paulo Esperança, "Integrated Outsourcing: A Tool for the Foreign Expansion of Small-Business Suppliers," in *Globalization and Entrepreneurship*, eds. Hamid Etemad and Richard Wright (Cheltenham, UK: Elgar, 2003), 38–58.

79. Reviews of research pertaining to the export behavior of entrepreneurial firms can be found in Erwin Dichtl, M. Leibold, Hans-Georg Koglmayr, and Stefan Muller, "The Export Decision of Small and Medium-Sized Firms: A Review," *Management International Review* 24, no. 2 (1984): 49–60; Kurt J. Miesenbock, "Small Business and Exporting: A Literature Review," *International Small Business Journal* 6, no. 2 (1988): 42–61; Aviv Shoham, "Export Performance: A Conceptualization and Empirical Assessment," *Journal of International Marketing* 6, no. 3 (1998): 59–81.

80. Panikkos Poutziouris, Khaled Soufani, and Nicos Michaelas, "On the Determinants of Exporting: UK Evidence," in *Globalization and Entrepreneurship*, eds. Hamid Etemad and Richard Wright (Cheltenham, UK: Elgar, 2003), 15–37.

81. Lu and Beamish, "The Internationalization and Performance of SMEs."

82. Daniele Dalli, "The Organization of Exporting Activities: Relationships Between Internal and External Arrangements," *Journal of Business Research* 34, no. 2 (1995): 107–115.

83. Poh-Lin Yeoh, "International Learning."

84. John H. Dunning, "Reappraising the Eclectic Paradigm in an Age of Alliance Capitalism," *Journal of International Business Studies* 26, no. 3 (1995): 461–492.

85. Sylvie Chetty and Colin Campbell-Hunt, "Paths to Internationalization among Small to Medium-Sized Firms: A Global versus Region Approach," *European Journal of Marketing* 37, no. 5/6 (2003): 796–820.

86. Sônia Dahab and José Paulo Esperança, "Integrated Outsourcing: A Tool for the Foreign Expansion of Small-Business Suppliers," in *Globalization and Entrepreneurship*, eds. Hamid Etemad and Richard Wright (Cheltenham, UK: Elgar, 2003), 38–58.

87. Dunning, "Reappraising the Eclectic Paradigm in an Age of Alliance Capitalism."

88. Dunning's eclectic paradigm, which has as one focus the firm's choice to utilize FDI to internationalize, can be reviewed in Dunning, "Reappraising the Eclectic Paradigm in an Age of Alliance Capitalism"; John H. Dunning, "The Eclectic Paradigm of International Production: A Restatement and Some Possible Extensions," *Journal of International Business Studies* 19, no. 1 (1988): 1–31; John H. Dunning, "Toward an Eclectic Theory of International Production: Some Empirical Tests," *Journal of International Business Studies* 11, no. 1 (1980): 9–31.

89. Lu and Beamish, "The Internationalization and Performance of SMEs."

90. Nicole E. Coviello and Kristina A.-M. Martin, "Internationalization of Service SMEs: An Integrated Perspective from the Engineering Consulting Sector," *Journal of International Marketing* 7, no. 4 (1999): 42–66.

91. Tatiana S. Manalova, "Small Multinationals in Global Competition: An Industry Perspective," in *Globalization and Entrepreneurship, Cheltenham*, eds. Hamid Etemad and Richard Wright (UK: Edward Elgar, 2003).

92. Ashish Arora, Andrea Fosfuri, and Alfonso Gambardella, "Markets for Technology and Their Implications for Corporate Strategy," *Industrial and Corporate Change* 10, no. 2 (2001): 419–451.

93. Margaret Webster and David Sugden, "Implementation of Virtual Manufacturing by a Technology Licensing Company," *International Journal of Operations and Production Management* 23, no. 5 (2003): 448–469.

94. Arora, Fosfuri, and Gambardella, "Markets for Technology and Their Implications for Corporate Strategy."

95. Davide Castellani and Antonello Zanfei, "Multinational Experience and the Creation of Linkages with Local Firms: Evidence from the Electronics Industry," *Cambridge Journal of Economics* 26, no. 1 (2002): 1–25.

96. Lorraine Eden, Edward Levitas, and Richard J. Martinez, "The Production, Transfer and Spillover of Technology: Comparing Large and Small Multinationals as Technology Producers," *Small Business Economics* 9, no. 1 (1997): 53–66, p. 57.

97. Ibid.

98. Peter J. Buckley, "International Technology Transfer by Small and Medium-Sized Enterprises," *Small Business Economics*, 9 (1997): 67–78.

99. Dave Crick and Marian V. Jones, "Small High-Technology Firms and International High-Technology Markets," *Journal of International Marketing* 8, no. 2 (2000): 63–85.

100. Hamid Etemad, "Managing Relations: The Essence of International Entrepreneurship," in *Globalization and Entrepreneurship*, eds. Hamid Etemad and Richard Wright (Cheltenham, UK: Elgar, 2003), 223–242.

101. Oliver Burgel and Gordon C. Murray, "The International Market Entry Choices of Start-up Companies in High-Technology Industries," *Journal of International Marketing* 8, no. 2 (2000): 33–62.

102. Poh-Lin Yeoh, "International Learning."

103. Marko Grünhagen and Robert A. Mittelstaedt, "Entrepreneurs or Investors: Do Multi-Unit Franchisees Have Different Philosophical Orientations?" *Journal of Small Business Management* 43, no. 3 (2005): 207–225.

104. Steven C. Michael, "Determinants of the Rate of Franchising among Nations," *Management International Review* 43, no. 3 (2003): 267–290.

105. Ibid.

106. John E. Clarkin, "Market maturation or opportunity recognition? An Examination of International Expansion by U.S. and Canadian Franchise Systems," in *International Franchising in Industrialized Markets: North America, the Pacific Rim and Other Countries*, eds. Dianne H. B. Welsh and Ilan Alon (Riverwoods, IL: CCH, 2002).

107. Dianne Welsh and Ilan Alon, eds., *International Franchising in Industrialized Markets: North America, the Pacific Rim, and Other Countries* (Riverwoods, IL: CCH, 2002); Dianne Welsh and Ilan Alon, eds., *International Franchising in Emerging Markets:*

Central and Eastern Europe and Latin America (Riverwoods, IL: CCH, 2001); Dianne Welsh and Ilan Alon, eds., *International Franchising in Emerging Markets: China, India, and Other Asian Countries* (Riverwoods, IL: CCH, 2001); Ilan Alon and Dianne Welsh, eds., *International Franchising in Industrialized Markets: Western and Northern Europe* (Riverwoods, IL: CCH, 2003), provide an extensive review of franchising in international markets.

108. Mason A. Carpenter, Timothy G. Pollock, and Myleen M. Leary, "Testing a Model of Reasoned Risk-Taking: Governance, the Experience of Principals and Agents, and Global Strategy in High-Technology IPO Firms," *Strategic Management Journal* 24, no. 9 (2003): 803–820.

109. Oliver Burgel and Gordon C. Murray, "The International Activities of British Start-up Companies in High-Technology Industries: Differences between Internationalizers and Non-Internationalizers," *Frontiers of Entrepreneurship Research* (1998).

110. Zoltan Acs, J. Randall Morck, J. Myles Shaver, and Bernard Yeung, "The Internationalization of Small and Medium-Sized Enterprises: A Policy Perspective," *Small Business Economics* 9, no. 1 (1997): 7–20.

111. Freek Vermeulen and Harry Barkema, "Learning through Acquisitions," *Academy of Management Journal* 44, no. 3 (2001): 457–476.

112. Harry G. Barkema and Freek Vermeulen, "International Expansion through Start-up or Acquisition: A Learning Perspective," *Academy of Management Journal* 41, no. 1 (1998): 7–26.

113. Jaideep Anand and Andrew Delios, "Absolute and Relative Resources as Determinants of International Acquisitions," *Strategic Management Journal* 23, no. 2 (2002): 119–134.

114. Bell, McNaughton, and Young, "'Born-Again Global' Firms."

115. Vermeulen and Barkema, "Learning through Acquisitions."

9

Entrepreneurial Exit

Monica Zimmerman Treichel and David L. Deeds

While much attention has been devoted to the start-up and growth of the entrepreneurial firm, the exit is an important and understudied aspect of the entrepreneurial process. Exit is the point at which the entrepreneur and her investors face the market in an attempt to realize the wealth they believe they have created during the venturing process, and as such, the manner in which the exit is handled can have a profound impact on the wealth realized as well as have ramifications for the future well-being of the venture. For some entrepreneurs, it is an event planned for from the start of the venture. For others it results from factors beyond their control. The exit is a paradox of the entrepreneurial process: "Build a great company but do not forget to harvest."[1] Few events in the life of the entrepreneur or the business are as important as the exit.[2] "If the entrepreneur is to take full advantage of an investment opportunity, it is essential not only to evaluate the merits of the opportunity at the outset but also to anticipate the options for exiting the business."[3]

An entrepreneurial exit is often referred to as a harvest. A harvest plan defines when and how owners and investors of an entrepreneurial venture will exit and realize an actual return on their investment.[4, 5] Fry compared the harvesting of a business to an agricultural harvest:

In agriculture, harvesting means reaping the crop at the end of the growing season. Similarly, growing businesses, like growing crops, need to be harvested to collect terminal after-tax cash flows on the investment that was initially "planted." Unlike agricultural crops, however, when a business is harvested, in most cases it continues to exist, since the entrepreneur or the initial investor may not necessarily leave the company. Instead, through harvesting, the ownership mix of the venture is changing in such a way that harvesting or exiting owners or shareholders extract tangible value from their investment in the form of money, stock, or other cash flow to be used for other purposes. In the case of parent entrepreneurs passing the business to their children without any financial benefits, the intangible value of succession can be rewarding in itself.[6]

For an entrepreneurial venture to be ultimately successful in the eyes of many entrepreneurs and investors there must be an effective and rewarding end. The presence and effectiveness of an exit strategy determines the economic and emotional value to be realized from a venture.[7] The exit is "more than simply leaving a company; it is the final piece necessary in creating the ultimate value to all the participants in the venture."[8] The motive for the exit, interests of the investors, and interest of the founder will dictate the nature of the buyer and the structure of the transaction.[9, 10] If the entrepreneurial venture is a lifestyle venture (i.e., designed to maximize the entrepreneur's life, rather than wealth), the focus of exit strategy maybe on the welfare and future operations of the business, that it be in "the right hands," rather than on the monetary outcome achieved by the exit. However, if the goal of the entrepreneurial venture is to create a high-growth business, the exit strategy is critical in achieving the financial returns expected by investors in high-growth ventures.[11] While the entrepreneur's exit is typically motivated primarily by financial considerations (i.e., to realize financial returns and create liquidity for investors in the case of good performance or stem losses in the case of poor performance), they also exit for other reasons, including personal motivations such as time, family constraints, age, health, opportunity to move onto the next venture; venture-related reasons such as changes in the industry; future entrepreneurial opportunities; or a combination of all the aforementioned.[12–14] The exit is critical to investors, since in the short run, they are likely to realize a return on their investment if the venture achieves a liquidity event, otherwise known as an exit.

The venture does not have the same personal significance for investors as it does for the founders, but is simply a means to achieve financial returns, which makes a successful exit a priority for investors.[15] As noted earlier, exit creates liquidity for investors, and in the case of professional investors (venture capitalists, VCs) it allows them to disperse the wealth realized in the exit to their investors and provides the seed and the incentive for additional investments by these investors in future funds and in turn in future ventures. In the realm of high-growth, venture capital (VC)-backed new venture, the ability to exit profitably is one of the keys to a fully functional new venture finance system. Without readily available exits, VC funds and angel investing become substantially less attractive investments since they can only realize returns through payouts from the cash flow generated by the venture. Under these circumstances substantially less investment capital will be made available for new ventures, which will in turn lead to a substantial decrease in new venture activity.

A clearly articulated exit strategy that investors view as reasonable dramatically increases the chance of investment and the terms the entrepreneur can negotiate.

An exit can take on a number of forms including initial public offerings (IPOs), acquisition, merger, reverse merger, direct public offering, employee stock option plans (ESOPs), management buyout (MBO), leveraged buyout (LBO), and liquidation.[16–18] However, these forms really fall into three broad categories: going public, being acquired, and liquidation. In general, it is the first two categories, going public and acquisitions, that represent a success in the world of venturing, success being defined as creating substantial wealth for entrepreneurs and investors. The other option, liquidation, generally represents a substantially less attractive outcome, particularly for professional venture investors. In the following sections, we review the current research and areas requiring research in these categories of entrepreneurial exits: going public, being acquired, and liquidation.

GOING PUBLIC

Among the means by which entrepreneurs and investors can exit their venture, the one that receives most attention by the press and has been studied most extensively is the IPO. An IPO is the sale of a portion of the company to the public through a stock offering, and is considered by many to be the preferred choice of exiting a firm.[19] For many there is an almost magical sound to "going public."[20] The frequency of dot-com IPOs during the bubble period of 1998 through 2000 made IPO almost a household term. An IPO, if successful, provides higher valuation for the exiting stockholders and at the same time may generate a major infusion of cash for the firm's future growth.[21] The higher valuation of the venture provided by IPOs is due to the increased legitimacy and visibility of the venture and the increased liquidity of the company's equity, making it a less risky and more accessible investment. Finally going public creates a much larger pool of potential investors for the venture, increasing demand for the venture's equities.

An IPO is an expensive and lengthy process. It requires a significant amount of time, effort, and financial resources to complete the many steps required by the Securities and Exchange Commission (SEC) to register the company; the underwriter to sell the stock; and the stock market to list the stock. In addition, an IPO requires the company to exhibit much greater transparency to the public and to regulators. Such transparency includes annual filings with the SEC containing information on the salaries, strategy, and financial performance of the public firm.

An IPO is a point of transition from the private to the public domain.[22] Although firms preparing for an IPO often attract investors' attention, the attention sometimes does not result in investment because IPO firms lack a publicly available record for their stock price and because IPO firms are riskier than larger more established firms.[23–25] They have no stock price record available to the public for evaluation, and in some industries, such as biotechnology, the potential of the firm to develop and market products are not clear.[26] They often face a "liability of market newness," meaning that investors may place a discount on

IPO firms because they "have not demonstrated an ability to cope effectively with the demands of public trading (e.g., market fluctuations, meetings with analysts, and so forth)."[27] Young firms lacking a history of operations face even greater difficulties going public than do established firms.[28, 29]

Major Research Questions Studied

IPOs have been the subject of a great deal of research, largely in the field of finance. Because the goal of an IPO is to raise money for the firm and/or the stockholders, the majority of the research focuses on IPO performance. Finance scholars narrowly define IPO performance as the returns to investors over various periods of time, up to and including one year after going public. The question driving this research is what influences the investment performance of IPO equities during the period immediately following the offering.

In contrast, management scholars are especially interested in the antecedents of IPO performance as a means to better understand the determinants of success in entrepreneurial firms. The IPO presents a unique opportunity to management scholars to analyze an objective market evaluation of the performance of an entrepreneurial venture. An IPO presents the management scholar with the financial market's judgment of the wealth created by the entrepreneurs over the life of the firm prior to the IPO and a detailed disclosure document (the prospectus) that provides a wealth of information on the internal activities of the firm and the entrepreneurs prior to the IPO.[30]

In order to address the question of venture success and performance, management scholars have used a range of performance measures other than ROI on equities, including capital raised by the firm in the IPO, market valuation of the IPO firm and the market value added by the firm, as measured at the time of the IPO. These are the measures chosen, because the focus of management scholars is on the impact of internal venture characteristics, such as top management team (TMT) demographics, scientific capabilities, product pipeline, and patent stock.

Theoretical Lenses

The most frequently used theory in IPO research is signaling theory, especially by finance scholars.[31] Signaling theory begins with the assumption that there is information asymmetry between buyer and seller, specifically that it is expensive and difficult for the buyer to determine the quality of the item being sold—in this case, the quality of the venture. Accordingly, IPO firms attempt to signal their quality to potential investors by undertaking specific actions that are more costly or difficult for low-quality ventures than high-quality ones. The classic example is the provision of a warranty in the market for used cars; however, since warranties are unavailable in the new venture market, firms engage in numerous other signaling mechanisms to convince investors that they are a quality firm and an economically rational investment that will perform well in the future.[32–34] These signals include board characteristics, underwriter prestige, equity retained in the firm, auditor reputation, firm size, and VC investment.[35]

Management scholars have generally applied two theoretical lenses to the study of IPOs. The most common is the resource-based view (RBV), which argues that firm-specific resources, including such things as scientific capabilities, management capabilities, patents, products, and the like are the basis of competitive value and in turn the market's valuation of a venture.[36] Research in this stream has focused on the activities and outcomes achieved by the firm as indicators of firm resources/capabilities and have been successful in establishing a link between resources and the value of a venture at IPO.[37]

The second lens that has been applied by management scholars is institutional theory. This theory posits that under conditions of uncertainty, ventures and emerging industries that are able to establish greater legitimacy in the eyes of their constituents will enhance the resource flows into the venture and the industry. Activities and outcomes, such as media coverage, partnerships with high-status organizations, regulatory success, government support, and so on enhance the legitimacy of the firms and industry and the subsequent resource flows into the industry and the firm.[38] Institutional theory provides unique insights by focusing the researcher on the relationship between the venture, its key constituencies, and the uncertainty present in new ventures and emerging industries. Enhancing our understanding of the legitimating processes in emerging industries presents an important opportunity for future research on new ventures.

Key Findings

The dominant IPO performance indicator in finance research is underpricing.[39] IPO underpricing is the difference between the opening price of the IPO, set by the underwriter, and the closing price of the equity at the end of the first day of trading, set by the market. Underpricing occurs with great regularity in IPOs.[40] Underpricing is beneficial to new investors purchasing the stock directly from the underwriter (e.g., institutional clients), but not to pre-IPO investors who are selling their stock at the IPO (e.g., founders). Underpricing has been characterized as a risk premium paid to investors willing to buy an unseasoned offering. This premium ensures that there will continue to be a market for unseasoned offerings, by creating a high probability that active IPO investors will receive some returns for their efforts. Empirically the persistence of underpricing in the market for IPOs has been well established. However, there is little consistency in the research predicting the magnitude and extent of underpricing, which may be due to the time periods studied, variation in methodologies used, and differences in the data sets.[41–43] Systematic analyses of the correlates of IPO underpricing through meta-analysis can be used to address some of these inconsistencies.[44]

A number of firm characteristics have been found to be related to IPO performance, including financial characteristics, networks, corporate governance, age, size, and the external environment. Financial characteristics of the firm that have been shown to influence performance include shareholders' equity and assets, profits, and the amount of equity sold through the IPO.[45-49] While financial characteristics have been studied, there is some question as to their value.[50] They tell only part of the story. Nonfinancial firm characteristics may have an equal if not greater influence on the performance of firms issuing an IPO.

One nonfinancial characteristic is the networks of the firm. VC backers, prominent strategic alliance partners, the underwriter and its syndicate, the auditor, and investors in the IPO firm's networks have been studied and shown to influence performance.[51-55] The interest in the role of networks in firm performance appears to be growing, especially as findings indicate that networks are positively related to several important outcomes for firms issuing an IPO, including time from inception to IPO, the amount of capital raised in the IPO, and the valuation of the firm at IPO. Networks provide resources, including financial and social capital, to IPO firms, which positively influence their performance. High quality and/or reputable network partners provide legitimacy for the firm.[56]

The corporate governance of IPO firms is another characteristic that has been found to be positively related to firm performance.[57-59] Corporate governance indicators include the current involvement, ownership position, and background of firm founders, as well as the ownership, background, and demographics of the TMT and board of directors. Corporate governance can be considered to be a secondary information source, and according to signaling theory, secondary information sources are of great importance when uncertainty is high, such as at the time of an IPO.[60] It is interesting to note that as the firm progresses through the life cycle, a number of corporate governance changes take place. These changes are often quite significant as the firm prepares for an IPO. Two such changes are the role of the founder(s) and the role of the top managers. The founder is often replaced in the preparation of an IPO, and TMT members are often replaced and/or additional members are added to strengthen the team, all in an effort to enhance firm performance.[61]

In addition, the influence of the CEO on IPO performance has also been found including the functional background and the role as founder.[62, 63] The presence of a founder-CEO and his/her equity in the firm has been shown to improve the IPO's performance and survival,[64, 65] perhaps because "the symbolic value, psychological commitment, ownership, structural authority, and tenure of founders may directly indicate and indirectly proxy the value of a firm's management to potential investors."[66] A founder-CEO may also be better able to lead the company through a period of transformation than a nonfounder-CEO.[67]

The board of directors of IPO firms has also been shown to influence performance. The board structure of IPO firms represents important nonfinancial information used by investors to make decision of whether or not to invest in the IPO.[68] The networks, prestige, background, equity holdings, and independence of the board members as well as the size of the board have been shown to be positively related to IPO performance.[69-73]

The age and the size of the IPO firm have also been studied in relationship to performance.[74–77] They are frequently used as control variables.[78–80] Age may positively influence performance by enabling the firm to acquire more information, resources, and experience, as well as establish more relationships. Characteristics external to the firm also influence IPO performance. Two external characteristics include "hot markets" and the industry. Given the level of risk and uncertainty surrounding the IPO market, investor's demand for equities in firms in particular markets (oil and gas, biotechnology, dot-coms, and so on) has been shown to vary dramatically over time. During certain periods, like the recent dot.com bubble, investor demand skyrockets driving prices up, creating a hot market for these IPOs. In contrast, during other periods, frequently following hot markets investor demand can drop off precipitously, tanking prices for these equities and making it nearly impossible to take a venture public. This cyclicality is well documented in the IPO literature and has been shown to significantly influence numerous measures of the performance of a firm's IPO. Specifically, firms can raise greater amounts of capital during hot markets, achieve higher valuations, as well as lower underpricing.[81–83] IPO performance has also been linked to conditions of the industry in which the firm operates. For example, firms operating in industries that were in the early stages of the industry life cycle, performed better than those in later stages.[84] The recent run up of the dot.com market is a classic example of a hot market but they are also well documented in resource industries, biotechnology, and computer hardware and software.

Future Research

There is a wealth of finance-based research, and the management-based IPO research is growing. Yet, much room remains to research IPOs. While we have learned a great deal about IPO performance using underpricing, there are other measures of performance that may be more appropriate. Underpricing, a stock-based performance measure is appropriate when examining investors because investors' primary reason for investing in IPOs is to make money from the increase in the stock price.[85] When the focus is on the firm and its ability to access resources, a more appropriate measure is the capital raised at IPO, especially since the most important reason for a company to go public is to infuse capital into the firm.[86] Capital raised has been used in only a few studies.[87–89] Researchers and practitioners alike would benefit from the study of the capital raised at IPO, since it has direct implications for raising funds not only in the public market, but in the private equity market as well. Improving our understanding of what enhances a venture's access to investor capital will have both operational and managerial implications for entrepreneurs and potential policy implications for agencies interested in increasing the flow of capital into entrepreneurial ventures.

Another area in need of research is IPOs in a global economy. While there is a growing body of research on entrepreneurial firms in a global economy, there is much more to learn. Research addressing the level of internationalization of IPO firms and the access to capital in equity markets across the globe would extend our knowledge of IPO firms. In addition, examining firm and environmental characteristics related to IPO performance across equity markets would be beneficial in understanding the impact of differences in structure and regulation of financial markets across countries and its impact on the rate of formation, survival, and growth of new ventures under these conditions. As the VC industry internationalizes, it is important to understand its impact on where firms are domiciled, where they chose to go public, and the impact of these choices on the performance and survival of ventures across various regions and of the rates of new venture formation in these regions.

Despite the wealth of information on IPOs, and the billions of dollars raised through public offerings, the process by which a privately held firm transforms itself into a publicly traded company is still not well understood.[90] The research currently provides very little insight into why one firm is able to, or chooses to, issue an IPO and another does not. While there is a wealth of practitioner-oriented material on how to take a company public, there is little empirical evidence to support much of the conjecture about how best to prepare a firm for going public. There is also little information on what type of firm makes a good IPO candidate and which type of firm is better off selecting another mode of exit. In fact, all the research to date begins with a sample bias by selecting firms, which have gone public. In order to better understand the lead up to IPO and who succeeds and who does not in issuing an IPO-mixed sample of firms, which issued an IPO and those that use other means are required.

Much of the IPO research is cross-sectional in nature. Longitudinal research would provide a better understanding of the transformation process over time. For example, we know little about the changes in the TMT over time from start-up through the IPO and post-IPO. We also know little about the operations of firms in this transformation process. Research on the changes in the supply chain, human resource management, and marketing of firms transitioning into the public market would be beneficial to scholars and practitioners alike.

The research on IPOs is beneficial to practitioners for several reasons. First, while there is a great deal of anecdotal information on preparing for an IPO, practitioners have little empirically derived information about the relationship between venture characteristics and the amount of capital raised, the valuation placed on the venture and the long-term performance and survival implications of going public. Recent research is rectifying this situation; it provides insight into the characteristics of the firm that are positively related to IPO performance, which practitioners can then use to prepare their own venture to maximize the benefit they realize from issuing an IPO. For example, using the knowledge that reputable underwriters are related to IPO performance should guide the entrepreneurs and/or top managers to seek a reputable underwriter to take their firm public. Second, practitioners can use knowledge about hot markets to determine the best time for a firm to initially offer its stock. Finally, research on firm characteristics, capabilities, and resources provides practitioners insights into what the market values and what resource and capability investments will provide significant returns.

So where are the holes in our knowledge of IPOs that provide opportunities for future research? The largest and most important is due to the sample bias of most of the IPO research; we only look at firms that successfully IPO. What we really do not understand that is of critical importance is what determines a firm's suitability for the public markets; at what point in its life and under what conditions should it use an IPO; and when would the prospects for the venture and the owners be enhanced by selecting another exit option? How do we explain the difference between firms that file for an IPO but later withdraw and those that go through the IPO process? What determines the probability of a given firm to IPO? All of these are important questions that require further study and can only be answered by creating either a database of matched pairs—public and non-public firms, or a comprehensive industry database that includes both IPO ventures and ventures that chose to stay private or be acquired.

ACQUISITIONS

A second exit strategy is to sell your firm. Being acquired allows the owner to exit the firm by selling its assets or stock. The firm can be acquired by outsiders: direct competitors, indirect competitors, and noncompetitors; foreign firms that seek a presence in a domestic market or to avoid tariffs; management of the firm through an MBO; employees using an ESOP; family members; and the like.[91]

While the concept of going public is for many entrepreneurs the ideal exit strategy because it provides an escape from bootstrapping and offers fame, respect, and a significant amount of cash, there are issues associated with IPOs that may make acquisitions a better option. The combination of the compliance costs of Sarbanes-Oxley for U.S. firms, Wall Street's lack of attention to small cap stocks, and investor distrust heightened by the dot.com bubble has lessened the appeal of an IPO. A small number of companies are "dual tracking"—simultaneously registering to go public and pursuing acquisition.[92] While costly, the dual strategy of pursuing both an IPO and acquisition expands the market for control/ownership of the firm and allows the firm to drive a harder bargain in negotiations with acquirers. George Rathman, one of the founders of Amgen, has stated that Genetech's IPO is one of the critical events in the history of the biotechnology industry, because it provided biotech firms an alternative source of capital and enhanced their ability to negotiate alliance and acquisition terms with the traditional pharmaceutical companies.[93]

Major Research Questions

Most of the research on acquisition addresses the question "Is value created by acquisitions and if so under what conditions is it captured by the acquiring another firm?" While a critical question for strategy scholars, it is only tangentially of interest to entrepreneurship scholars trying to understand exits. It is clear that on the whole, if an acquisition creates value then it is beneficial to society. However, in the case of exits, acquisition is the appropriate strategy only if it allows the investors and entrepreneurs to capture the value that has been created through the venture.[94] This leads to two important but understudied questions for entrepreneurship scholars; under what conditions does being acquired allow the investors and the entrepreneurs to maximize the wealth that they capture? How can the current owners of a venture prepare a firm for acquisition, such that it maximizes the wealth they realize from the acquisition?

The advantages of acquisitions for the entrepreneur frequently include instant liquidity, enhanced estate planning, and the ability to diversify their wealth. The advantages of being acquired for the venture can include the access to resources to grow the firm, achieving economies of scale and scope, and broader market access. Following an acquisition, the acquiring firm often provides security and resources for the acquired firm and its members. For the acquiring firm, acquisition often facilitates growth.[95] It can be cheaper, smarter, and faster to buy a firm than to build one.[96] Opportunities to consolidate the functions of the acquired firm may create cost savings, and acquisitions often provide clout in the marketplace and critical mass (i.e., economies of scale and scope).[97] Acquisitions also can facilitate the consolidation of highly fragmented industries, such as early on in the automobile industry, increasing the economies of scale in the industry, lowering costs and decreasing the price to the consumer.[98] Standard Oil provides an example of the benefits of the consolidation of a fragmented entrepreneurial industry to society. By consolidating refining and the production of kerosene, Standard Oil was able to lower the price of kerosene by approximately 90 percent, which is why it is often said that it was Rockefeller, not Edison, that brought light to the country.

Theoretical Lenses

Almost all of the research on acquisitions has focused on the question of the conditions under which acquisitions create value. Most of this literature is grounded in the core theories of strategic management, such as Porter's I/O paradigm, transaction cost economics, the resource-based view of the firm, dynamic capabilities, and the knowledge-based view of the firm. In general, these theories focus on two explanations for value creation through acquisition. The first revolve around economies of scale and scope and market power arguments. These follow traditional economic rationales from industrial organization economics and Porter's five forces theory. The second explanation for the value creation of acquisitions comes from synergies, defined as uniquely valuable combination of resources, created by merging the acquirer and the acquired. While this research is important to managers and informative to entrepreneurs, it provides little guidance on when being acquired is the wealth maximizing choice for the owners of a venture.

Key Findings

Value Creation

Research has found that for the acquiring firm, the best chance for rapid growth through acquisition takes place in fragmented service industries, which do not require a huge investment in plant and equipment, and the most successful acquisitions are those within the acquiring firm's industry.[99] Evidence indicates that acquirers of young firms prefer public rather than private ones. Research has also found that acquirers prefer young firms when reaching beyond the boundaries of their current industry.[100]

Research has also highlighted the disadvantages of acquisitions for the acquirer, including expense, difficulty in valuing the firm, structuring the payment, managing the entrepreneur's emotional investment in their firm and in the sale. While acquisitions are often cheaper, smarter, and faster than building a firm, they often require considerable outlays up front and may, in some cases, be much more costly in the long run.[101–103] Sellers often demand a premium price for their inflated view of the firm they worked hard to build over many years, which may lead buyers to over pay.[104] In the acquisition of a small firm, one of the biggest problems a buyer faces is dealing with the entrepreneur.[105] Entrepreneurs often have difficulty viewing the firm in purely economic terms and perceive their firm as being more valuable and having more potential than it really has.[106] When the entrepreneur continues with the firm after the sale, there is a potential for her disillusionment and/or disappointment with the new firm due to changes in the operations and strategy of the firm, and/or their loss of control over the venture.[107]

The timing of the sale appears to be important, based on anecdotal evidence. Many entrepreneurs do not sell until they face financial difficulties at which point, it may be difficult to find a buyer and their negotiating position is substantially weaker. Under these circumstances, the entrepreneur's ability to capture value through an acquisition has declined and in turn the value she is able to get for the firm has probably decreased. There are numerous examples of entrepreneurs who failed to take an offer in hopes of receiving a higher one only to sell later at a lower price. The timing of the sale and the conditions under which the entrepreneurs and owners maximize their returns is an area in need of much greater study and one, which is important for the field of entrepreneurship.

In addition to the aforementioned challenges, acquirers must be aware of the many noneconomic factors not evident, using traditional valuation methods that can influence the value of an entrepreneurial firm.[108] During the process of acquisition, key employees may be lost and key initiatives may be stalled, substantially weakening the competitive position of the acquired firm. In addition, acquisition frequently causes a loss of customers, since the change signals to the customer the potential need to reevaluate the relationship with the acquired firm. This is particularly problematic when the entrepreneur's reputation is difficult to separate from the venture. In other words, customers view the firm as an extension of the entrepreneur, not as a stand-alone entity.

Acquisition Process

The steps in the process of exiting through acquisition should begin early with a conscious choice of this as an exit strategy. This allows the entrepreneur to prepare the firm for sale and start marketing the firm. Once an acquisition is initiated, a slew of activities is undertaken, including due diligence on the firm being sold, negotiations, signing a letter of intent (i.e., a letter expressing the intention of the parties to sell/buy the firm), and the agreement of sale. Preparing a firm for sale is analogous to preparing a house for sale, but rather than paint, much of the work is done through documenting and cleaning up prior transactions, preparing solid financial statements, and getting accounts receivable, inventory and other documents and in order. A successful acquisition typically involves a number of experts, including a lawyer, accountant, investment banker or business broker, and tax experts such as a tax lawyer and tax accountant. In smaller and simpler transactions, generally, when the value of the firm is less than US$1 million and the bulk of the assets to be transferred are tangible and well documented, owners may be able to sell the firm with little or no outside assistance. In larger and more complex deals, conventional wisdom is that it is unwise to attempt such a transaction without significant assistance. However, the implications of the use of advisors (amount, type, quality, and so on) during a sale on the wealth realized by the entrepreneur have not been researched, which presents an interesting opportunity for those interested in the area.

In general, owners looking to sell a venture have a choice of engaging some variety of broker or marketing the business themselves. There are a number of ways to identify buyers without using a broker or investment banker. These include advertising in trade journals, Web sites, business papers, and the like; informing those that might have an interest in purchasing the firm (e.g., employees, managers, competitors, strategic partners, and clients); as well as professional sources, such as attorneys, accountants, and consultants. The key to marketing it oneself, appears to be getting the word out to potential acquirers through personal and business networks and the use of selective advertising. There are clear tax advantages to selling the business through an ESOP, but again the implications of this on the owner's wealth is unknown and in need of further study.

Business brokers are typically used in the sale of firms with revenue under US$10 million. An investment banker is used for larger firms with the minimum size dependent on the size and prestige of the investment bank.[109] Advantages of using a broker or investment banker is their knowledge of potential buyers, means of contacting potential buyers, screening capabilities, and ability to maintain confidentiality of the sale, and negotiating skills.[110, 111] Fees charged by bankers and brokers are typically a percentage of the sale price. For large firms, the fee is often based on the Lehman formula: 5 percent of the first US$1 million, and decreasing percentages on each million above the first. There may also be a fixed consulting fee due whether or not the firm is sold.[112, 113] However, as mentioned earlier, the implications of employing either brokers or investment bankers on the wealth and satisfaction of the entrepreneur with the process have not been subject to rigorous study and this presents an opportunity for future research.

Valuation

To prepare for the sale of a firm, a valuation is made of the firm. The determination of value is influenced by who is doing the valuation. There are a number of ways to value a firm, including book value, adjusted book value (e.g., tangible and economic), income capitalization, discounted earnings, free cash flows, discounted cash flows, multiple of sales (price/earnings ratio), multiple of earnings, comparable firm method, comparable transaction method, asset accumulation, excess earning, earnings before interest taxes deprecation and amortization (EBITDA), liquidation value, and dividend capitalization.[114–117]

For firms generating US$5 million or more, the EBITDA method combined with a comparable transaction analysis is often used. In a firm with no significant earnings, a discounted cash flow method is often used. For smaller firms, say under US$5 million, a rule-of-thumb formula may be used, but choice of the rule of thumb is industry specific. An example of the use of a rule-of-thumb formula is in the cable TV industry where the number of subscribers is used to value the firm.[118] The goal is to get at a metric that actually reflects the underlying value drivers of the business. In the previous example, and in the burglar alarm and cell phone business that is reflected by the size of the network, number of customers is a good metric. In other businesses, it may be something completely different, such as measure of traffic on a Web site. Financial information is often not relied upon as much for small firms as it is for large firms, because of a perception that financial information is not completely reliable due to intermingling of the owner's personal and business expenses and/or because the business model will be changed after acquisition to conform to the acquiring firm's model, thus making the seller's accounting of income irrelevant.[119]

The most common structures for acquisitions include sale of assets, sale of stock, and mergers (which is the combination of the equity of the two firms). Sellers prefer the sale of stock to sale of assets. In a sale of stock, the seller can generally obtain long-term capital gain treatment on the stock sale. Proceeds from the sale of a private firm usually consist of cash, shares of the acquiring firm, or a combination of cash and shares.[120] The sellers' advisors argue for a cash sale over an exchange of stock, because the former provides cash up front and is more liquid. An exchange of stock is a tax-free transaction, but it is subject to the volatility and unpredictability of the purchasing firm's stock price. Buyers prefer the sale of assets to sale of stock because they can select the assets (and liabilities, especially those that are undisclosed or even unknown at the time of sale) they want to acquire. When assets are sold, there may be a premium offered for goodwill often in the form of employment contract.[121]

A merger is the combination of two companies and is often used to describe the purchase of all the assets and liabilities of a company by a buyer. In a merger, all of the assets and liabilities of one firm are transferred to that of another. The merged firm may, however, not want all of the assets and liabilities.[122] A merger provides an alternative to selling the firm or a portion of it.[123] It can provide instant product diversification, quick completion of product lines, increased technical expertise, economies of scale, greater executive depth, improved access to financing, vertical integration, entry into otherwise closed markets, and enhanced marketing capabilities.[124]

Employee Stock Option Plans

Many entrepreneurs sell stock to their employees using an ESOP. In closely held companies, ESOPs are often used to create a market for the entrepreneurs' stock.[125] When the ESOP is used primarily for a retirement plan for the employees, the firm makes an annual contribution to the ESOP; the ESOP purchases stock in the firm, and then uses the money to buy stock from the firm and from stockholders. This is an attractive means of exit for an entrepreneur for a number of reasons including continuation of the business and tax ramifications.[126] An ESOP provides ownership to employees of their firm and allows the owners to gradually exit the firm. There are ordinary ESOPs, leveraged ESOPs, and transfer of ownership ESOPs.[127] However, while there is substantial research on the implications of ESOPs for future performance, human resource policies, employee satisfaction, productivity, and the like, there has been no research on the implications of ESOPs on the wealth and satisfaction of the prior owners.

Management Buyout

An MBO is a means by which an entrepreneur can exit by selling to partners or key managers of the firm. One advantage of an MBO is that it aligns the interest of the managers and owners and thus avoids the agency problem.[128, 129] Disadvantages may relate to the financing of the buyout. When debt is used to finance the buyout (i.e., an LBO), the firm may struggle to cover the debt charges; however, in firms that generate substantial free cash flow, the leverage may lead to improved efficiencies, limit the agency problems and enhanced firm value. When the founder allows the managers to pay a portion of the purchase price upfront and the balance over time, the managers may struggle to pay the founder, thus putting the founder's payout at risk. The use of MBOs as an exit vehicle remains understudied. While substantial research has looked at venture-backed MBOs and the movement of firms via MBO and IPO from public to private and back to public, the condition under which an MBO is the preferred vehicle for exit, the wealth implications of MBOs for founders, and the characteristics of firms that are well suited to use an MBO as an exit vehicle remain questions for future research.

Future Research

Much of the knowledge we have about acquisitions as a means of entrepreneurial exit is anecdotal and much of the literature is prescriptive in nature. We know relatively little about the relationship of nonfinancial firm characteristics and the value of the acquisition. For example, while we know the importance of networks and governance to IPO performance, we do not know if these things influence the valuation of acquisitions. It would be interesting to learn if networks and governance are important in all types of entrepreneurial exits or only in IPOs. It would appear that governance would influence acquisitions in that the management-team influence on firm performance has been demonstrated, and that firm performance is used to value the firm, then the management team characteristics, directly or indirectly, should be related to the valuation of the acquired firm. The relationship of the founder-CEO to IPO performance suggests the importance of founder-CEOs in the valuation of acquired firms. This may be especially important in valuing privately held companies because the founder is often instrumental in the sale of the firm.

Future research might also address the importance of networks in acquisitions. We know that networks are positively related to IPO performance, and so the same might be true for acquisitions. Networks of the firm, the founder, and the manager, may be called upon to identify potential buyers, may influence the valuation of the firm, and may also influence the success of the acquisition process by screening the acquisition targets. Another area for future research on acquisitions is the entrepreneur. Because an acquisition does not involve the regulation of an IPO, the entrepreneur is often more actively involved in an exit through an acquisition. For many ventures, the exit results in the founder leaving the company, while in other cases the entrepreneur may continue to be involved with the business and may face disappointed following the exit.[130] Examining the entrepreneur's influence on the selection of a buyer, the completion of the acquisition, the valuation of the firm, and the postacquisition performance of the firm are four areas for future research on the entrepreneur. A third area for future research is the role of investors in the acquisition process. Professional investors (rather than other companies) expect a return on their investment typically within five to seven years, and so they expect a plan for cash liquidity for themselves.[131] This would influence not only investment in a firm but also the exit including the speed with which the firm is sold.

LIQUIDATION

A third exit strategy is liquidation. This exit strategy involves converting the firm's assets (e.g., inventory, accounts receivable, and equipment) into cash to pay off the firm's debt. There are multiple reasons for liquidation, but the most frequent one is organizational failure. Organizational failure is a significant problem for start-ups. According to the Small Business Administration, one-third of new firms (with employees) survive less than two years. In 2004, there were 580,900 new firms and 576,200 closures.[132] Many new firms face a liability of newness, which threatens their existence.[133]

There is a significant body of research addressing organizational failure, including factors that are related to failure. Such factors include crisis recognition, symptoms of failure, TMT credentials, capital structure, industry conditions, and strategy.[134–142] Moreover, what is considered failure in the literature is broad and often includes all cessation of business activity no matter what the cause is (e.g., insolvency, liquidation, merger, and acquisition).[143]

When organizational failure is due to its inability to meet its financial obligations (i.e., insolvency), a firm may file for bankruptcy protection. Bankruptcy protection is sought if the firm fails to meet its obligations and petitions the court to reorganize (Chapter 11) or to liquidate (Chapter 7). The debtor's property is taken over by a trustee or receiver for the benefit of the creditors.[144] Chapter 7 "may be the best choice when the firm has no future, it has no substantial assets or qualities that cannot be reproduced after bankruptcy, or the debts are so overwhelming that restructuring them is not feasible."[145] Liquidation is especially challenging in that it not only seeks to honor the legal rights of the creditors but also minimize the damage to the founders and employees.[146] Struggling firms can go out of business without filing for bankruptcy (i.e., they liquidate their assets, pay creditors, and cease operations). However, filing for bankruptcy may protect assets from creditors and preserve some assets to pay the taxes and employees.[147]

Future Research

As in the case of acquisitions, most of what we understand about liquidation as a means of entrepreneurial exit is anecdotal in nature. A number of studies have examined firm failure and some have addressed failure of entrepreneurial ventures, but little research addresses the liquidation of entrepreneurial ventures. The dearth of research addressing liquidation may be because of the percentage of liquidations that are privately held. Research addressing the factors leading to liquidation, including financial position, governance characteristics, networks, as well as economic conditions would be valuable to researchers and practitioners alike. Based on the finding of IPOs, researchers might consider the importance of governance characteristics, such as the involvement of the founder, the management team, and the board of directors. Because many of the firms that liquidate do so as a result of failure and because many failures take place within the first two years of the firm's inception, one would anticipate that the founder is actively involved in the firm. For small start-ups, the role of the board may not be as well developed as in larger start-ups. In addition, examining the process of liquidation would be informative.

CONCLUSION

This chapter addressed entrepreneurial exit—an inevitable, but underre-searched, part of the entrepreneurial process. In addition, in emphasizing the need for an exit plan, three of the more frequently used means of exit were addressed: IPOs, acquisitions, and liquidations. Much more could be written about the exit strategy, including the other means of exit not addressed in this chapter, such as succession plans for family-owned businesses, reverse merg-ers for businesses seeking a public market for their stock, and direct public of-fering.

While there has been extensive research on IPOs of entrepreneurial firms, less is known about other means of entrepreneurial exit. While we infer some im-plications from the research on the exit of established firms (e.g., acquisitions and failure) for entrepreneurial firms, it is clear that research focused on the acqui-sition and liquidation of entrepreneurial firms among other forms of exit would benefit entrepreneurs and scholars alike.

Exit is frequently the last and most important strategic decision made by the founding entrepreneur, but as it stands today, aside from work on IPOs, the field can provide very limited guidance on the wealth-maximizing, or perhaps better, utility-maximizing choice among the various exit options. Topics, such as the implications of exit using MBOs and ESOPs for the wealth of entrepreneurs, the conditions under which acquisition is preferred to IPO, or the conditions under which different types of liquidation alternative maximize investors wealth (min-imize loss) are ripe for further research. While research in the field of entre-preneurship has advanced our understanding of much of the entrepreneurial process, entrepreneurial exit remains to be explored.

NOTES

1. Jeffry A. Timmons and Stephen Spinelli, *New Venture Creation: Entrepreneurship for the 21st Century*, 6th ed. (New York: McGraw-Hill Irwin, 2004), 606.

2. Richard D. Dorf and Thomas H. Byers, *Technology Ventures: From Idea to En-terprise* (New York: McGraw-Hill, 2005).

3. J. W. Petty, "Harvesting Firm Value: Process and Results," in *Entrepreneurship 2000*, eds. D. L. Sexton and R. W. Smilor (Chicago: Upstart, 1997), 416

4. Richard D. Dorf and Thomas H. Byers, *Technology Ventures: From Idea to En-terprise* (New York: McGraw-Hill, 2005).

5. J. W. Petty, "Harvesting Firm Value: Process and Results," in *Entrepreneurship 2000*, eds. D. L. Sexton and R. W. Smilor (Chicago: Upstart, 1997).

6. Prasad, G. S. Vozikis, G. D. Bruton, and A. Merikas, " 'Harvesting' through Initial Public Offerings (IPOs): The Implications of Underpricing for the Small Firm," *Entrepreneurship: Theory and Practice* 20, no. 2 (1995): 31–41.

7. J. W. Petty, "Harvesting Firm Value: Process and Results," in *Entrepreneurship 2000*, eds. D. L. Sexton and R. W. Smilor (Chicago: Upstart, 1997), 416–417.

8. J. W. Petty, "Harvesting Firm Value: Process and Results," in *Entrepreneurship 2000*, eds. D. L. Sexton and R. W. Smilor (Chicago: Upstart, 1997).

9. Richard D. Dorf and Thomas H. Byers, *Technology Ventures: From Idea to Enterprise* (New York: McGraw-Hill, 2005).

10. F. D. Lipman, *The Complete Going Public Handbook* (Roseville, CA: Prima Publishing, 2000).

11. J. W. Petty, "Harvesting Firm Value: Process and Results," in *Entrepreneurship 2000*, eds. D. L. Sexton and R. W. Smilor (Chicago: Upstart, 1997).

12. R. Ronstadt, "Exit, Stage Left: Why Entrepreneurs End Their Entrepreneurial Careers before Retirement," *Journal of Business Venturing* 1, no. 3 (1986): 323–338.

13. Robert A. Baron and Scott A. Shane, *Entrepreneurship: A Process Perspective* (Mason, OH: Thomson South-western, 2005).

14. Jeffry A. Timmons and Stephen Spinelli, *New Venture Creation: Entrepreneurship for the 21st Century*, 6th ed. (New York: McGraw-Hill Irwin, 2004).

15. J. W. Petty, "Harvesting Firm Value: Process and Results," in *Entrepreneurship 2000*, eds. D. L. Sexton and R. W. Smilor (Chicago: Upstart, 1997).

16. Prasad et al., 1995.

17. R. Ronstadt, "Exit, Stage Left: Why Entrepreneurs End Their Entrepreneurial Careers before Retirement," *Journal of Business Venturing* 1, no. 3 (1986): 323–338.

18. Jeffry A. Timmons and Stephen Spinelli, *New Venture Creation: Entrepreneurship for the 21st Century*, 6th ed. (New York: McGraw-Hill Irwin, 2004).

19. Prasad et al., 1995.

20. D. L. Deeds, D. DeCarolis, and J. E. Coombs, "The Impact of Firm-Specific Capabilities on the Amount of Capital Raised in an Initial Public Offering: Evidence from the Biotechnology Industry," *Journal of Business Venturing* 12, no. 1 (1997): 31–46.

21. Prasad et al., 1995.

22. S. T. Certo, "Influencing Initial Public Offering Investors with Prestige: Signaling with Board Structures," *Academy of Management Review* 28, no. 3 (2003): 432–447.

23. R. P. Beatty and E. J. Zajac, "Managerial Incentives, Monitoring, and Risk Bearing: A Study of Executive Compensation, Ownership, and Board Structure in Initial Public Offerings," *Administrative Science Quarterly* 39, no. 2 (1994): 313–335.

24. T. Nelson, "The Persistence of Founder Influence: Management, Ownership, and Performance Effects at Initial Public Offering," *Strategic Management Journal* 24, no. 8 (2003): 707–724.

25. T. M. Welbourne and A. O. Andrews, "Predicting the Performance of Initial Public Offerings: Should Human Resource Management Be in the Equation?" *Academy of Management Journal* 39, no. 4 (1996): 891–919.

26. T. Nelson, "The Persistence of Founder Influence: Management, Ownership, and Performance Effects at Initial Public Offering," *Strategic Management Journal* 24, no. 8 (2003): 707–724.

27. S. T. Certo, "Influencing Initial Public Offering Investors with Prestige: Signaling with Board Structures," *Academy of Management Review* 28, no. 3 (2003): 433.

28. W. G. Sanders and S. Boivie, "Sorting Things Out: Valuation of New Firms in Uncertain Markets," *Strategic Management Journal* 25, no. 2 (2004): 167–186.

29. M. A. Zimmerman and G. J. Zeitz, "Beyond Survival: Achieving New Venture Growth by Building Legitimacy," *Academy of Management Review* 27, no. 3 (2002): 414–431.

30. M. Daily, S. T. Certo, D. R. Dalton, and R. Roengpitya, "IPO Underpricing: A Meta-Analysis and Research Synthesis," *Entrepreneurship: Theory and Practice* 27, no. 3 (2003): 271–295.

31. Ibid.

32. S. T. Certo, "Influencing Initial Public Offering Investors with Prestige: Signaling with Board Structures," *Academy of Management Review* 28, no. 3 (2003): 432–447.

33. Deeds et al., 1997.

34. M. A. Zimmerman and G. J. Zeitz, "Beyond Survival: Achieving New Venture Growth by Building Legitimacy," *Academy of Management Review* 27, no. 3 (2002): 414–431.

35. Daily et al., 2003.

36. DeCarolis and D. L. Deeds, "The Impact of Stocks and Flows of Organizational Knowledge on Firm Performance: An Empirical Investigation of the Biotechnology Industry," *The Strategic Management Journal* 20, no. 10 (1999).

37. Deeds et al., 1998.

38. Deeds et al., 2004.

39. Daily et al., 2003.

40. R. P. Beatty, "Auditor Reputation and the Pricing of Initial Public Offerings," *Accounting Review* 64, no. 4 (1989): 693–710.

41. Daily et al., 2003, p. 272.

42. Prasad et al., 1995.

43. Ibid.

44. Daily et al., 2003.

45. T. G. Pollock, J. F. Porac, and J. B. Wade, "Constructing Deal Networks: Brokers as Network 'Architects' in the U.S. IPO Market and Other Examples," *Academy of Management Review* 29, no. 1 (2004): 50–72.

46. Deeds et al., 1997.

47. Pollock et al., 2004.

48. M. McBain and D. S. Krause, "Going Public: The Impact of Insiders' Holdings on the Price of Initial Public Offerings," *Journal of Business Venturing* 4, no. 6 (1989): 419–428.

49. W. G. Sanders and S. Boivie, "Sorting Things Out: Valuation of New Firms in Uncertain Markets," *Strategic Management Journal* 25, no. 2 (2004): 167–186.

50. S. T. Certo, "Influencing Initial Public Offering Investors with Prestige: Signaling with Board Structures," *Academy of Management Review* 28, no. 3 (2003): 432–447.

51. R. Gulati and M. C. Higgins, "Which Ties Matter When? The Contingent Effects of Interorganizational Partnerships on IPO Success," *Strategic Management Journal* 24, no. 2 (2003): 127–145.

52. T. E. Stuart, H. Hoang, and R. C. Hybels, "Interorganizational Endorsements and the Performance of Entrepreneurial Ventures," *Administrative Science Quarterly* 44, no. 2 (1999): 315–349.

53. R. Carter and S. Manaster, "Initial Public Offerings and Underwriter Reputation," *Journal of Finance* 45, no. 4 (1990): 1045–1068.

54. R. P. Beatty, "Auditor Reputation and the Pricing of Initial Public Offerings," *Accounting Review* 64, no. 4 (1989): 693–710.

55. Stuart et al., 1999.

56. M. A. Zimmerman and G. J. Zeitz, "Beyond Survival: Achieving New Venture Growth by Building Legitimacy," *Academy of Management Review* 27, no. 3 (2002): 414–431.

57. W. G. Sanders and S. Boivie, "Sorting Things Out: Valuation of New Firms in Uncertain Markets," *Strategic Management Journal* 25, no. 2 (2004): 167–186.

58. Fisher and Pollock, 2004.

59. T. M. Welbourne and L. A. Cyr, "The Human Resource Executive Effect in Initial Public Offering Firms," *Academy of Management Journal* 42, no. 6 (1996): 616–629.

60. W. G. Sanders and S. Boivie, "Sorting Things Out: Valuation of New Firms in Uncertain Markets," *Strategic Management Journal* 25, no. 2 (2004): 167–186.

61. D. Ucbasaran, A. Lockett, M. Wright, and P. Westhead, "Entrepreneurial Founder Teams: Factors Associated with Members Entry and Exit," *Entrepreneurship: Theory and Practice* 28, no. 2 (2003): 107–127.

62. T. A. Finkle, "The Relationship between Boards of Directors and Initial Public Offerings in the Biotechnology . . . ," *Entrepreneurship: Theory and Practice* 22, no. 3 (1998): 5–30.

63. T. Nelson, "The Persistence of Founder Influence: Management, Ownership, and Performance Effects at Initial Public Offering," *Strategic Management Journal* 24, no. 8 (2003): 707–724.

64. Fisher and Pollock, 2004.

65. T. Nelson, "The Persistence of Founder Influence: Management, Ownership, and Performance Effects at Initial Public Offering," *Strategic Management Journal* 24, no. 8 (2003): 707–724.

66. Ibid., 712.

67. H. M. Fischer and T. G. Pollock, "Effects of Social Capital and Power on Surviving Transformational Change: The Case of Initial Public Offerings," *Academy of Management Journal* 47, no. 4 (2004): 463–481.

68. S. T. Certo, "Influencing Initial Public Offering Investors with Prestige: Signaling with Board Structures," *Academy of Management Review* 28, no. 3 (2003): 432–447.

69. Ibid.

70. S. T. Certo, C. M. Daily, and D. R. Dalton, "Signaling Firm Value through Board Structure: An Investigation of Initial Public Offerings," *Entrepreneurship: Theory and Practice* 26, no. 2 (2001): 33–50.

71. Filatotchev and Bishop, 2002.

72. Finkle, 1998.

73. W. G. Sanders and S. Boivie, "Sorting Things Out: Valuation of New Firms in Uncertain Markets," *Strategic Management Journal* 25, no. 2 (2004): 167–186.

74. J. R. Ritter, "The Long-Run Performance of Initial Public Offerings," *Journal of Finance* 46, no. 1 (1991): 3–27.

75. Pollock et al., 2004.

76. T. G. Pollock and V. P. Rindova, "Media Legitimation Effects in the Market for Initial Public Offerings," *Academy of Management Journal* 46, no. 5 (2003): 631–642.

77. Ibbotson, "Price Performance of Common Stock New Issues," *Journal of Financial Economics* 2, no. 3 (1995): 235–272.

78. R. P. Beatty, "Auditor Reputation and the Pricing of Initial Public Offerings," *Accounting Review* 64, no. 4 (1989): 693–710.

79. R. P. Beatty and E. J. Zajac, "Managerial Incentives, Monitoring, and Risk Bearing: A Study of Executive Compensation, Ownership, and Board Structure in Initial Public Offerings," *Administrative Science Quarterly* 39, no. 2 (1994): 313–335.

80. R. Gulati and M. C. Higgins, "Which Ties Matter When? The Contingent Effects of Interorganizational Partnerships on IPO Success," *Strategic Management Journal* 24, no. 2 (2003): 127–145.

81. Deeds et al., 1997.

82. Finkle, 1998.

83. J. R. Ritter, "The Long-Run Performance of Initial Public Offerings," *Journal of Finance* 46, no. 1 (1991).

84. W. D. Bygrave, G. Johnstone, J. Lewis, and R. Ullman, "Venture Capitalists' Criteria for Selecting High Tech Investments: Prescriptive Wisdom Compared with Actuality," in *Frontiers of Entrepreneurship Research* (1998).

85. T. M. Welbourne and L. A. Cyr, "The Human Resource Executive Effect in Initial Public Offering Firms," *Academy of Management Journal* 42, no. 6 (1996): 616–629.

86. Deeds et al., 1997, p. 31.

87. L. Deeds, Y. Mang, and M. L. Frandsen, "The Influence of Firms' and Industries' Legitimacy on the Flow of Capital into High-Technology Ventures," *Strategic Organization* 2, no. 1 (2004): 9–34.

88. Finkle, 1998.

89. Gulati and Higgins, 2003.

90. Filatotchev and K. Bishop, "Board Composition, Share Ownership, and 'Underpricing' of U.K. IPO Firms," *Strategic Management Journal* 23, no. 10 (2002): 941–955.

91. Robert A. Baron and Scott A. Shane, *Entrepreneurship: A Process Perspective* (Mason, OH: Thomson South-western, 2005).

92. Ian Mount, "Death of the IPO Dream," *Fortune Small Business* 15, no. 3 (2005): 16–18.

93. Deeds, 1994.

94. J. W. Petty, "Harvesting Firm Value: Process and Results," in *Entrepreneurship 2000*, eds. D. L. Sexton and R. W. Smilor (Chicago: Upstart, 1997).

95. Joao C. Neves, "The Value of Financial Freedom and Ownership in Opportunities of Entrepreneurial Harvest," *International Journal of Entrepreneurship and Innovation Management* 5, no. 5/6 (2005).

96. Nathaniel Gilbert, "The M&A Cradle Game for Young Companies on the Fast Track," *Management Review* 78, no. 11 (1989): 1–28.

97. Ibid.

98. Neves, 2005.

99. Gilbert, 1989.

100. Jung-Chin Shen and Jeffrey Reuer, "Adverse Selection in Acquisitions of Small Manufacturing Firms: A Comparison of Private and Public Targets," *Small Business Economics* 24, no. 4 (2005): 393–407.

101. Gilbert, 1989.

102. Neves, 2005.

103. Gilbert, 1989.

104. Ibid.

105. Ibid.

106. Robert A. Baron and Scott A. Shane, *Entrepreneurship: A Process Perspective* (Mason, OH: Thomson South-western, 2005).

107. J. W. Petty, "Harvesting Firm Value: Process and Results," in *Entrepreneurship 2000*, eds. D. L. Sexton and R. W. Smilor (Chicago: Upstart, 1997).

108. Neves, 2005.

109. F. D. Lipman, *The Complete Going Public Handbook* (Roseville, CA: Prima Publishing, 2000).

110. Jack M. Kaplan, *Patterns of Entrepreneurship* (Hoboken, NJ: John Wiley, 2003).

111. Lipman, 2000.

112. Kaplan, 2003.

113. Lipman, 2000.

114. Baron and Shane, 2005.

115. Bygrave, 1997.

116. Donald F. Kuratko and Richard M. Hodgettes, *Entrepreneurship: Theory, Process, and Practice*, 6th ed. (Mason, OH: Thomson South-western, 2004).

117. Lipman, 2000.

118. Other rules of thumb include insurance agencies at 1 to 2 times annual gross commissions, travel agencies at .05 to .1 times annual gross sales, real estate agencies at .2 to .3 times annual gross commissions, and restaurants at .3 to .5 times annual gross sales.

119. Lipman, 2000.

120. Richard D. Dorf and Thomas H. Byers, *Technology Ventures: From Idea to Enterprise* (New York: McGraw-Hill, 2005).

121. Gilbert, 1989.

122. Lipman, 2000.

123. Kaplan, 2003.

124. Ibid.

125. J. W. Petty, "Harvesting Firm Value: Process and Results," in *Entrepreneurship 2000*, eds. D. L. Sexton and R. W. Smilor (Chicago: Upstart, 1997), 431.

126. Ibid., 432.

127. Baron and Shane, 2005.

128. Berle and C. Means, *The Modern Corporation and Private Property* (New York: Commerce Clearing House, 1932).

129. M. Jensen and W. Meckling, "Theory of the Firm: Managerial Behavior, Agency Costs and Ownership Structure," *Journal of Financial Economics* 3, no. 4 (1976): 305–360.

130. Petty, 1997.

131. Richard D. Dorf and Thomas H. Byers, *Technology Ventures: From Idea to Enterprise* (New York: McGraw-Hill, 2005).

132. http://app1.sba.gov/faqs/faqindex.cfm?areaID=24.

133. L. Stinchcombe, "Social Structure and Organization," in *Handbook of Organizations*, ed. J. G. March (Chicago: Rand McNally, 1965), 142–193.

134. Matthias Almus, "The Shadow of Death—An Empirical Analysis of the Pre-exit Performance of New German Firms," *Small Business Economics* 23 (2004): 189–201.

135. G. D. Bruton and Y. T. Rubanik, "Turnaround of High Technology Firms in Russia: The Case of Micron," *Academy of Management Executive* 11, no. 2 (1997): 68–79.

136. J. G. Covin and D. P. Slevin, "New Venture Strategic Posture, Structure, and Performance: An Industry Life Cycle Analysis," *Journal of Business Venturing* 5 (1990): 123–135.

137. Richard A. D'Aveni, "The Aftermath of Organizational Decline: A Longitudinal Study," *Academy of Management Journal* 32, no. 3 (1989): 577–606.

138. Donald C. Hambrick and Richard A. D'Aveni, "Large Corporate Failures as Downward Spirals," *Administrative Science Quarterly* 33 (1988): 1–23.

139. R. Ronstadt, "Exit, Stage Left: Why Entrepreneurs End Their Entrepreneurial Careers before Retirement," *Journal of Business Venturing* 1, no. 3 (1986): 323–338.

140. K. H. Vesper, "New Venture Planning," *Journal of Business Strategy* 1, no. 2 (1980): 72–74.

141. J. Welsh and J. White, "A Small Business Is Not a Little Big Business," *Harvard Business Review*, 59, no. 4 (1981): 18–33.

142. W. Wucinich, "How to Finance Small Business," *Management Accounting* 6, no. 15 (1979): 16–18.

143. Ronstadt, 1986.

144. http://www.sba.gov/starting_business/startup/guide8.html.

145. http://www.moranlaw.net/struggling.htm.

146. http://www.moranlaw.net /failing-startup.htm.

147. Ibid.

Index

About the Set Editors

Timothy G. Habbershon is Founding Director of the Institute for Family Enterprising at Babson College, where he holds the President's Term Chair in Family Enterprising, developing Babson's emphasis on family-based entrepreneurship. Additionally, he is a founding partner in The TELOS Group, providing transition and strategy consultations to large family firms worldwide. Formerly, Tim was the founding director of family business programs in the Snider Entrepreneurship Center at the Wharton School of the University of Pennsylvania and in the Freeman Institute for Rural Entrepreneurship in the School of Business, University of South Dakota. Tim presents executive education programs to family ownership and management teams on entrepreneurial strategy and relationships issues through universities around the world. His research on family business has appeared in such journals as the *Journal of Business Venturing, Family Business Review,* and *Entrepreneurship Theory and Practice.* He has a regular column—Family, Inc.—in *BusinessWeek's Small Biz* magazine, and has been cited in the *Financial Times, Newsweek,* and the *New York Times.* Prior to moving into entrepreneurship, Tim was a minister in the Presbyterian Church, where he started churches.

Maria Minniti is Professor of Economics and Professor of Entrepreneurship at Babson College. She has published numerous articles on entrepreneurship, economic growth and complexity theory, as well as book chapters and research monographs. Her articles have appeared in such publications as the *Journal of Economic Behavior and Organizations, Small Business Economics,* the *Journal of Business Venturing, Small Business Economics Journal, Comparative Economics Studies,* and *Entrepreneurship Theory and Practice.* Dr. Minniti is the Research Director of the Global Entrepreneurship Monitor (GEM) project and an associate editor of the *Small Business Economics Journal*. She is currently working on a book about entrepreneurial behavior.

Mark P. Rice is the Murata Dean of the F. W. Olin Graduate School of Business and the Jeffry A. Timmons Professor of Entrepreneurial Studies at Babson College. His research on corporate innovation and entrepreneurship has been published widely in academic and practitioner journals, including *Organization Science, R&D Management*, the *Journal of Marketing Theory and Practice, IEEE Engineering Management Review, Academy of Management Executive*, and *California Management Review*. Dean Rice has been a director and chairman of the National Business Incubation Association, which honored him in 1998 with its Founder's Award, and in 2002 he received the Edwin M. and Gloria W. Appel Entrepreneurship in Education Prize. He is co-author of *Radical Innovation: How Mature Companies Can Outsmart Upstarts*, and, with Jana Matthews, of *Growing New Ventures, Creating New Jobs: Principles and Practices of Successful Business Incubation* (Quorum, 1995).

Stephen Spinelli Jr. is Babson College's Vice Provost for Entrepreneurship and Global Management. An Associate Professor, Spinelli holds the Paul T. Babson Chair in Entrepreneurship and the Alan Lewis Chair in Global Management. In his role as Vice provost, Spinelli is responsible for developing entrepreneurship initiatives within the college and for extending Babson's entrepreneurial brand worldwide. A recognized leader in defining the field of entrepreneurship, prior to his academic career he cofounded Jiffy Lube International and subsequently founded and served as Chairman and CEO of American Oil Change Corporation, which he sold in 1991. As an educator, he has researched, written, and lectured extensively on various aspects of entrepreneurship. His work has appeared in such publications as the *Journal of Business Venturing* and *Frontiers of Entrepreneurship*. Spinelli has also been featured in the popular press such as the *Wall Street Journal, Financial Times*, the *Boston Globe, Entrepreneur*, and *Inc.* He has authored numerous business cases and recently coauthored the following books: *Business Plans That Work, Franchising: Pathway to Wealth Creation*, and *New Venture Creation*. Spinelli has consulted for major corporations such as Fidelity Investments, Intel Corporation, IBM Corporation, and Allied Domecq. He has served in leadership roles for a number of community, business, and professional associations. He is cofounder and codirector of the Babson/Historically Black Colleges and Universities Consortium, a partnership dedicated to improving the quality, quantity, and longevity of African American businesses. He is a fellow of the PriceBabson College Fellows Program.

Andrew Zacharakis is the John H. Muller Jr. Chair in Entrepreneurship at Babson College, where he previously served as Chair of the Entrepreneurship Department and Acting Director of the Arthur M. Blank Center for Entrepreneurship. In addition, Zacharakis was the President of the Academy of Management,

Entrepreneurship Division, from 2004 to 2005. He has also served as an associate editor of the *Journal of Small Business Management* since 2003. Zacharakis's primary research areas include the venture capital process and entrepreneurial growth strategies. Zacharakis is the coeditor, with William Bygrave, of *The Portable MBA in Entrepreneurship*, Third Edition, and coauthor, with Jeffrey Timmons and Stephen Spinelli Jr., of *Business Plans That Work* and *How to Raise Capital*. Zacharakis has been interviewed in newspapers nationwide, including the *Boston Globe*, the *Wall Street Journal*, and *USA Today*. He has also appeared on Bloomberg Small Business Report and been interviewed on National Public Radio. Zacharakis has taught seminars to leading corporations, such as Boeing, Met Life, Lucent, and Intel. He has also taught executives in countries worldwide, including Spain, Chile, Australia, China, Turkey, and Germany. Professor Zacharakis actively consults with entrepreneurs and small business start-ups. His professional experience includes positions with the Cambridge Companies (investment banking/venture capital), IBM, and Leisure Technologies.

About the Contributors

Frances M. Amatucci is Associate Professor in the School of Business at Robert Morris University in Pittsburgh. Her research interests are minority and women entrepreneurship, entrepreneurship and regional economic development, and change management. She has presented her research at several national and international conferences, and published in *Venture Capital* and *Entrepreneurship Theory and Practice*. She served as Vice President of the Women and Minority Division of the U.S. Association for Small Business and Entrepreneurship.

Gaylen N. Chandler is the Robert B. and Beverlee Zollinger Murray Professor of Entrepreneurial Studies at Utah State University. Prior to joining the faculty at Utah State University in 1993, he was a faculty member at Penn State–Erie. His research interests include opportunity recognition processes, the role of ongoing learning in new venture development, and new venture teams. During his professional career, Dr. Chandler has authored or coauthored over seventy articles and papers that have been published in academic journals or presented at professional meetings. His articles have appeared in journals such as the *Journal of Business Venturing,* the *Journal of Management, Entrepreneurship Theory and Practice,* and the *Academy of Management Learning and Education Journal.* He is a member of the editorial board of the *Journal of Business Venturing* and a frequent ad hoc reviewer for the *Journal of Management.* He spent the 2001–2002 academic year as a Visiting Professor of Entrepreneurship at the Jönköping International Business School in Sweden.

Andrew C. Corbett is Assistant Professor of Entrepreneurship and Strategic Management at the Lally School of Management and Technology at Rensselaer Polytechnic Institute. His writing and research examine cognitive perspectives of the entrepreneurial process and the role of individuals within strategic renewal. Specifically, he explores issues such as learning, schemas, action, emotions, environment, and improvisation. Prof. Corbett's research has been published in the *Journal of Business Venturing, Entrepreneurship: Theory and Practice, Management Communications Quarterly*, and the *Journal of Small Business Management*. In addition to his scholarly work, he has written a number of practitioner articles and published a book on strategic management. Prof. Corbett has been recognized for his excellence in teaching on numerous occasions. Most recently, he was awarded the 2005 McGraw-Hill Innovation in Entrepreneurship Pedagogy Award by the Academy of Management for his development and delivery of entrepreneurship courses. In 2004, he was named Outstanding Teacher of the Year by the Lally School's MBA Class.

David L. Deeds is currently Associate Professor at the School of Management at the University of Texas at Dallas. Prior to coming to the University of Texas at Dallas, he held faculty positions at the Weatherhead School of Management at Case Western Reserve University and the Fox School of Business at Temple University. He received a PhD from the University of Washington in Seattle in 1994. His articles have appeared in *Inc.* magazine, the *Journal of Business Venturing, Entrepreneurship: Theory and Practice*, the *Journal of Management Studies*, the *Strategic Management Journal, Research Policy*, the *Journal of Engineering and Technology Management*, and the *Journal of Product Innovation Management*. He received the Mescon Award for best empirical research in Entrepreneurship at the National Academy of Management meetings in 1996, was awarded the NASDAQ Fellowship in Capital Formation in 1997, and received the *Fast Company* Award for best paper on high-growth firms at the National Academy of Management meetings in 2000. His current research interests include the management of strategic alliances, entrepreneurial finance, and the management of high-technology ventures. Prior to pursuing a career as an academic, Dr. Deeds was cofounder and president of LightSpeed Corporation, a computer hardware and software developer specializing in custom CAD/CAM computer systems, from 1983 to 1989.

Pat H. Dickson is an Associate Professor of Business in the Wayne Calloway School of Business and Accountancy at Wake Forest University. Previously, Dickson held faculty positions at the Georgia Institute of Technology and the University of Louisville. His research, which focuses on the strategic alliance behavior of entrepreneurial firms, has appeared in various journals including the *Academy of Management Journal* and the *Journal of Business Venturing*. His work, as cofounder of the Strategic Alliance Research Group, has resulted in a research program involving fifteen international researchers and data collected from over 3,500 entrepreneurial firms in ten countries. Dickson served for three years as Proceedings Editor for the United States Association of Small Business and Entrepreneurship and for the International Council for Small Business in 2005. He was elected in 2002 to a three-year term on the Executive Board of the Academy of Management Entrepreneurship Division. Dickson's teaching has focused on venture creation, technology and strategic management, and technology entrepreneurship. In addition to his teaching in the United States, he has taught venture creation and strategic management in Singapore, Hong Kong, El Salvador, and Costa Rica. Dickson spent fifteen years as an entrepreneur, co-founding companies in the automotive parts and service industry, and as a corporate entrepreneur serving as Director of Franchising for a superregional services and manufacturing company.

Dimo Dimov is Assistant Professor of Entrepreneurship at the University of Connecticut. He previously held a faculty position at Instituto de Empresa. His research focuses on both sides of entrepreneurial opportunities—how potential entrepreneurs create them and how investors select them. His work has been published in *Journal of Business Venturing, Entrepreneurship Theory and Practice,* and *Venture Capital* and presented numerous conferences including the Academy of Management, the Babson College Entrepreneurship Research conference, and INFORMS. Prior to entering academia, Dimo was CFO for two Marriott hotel businesses in Budapest, Hungary.

Matthias Eckermann is working in investment banking in London, focusing primarily on merger and acquisition transactions in Europe. Matthias holds a PhD in Finance and a diploma in Finance and Engineering from Dresden University of Technology, Germany, specializing in analyzing exit strategies of venture capital investors and the impact of asymmetrical information on exits. He also spent some time at Columbia Business School and Babson College as DAAD scholar.

Jeffery S. McMullen is Assistant Professor of Management and Entrepreneurship at Baylor University. His current research interests involve entrepreneurial decision making and action, self-regulation, and institutional economics. Dr. McMullen's research has been presented at conferences around the world. He was the 2002 winner of the Academy of Management's Best Conceptual Paper in the Entrepreneurship division, has published articles in the *Academy of Management Review,* the *Journal of Management Studies,* and the *Journal of Business Venturing,* and serves on the editorial board of the *Journal of Business Venturing.* Dr. McMullen has taught strategic management, entrepreneurship, and social entrepreneurship at Baylor University and the University of Colorado. In addition to his teaching and research, he has consulted and created new ventures in the Boulder Valley and has worked in the Information, Communications, and Entertainment division of KPMG, Denver. As a CPA, he specialized in emerging enterprises and played a significant role in a number of initial public offerings.

Heidi M. Neck is Assistant Professor of Entrepreneurship and holds the Babson Family Term Chair at Babson College. Her research interests include corporate entrepreneurship, radical innovation, and entrepreneurship education. She has presented at numerous conferences including the Academy of Management, the Babson Entrepreneurship Research conference, and the United States Association for Small Business and Entrepreneurship, and has several refereed publications and book chapters. Neck is the Faculty Coordinator of the Babson SEE Reflect, a reunion program for alumni of the Price-Babson Symposium for Entrepreneurship Educators as well as a program designer and faculty member of the Babson-Olin Symposium of Engineering Entrepreneurship Educators. At Babson, she teaches entrepreneurship classes at the undergraduate and graduate levels and has been involved in several custom executive education programs for companies such as EMC, Siemens, and Intel. Neck was recently awarded Babson's Deans' Award for Excellence in Teaching.

Jeffrey E. Sohl is Director of the Center for Venture Research at the Whittemore School of Business and Economics at the University of New Hampshire. Prior to joining the Whittemore School, he was a consultant to the Department of Energy in the area of public policy analysis. His current research interests are in early-stage equity financing for high growth ventures. He currently serves on the advisory board of the New Hampshire Community Loan Fund, the eCoast Technology Roundtable and MerchantBanc, and the editorial board for *Venture Capital, Entrepreneurship Theory and Practice,* and *Frontiers of Entrepreneurship Research.* He also serves on the New Hampshire Governor's Advisory Committee on Capital Formation and is on the board of directors for NetworkNH. He has presented his angel research in academic and practitioner forums in the United States, Europe and Asia, and in briefings for several government agencies and scholars from the United States, Europe, Scandinavia, Australia, Asia, and Africa. He has appeared on CNBC, MSNBC, National Public Radio, NHPTV's NH Outlook, and has been quoted in *Inc., Forbes, Fortune,* the *Wall Street Journal, Red Herring, Newsweek, Business Week, Newsweek-Japan, Financial Times, New York Times, Chicago Tribune, Los Angeles Times,* and the *Financial Times-France.* He has written many articles which have been published in academic and business journals, including *Venture Capital: An International Journal of Entrepreneurial Finance,* the *Social Science Journal,* the *Journal of Forecasting, Frontiers of Entrepreneurship Research, Entrepreneurship and Regional Development, Entrepreneurship: Theory and Practice, Entrepreneurship 2000,* and the *Journal of Business Venturing.*

Jeffry A. Timmons is Franklin W. Olin Distinguished Professor of Entrepreneurship, Babson College. Known internationally for his research, innovative curriculum development, and teaching in entrepreneurship, new ventures, entrepreneurial finance and venture capital, Jeff Timmons held simultaneous professorships at Babson and Harvard Business School. He returned to Babson full time, and in 1995 was named the first Franklin W. Olin Distinguished Professor of Entrepreneurship. Timmons' friends and supporters endowed the Jeffry A.

Timmons Professorship in the mid-1990s in recognition of his contributions to Babson College and to the field of entrepreneurship. In 1984, Timmons collaborated with the Price Institute for Entrepreneurial Studies to launch the Price-Babson Symposium for Entrepreneurship Educators (SEE), aimed at improving teaching and research by teaming faculty with highly successful entrepreneurs wishing to teach. *Inc.* magazine called him "The Johnny Appleseed of Entrepreneurship Education" and noted that the Price-Babson programs "changed the terrain of entrepreneurship education." Dr. Timmons served as a charter board member of the Kauffman Center for Entrepreneurial Leadership at the Ewing Marion Kauffman Foundation in developing and implementing their mission and strategy. He is the creator and dean of faculty for the Kauffman Fellows Program. Dr. Timmons has authored several books, including the leading textbook *New Venture Creation*, Seventh Edition (2007); *Venture Capital at the Crossroads*, with Babson colleague William D. Bygrave (1992); and the groundbreaking *The Entrepreneurial Mind* (1989). He has recently coauthored *Business Plans That Work* (2004) and *How to Raise Capital: Techniques and Strategies for Financing and Valuing Your Small Business* (2005) with Stephen Spinelli and Andrew Zacharakis. He has published more than 100 articles and papers in publications such as *Harvard Business Review* and *Journal of Business Venturing*, as well as numerous teaching cases. Dr. Timmons has earned a reputation for practicing what he teaches. For over thirty years, he has been immersed in the world of entrepreneurship as an investor, director, or advisor in private companies and investment funds.

Monica Zimmerman Treichel is a faculty member in the Fox School of Business and Management at Temple University, where she teaches graduate and undergraduate courses in entrepreneurship and strategic management. Her research focuses on the initial public offering of technology firms, top management teams, women entrepreneurs, and legitimacy. Her work has been published in the *Academy of Management Review*, the *Journal of Business Venturing*, and *Venture Capital*. Monica is the undergraduate entrepreneurship program chair at the Fox School. She was awarded a Coleman Foundation/United States Association of Small Business and Entrepreneurship Entrepreneurship Awareness and Education grant, which she used to create an interdisciplinary entrepreneurship program at Temple University. In 2002, Monica was selected as an outstanding junior entrepreneurship faculty member by the Coleman foundation. She cofounded and cochairs Temple University's League for Entrepreneurial Women and served as the faculty lead on the Temple CIBER's Developing Women Entrepreneurs for a Global Marketplace project. Monica is a member of many professional and civic organizations/programs including the Academy of Management, the American Institute of Certified Public Accountants (AICPA), the Pennsylvania Institute of Certified Public Accountants (PICPA), Women's Investment Network (WIN), National Association of Women Business Owners (NAWBO), Women's Regional Business Council, and Friends of the American

Red Cross, Interfaith Hospitality Network, and the Optimist Club. Monica serves on the board of the Women's Investment Network and on the advisory board of Temple University's Center for Excellence on Women's Health Research, Leadership, and Advocacy.

Johan Wiklund is Professor of Entrepreneurship at Jönköping International Business School, Sweden. His research interests include: small business growth, the decision to be self-employed, new venture creation, and corporate entrepreneurship. He is chairman of the International Award for Entrepreneurship and Small Business Research and a member of the FSF scientific board. Wiklund is frequently invited as a speaker in Sweden and internationally. He is also Associate Editor for *Small Business Economics,* editorial board member of *Journal of Business Venturing, Journal of Management Studies, Entrepreneurship Theory and Practice,* and *International Entrepreneurship and Management Journal.* His research appears in the *Strategic Management Journal, Journal of Management, Journal of Management Studies, Journal of Business Venturing,* and *Entrepreneurship Theory and Practice,* among other journals.